THE SOURCES OF WEALTH

AND

THE CAUSES OF POVERTY

Paul C. Goelz

Editor

St. Mary's University Press

San Antonio, Texas

THE SOURCES OF WEALTH

AND

THE CAUSES OF POVERTY

Proceedings of the Sixth
National Symposium on the
Philosophy of Free Enterprise

Conducted by

St. Mary's University of San Antonio

1988

Paul C. Goelz

Editor

St. Mary's University Press

San Antonio, Texas

Library of Congress 90-63055
ISBN 0-945632-02-9
Printed by Best Printing Co., of Austin, Texas
Bound by Custom Bookbinders, Austin, Texas
Printed in the United States of America

Appreciation

We gratefully acknowledge the financial assistance of Dennis W. and Del McCarthy of Houston, Texas which made possible the publication of this volume.

Their loyalty to St. Mary's University has been constant and meaningful.

Mr. McCarthy graduated from St. Mary's University in 1951 with a Bachelor of Business Administration degree.

CONTENTS

Rights – Personal Liberty versus Institutions – Principles for the Formulation of Policy – Philosophy in an Economic Structure – Values Outside the Structure – Material Goals versus Spiritual Goals – Discussion

PANELISTS

David Jacobson
Rabbi Emeritus
Tempel Beth-El

Charles H. Miller – Dean
School of Humanities and Social Sciences
St. Mary's University

W. Francis Schorp – Professor
Philosophy Department
St. Mary's University

Preface

Since 1973, the Golden Anniversary of the establishment of the School of Business and Administration, St. Mary's University has brought to the professional and civic communities of South Texas national and international leaders in thought and action. Their principal message has been the moral superiority of the philosophy of the Free Market approach to the allocation of resources and to the refining of national economic policy.

Material resources exist for the well-being of humanity. Developing resources and the creation of wealth make possible advancing society's cultural and spiritual heritage. Articulating at the podium and through publications the values and principles of the American ethos is a cause toward which St. Mary's University feels a responsibility.

Our commitment finds expression throughout the United States, Mexico, Argentina, Uruguay, and Europe.

This Seventh Symposium, whose discussions these Proceedings record, analyzes the nature of "Wealth" in the late Twentieth Century, the means of creating wealth, and the processes of wealth distribution. Similarly analyzed is the nature of "Poverty," the causes of low income for segments in our society, and means of assisting poor individuals.

To the many friends of St. Mary's who assist us in fulfilling our commitment we are indebted.

Paul C. Goelz, SM, Ph.D.
Director
Algur H. Meadows Center
for Entrepreneurial Studies

St. Mary's University
of San Antonio

Acknowledgments

Appreciation is extended to Baldemar G. Garza, Jr. for his continuous highly professional assistance in the photographic coverage of this and our other scholarly convocations.

The success of the Symposium and the attractiveness of this publication are due in great measure to Louise Lagutchik whose extensive contributions overseeing the infinite details associated with the lectures and printing the Proceedings made everything possible.

ERIK RITTER VON
KUEHNELT-LEDDIHN

ERIK RITTER VON KUEHNELT-LEDDIHN

Erik Ritter von Kuehnelt-Leddihn is referred to by William F. Buckley, Jr. as "the world's most fascinating man." His broad intellectual and cultural interests, encompassing the full spectrum of universal knowledge, qualify him as an eminent exemplar of the "Renaissance Man."

Born in Austria he studied theology, civil and canon law at the University of Vienna, and later political science at the University of Budapest where he earned the Doctorate.

He speaks fluently eight languages and has a reading knowledge of eleven others. At sixteen he began to write for newspapers and periodicals, the first being the London Spectator, and at the age of twenty was sent to Russia as a special correspondent for a Hungarian daily.

In 1937 he taught at Georgetown University. After a visit to Spain during the Civil War he returned to the United States and was made head of the Department of History and Sociology at St. Peter's College in Jersey City. He taught Japanese at Fordham University. Later he joined the faculty of Chestnut Hill College in Philadelphia. In the summer of 1947 he resettled in Austria to devote himself to reading, writing, and further studies – visiting America every year since. He has regularly alternated periods of study with periods of travel to the Southern Hemisphere, the

Subarctic, and around the world in order to gain first-hand information about every part of the globe.

Among his novels are *Gates of Hell*, *Night Over the East*, *Moscow 1979*, *Black Banners*, and *Die Gottlosen*, each published in various countries. His numerous theoretical writings include *Liberty or Equality?*, *America's Founding Fathers*, *Catholicism in America*, *Wanderwege*, *Lateinamerika*, *Zwischen Ghetto und Katakombe*, *From Sade and Marx to Hitler and Marcuse*, *Das Ratsel der Liebe*, and *Herz, Hirn und Ruckgrat* (illustrated with his own paintings).

In journalism he has written for many publications including: *America*, *The Catholic World*, *The Commonweal*, *The Geographic Review*, *Modern Age*, *Journal of Central European Affairs*, *The National Review* (for which he is foreign correspondent), *The Dublin Review*, *The Tablet*, *Frankfurter Hefte*, *Una Sancta*, *Humanitas* (Italy), *Criterio* (Argentina), *Credo and Samtid och Framtid* (Sweden), *Farmand* (Norway), *Seike* (Japan), and *Quadrant* and *The Advocate* (Australia).

His lectures cover the spectrum: "The Far East Today," "Soviet Man Today," "The Five Wounds of Latin America," "Work Ethics and Commercialism: a World Problem," "What to Think of South Africa," "The Germans and the Germanies," and "The Irish Problem."

From all of this it is evident Dr. Kuehnelt-Leddihn dislikes specialization. He has repeatedly altered the line of his activities in order to attain and retain a comprehensive view of the humanities. Studies in political theory and practice have been largely directed toward finding ways to strengthen the great Western tradition of human freedom, now under attack from many sides. Recently his interests have been channeled toward the spiritual problem of Eros as distinguished from sex.

The Baron is married to Countess Christiane Goess (Ph.D.). They have three children and seven grandchildren and live in a mountain village near the capital of the Austrian Tyrol. His hobbies are photography, hiking, music, bridge, stamp collecting, the writing of satirical essays, and painting. He had his first exhibition in 1971; and says he enjoys much more wielding the brush than the pen.

WORK ETHICS AND COMMERCIALISM: A WORLD PROBLEM

Dr. Erik von Kuehnelt-Leddihn
Austria

BIBLICAL PERSPECTIVES

Work ethics and commercialism need to be analyzed in a global fashion. Work, we have to bear in mind, was according to the Bible a real curse directed more to Adam than to Eve. Antiquity took a similar stand. Aristotle considered it degrading, and this though he was a very hard intellectual worker. The Middle Ages, by modern standards, had rather limited work ethics. On the Continent we had, if we include the Sundays, between 130 and 160 days when no "menial" work was done; the feast days abounded. The guilds, moreover, by flying commissions, saw to it that no work was done by artificial light. Also the number of apprentices and journeymen was strictly curtailed.

Free enterprise on a larger scale began only at the end of the Middle Ages; but well before the Reformation. In the High Middle Ages the laws against usury (that is, the taking of any interest) were handled very strictly; only the Jews were permitted to take interest, but later many ways were found to get legally around the prescriptions. "Formally" the taking of interest was only permitted by the Codex of Canonic Law issued in May 1918.

We see the rise of free enterprise actually in Lombardy. The Lombard merchants and bankers also settled in London, and

Lombard Street in the heart of the city is named after them. At the very end of the Fifteenth Century Fra Luca di Paioli, a Franciscan, invented double-entry bookkeeping. Spain soon followed in this "capitalistic" development. Margaret Gryce-Hutchinson, a pupil of F. A. von Hayek, has written a brilliant study about the role of Sixteenth Century Spain in the development of free enterprise.

It did not start with the Reformation but Luther and Calvin did bring a radical change in European economics with the "Protestant Work Ethic," a term coined by Max Weber.

I, personally, never use the word "Protestant" because it is a pejorative term formulated by Catholics in 1529 and, although used colloquially, it has no official standing on the Continent. The official label for the Reformation faiths is "Evangelical," a term used with a different meaning in the United States.

As one can see, the reason for the dynamic development of commerce and the rise of material standards in the world of the Reformation was not the total freedom of enterprise but rather the work ethics. The abolition of countless feast days alone resulted in a marked increase in merchandise.

I have in my collection a handbill distributed in Massachusetts in the early Eighteenth Century which menaces everybody celebrating Christmas by non-work with a fine of 5 shillings; still, at the beginning of this century to celebrate Christmas in Presbyterian communities in Scotland was considered a sign of "popery." An even more potent reason for working hard was the new emphasis in the Bible, whose much larger part is the Old Testament. Among the old Israelites the notion of a life everlasting was dawning only gradually and very slowly. If we read carefully the Fourth Commandment exhorting us to honor father and mother "so that you should live long and be happy on the land," we realize the original belief. At the time of Christ the conservative, the Sadducees, still had no belief in an afterlife; only the Pharisees did. (St. Paul even prides himself to be a

Pharisee – Christ only criticized the hypocritical Pharisees, not all of them.)

Thus in the Old Testament you get the notion that if you are really beloved by God, you will prosper right here on earth. The four great curses among the Jews were poverty, childlessness, blindness, and leprosy. And these curses were signs that God did not bless you, that you were "cursed by the Lord."

One can imagine that Israelites and, much later on, followers of the Reformation faiths made efforts to prove not only to themselves but also to their neighbors that they were among the elect. This means that they worked as hard as possible and avoided spending money on luxuries. Believing also in predestination one wanted salvation to be heralded right here on Earth. And Puritanism was the logical result of this attitude.

THE MIDDLE AGES

On the other hand, we saw in the Medieval World the rise of the mendicant, that is, the begging orders. In the lecture I gave here a few years ago I pointed out that these orders were partly responsible for the "proletarianization" of Christ who, quite to the contrary, was in the eyes of the Israelites a prince of royal blood. Therefore His insistence: "My kingdom is not of this world." As a possible candidate for the throne of Judea and, perhaps, of all of Israel, this pronouncement was all important. Some people seem to equate nobility with wealth, which of course is a great sociological error. Still, Joseph, according to the Bible, as a *Tekton*, could have been a carpenter as well as a contractor or an architect. There can be no doubt that he owned real estate in Bethlehem.

It is then in the Catholic world where we have the tradition of poverty and also the respect for poverty. I could hardly imagine this happening in an Evangelical country: it was Spain where Professor Allison Piers was solicited by a beggar with the words: "Dear little brother (*hermanito*) do give me some alms for the love of God, who in the fullness of my youth had taken away from me the disposition for work!"

So we are, thanks to the praise of poverty, dealing in the Catholic rather than in the Evangelical world, with the lacking *gana de trabajar*, the enthusiasm for work. We also find this situation, quite obviously, in the lands of the Eastern Church. In Russia we had the *startsy*, migrating pious men, praying, begging, and preaching.

LATIN AMERICA

Here, of course, we are touching upon the main problem of Latin America with its mass aversion for hard work. (Remember the early Spanish settlers who had to import African slaves because the Indians worked only under the greatest duress.) In Guatemala City, for instance, we find 15,000 licensed lottery-ticket vendors. (How many unlicensed ones there are we do not know.)

I shall never forget my discussion with Senor Zimmermann, the Secretary of Peru's Christian Democratic Party prior to the Leftist military dictatorship which confiscated all landed properties above 250 acres. Zimmermann told me that 78 percent of all lands belong to big landowners. The lack of distributive justice was a real crime. I immediately inquired how large the remaining 22 percent were and how many farmers were to benefit from that area. We used paper and pencil. "That's not bad," I said. "That's much better than where I live in the Tyrolean mountains."

He protested violently. "These people live in poverty and have no chance to rise."

"Look here," I replied. "Take the telephone book of Lima, a rather thin booklet, and see who the people under the letter 'K' are, obviously a letter which does not exist in Spanish. There you find a few Germans, a few Britishers but almost a majority of Japanese. And these Japanese, as you well know, came without a penny in their pockets, not knowing a word of Spanish and they took the toughest and dirtiest jobs. Then they bought one acre, a second, and third acre and raised vegetables. Today the whole vegetable market of Peru is in Japanese hands. Now, they not only have a house and a car but even a telephone which is very expensive and a real status symbol. They also send their children to good schools and pay for it. Isn't that a success story right here in your country?"

The man now was furious. "You don't really expect that our noble Peruvian people would engage in such back-breaking work like these dirty Japs?", he fairly shouted.

"That comment I exactly expect from you," was my reaction.

THE THIRD WORLD

I am sure that you now see the problem of the so-called Third World. If you visit Uganda you will discover that the average male farmer works about two hours a day and his wife four to five hours. (The climate at an altitude of about 4,000 to 6,000 feet is excellent.) Of course, the women are considered to be the real work-horses in Black Africa. They "exist" to produce children and to work, work hard. Often they are physically stronger than the males.

I still well remember a woman on the "Congolia," a boat traveling between Brazzaville and Kinshasa on the Zaire River. She carried a basket, or rather, a sheet metal tub with an enormous amount of grapefruit on her head and asked the men squatting on deck to help her to put it down. After she disappeared I tried to lift it and succeeded beautifully — I held it for two seconds three inches above the ground.

Shocked I asked the men — "How would you carry this load?" They did not understand.

"Don't you speak any French?" They did and I repeated my question. "We?" They looked at me with amazement. "We're men. We could not carry anything of this sort!" As you can see female emancipation in Africa has a long way to go.

INDIA

Or take a country like India. A Viennese lady, married to a "casteless" Sikh, told me about the problems they had with their servants because they would work only in certain capacities. So when their sweeper, who was "untouchable," became ill, the Brahman cook refused to clean the floor of the kitchen. (Brahmans are frequently cooks, chauffeurs, etc. because they do not defile the food ritually, nor persons sitting too close to them.)

She had a violent discussion with this noble man and, finally, she said: "If you don't clean the floor, then I will."

The Brahman hit the ceiling. "Listen, lady," he said, "as a foreigner you are to me anyhow unclean. But somewhere I do draw the line. I certainly would not cook for a woman who sweeps the floor. If you do that I'll quit immediately!"

They found a way out by emptying buckets of water on the floor of the kitchen and the fluid carried out the dirt into the garden. (But no broom could be used. That meant "Sweeping"!)

Once they spent a summer in Udhaipur and rented there a house with servants. Two days later the "headboy" declared to them that she had to send the sweeper away who did not know how to behave properly. He got too near to the other servants and then they needed ritual purification in the temple. If she did not comply they all would leave. "Well," she said, "I will send my sweeper back to Delhi and give him money to feed himself, but who would do his job?"

"We'll find somebody," they replied. "You give us the money and we get a man who knows his place."

She saw that everything was well swept, but could not see a sweeper. "Where is he?" she asked. "Ah," they said, "he comes every night and climbs into the house through the window of the lavatory. No touching of the entrance gate! Then he works, leaves through the window of the lavatory and we throw the money after him."

I once spent several days in Delhi in a boarding house as all hotels were full. (Day of the Republic, January 26th) That place had three rooms with one, two, and three beds, six beds altogether. Yet they had a cook, a waiter, a room-boy, a nightwatchman (a so-called *chokidar*), a sweeper, and a gardener. (The "garden" was at best 150 square yards.) Of course, there was also a manager. On the average half the beds were occupied. When I left I also gave a tip to the sweeper who accepted it crouching with open palms to accept the coins so I did not have to touch him. All this happens in the late Mrs. Indira Ghandi's "Biggest Democracy."

If, however, one goes to a Christian church in India, one sees the men usually in Western clothes (and not with a *dhoti*), the women in nice saris and outside pagan beggars displaying frightening diseases and physical shortcomings. One gets the impression that the Christians form a middle-class, a "bourgeois" community which is, in a way, respected but rather disliked. If, however, one asks the priest or the minister what the social origin of their flock is like, you will be told that they, their parents or grandparents, were mostly untouchables. But they went to Christian schools where they were not only properly instructed but also given a strict moral education. (One finds, therefore Goan Catholic cashiers and pursers all over India.)

Once the Indian Cultural Association gave me for a full week a car and a driver, and usually I got a slovenly driver and a rather dirty car. Yet at the end of the week I got a neatly dressed, intelligent, and circumspect driver with a shining car. He was an excellent organizer, rang up the people when late. When I finally took leave from him I asked him whether he was a Muslim or a Christian. "I am a Methodist," he said proudly. And that was it!

This happened to me again and again. Talking to somebody I always found out after a while without touching the subject of religion whether he was a polytheist or a monotheist. A communicant of the "Church of Southern India" (an Anglican-Presbyterian-Methodist combine), I had met in a plane, told me that he was an architect and a contractor: all his white collar employees had to be Christians. "We're on the same wavelength," he explained.

Yet it is also a fact that Hindus who emigrate – to Malaysia, South Africa, Polynesia – and escape the religious pressures of their country can be very efficient, very prosperous. (Now with apartheid in South Africa practically terminated, they even are sometimes very rich.)

EUROPEAN COLONIES

Americans are very rarely aware that the vast majority of the colonies once owned by the European powers were usually in the red. (It is the loss of the colonies which started the great European prosperity.) Of the colonies of the German *Reich* prior to 1914 only little Togo was in the black. The British before 1939 used to say: "We can lose India any time. It would not hurt us in the least. But if we lose Argentina, it would be a catastrophe." (Who then were the people who became rich in India? The Parsees.)

It was *decolonialization* which largely created (outside of Latin America) the "Third World." Before the end of World War II London, Paris, Amsterdam, Brussels, and Lisbon were responsible for the welfare of the world's "underdeveloped" areas. Today we see Washington and, to a much lesser degree, Moscow being blackmailed by the "liberated nations" who have the greatest difficulty to stand on their own feet. (Latin America is in an agony ever since the 1820's.)

In Brazil I stayed with a friend who had become a refugee from Czechoslovakia and came to Brazil with a very few thousand dollars. With this modest sum he established a "factory" in a quonset hut where he "manufactured" primitive paper bags for air passengers suffering from nausea.

I watched him "presiding" in that shed. He had about ten employees and intervened constantly in their work. "Glue together only three sides!" he had to shout. "Cut that paper straight!" "Put that pot with glue over to the other side!" "You want to go to the toilet? OK. I'll give you five minutes, if you're not back, you're fired." Needless to say that he could never take a vacation. An overseer? He would pay him five times what he pays to a worker, but if he is good, he would be snatched away from him by a bigger company.

THE EUROPEAN COUNTRIES

Commercialism? Industriousness? There are nations gifted for it, as, for instance, the Chinese or, this might surprise you, the Italians. Italy, at the present moment, is economically perhaps one of the soundest countries in Europe even if her government owes money right and left. Italy has a huge number of family businesses and Italy's economic center, the Milan stock exchange, shows a stock index 46 percent over that prior to the October shock of 1987. (This was in Fall 1988.) These family enterprises are small or only medium size, but the "family" is not just dad and mom, but also the children, aunts and uncles, cousins of the first, second, and third degree with their spouses, godfathers, and godmothers. There might be no unions. Everybody trusts everybody else, but one is certainly not over-honest about the taxable revenues. To a south, central or east-European the State is the enemy. The time of beloved monarchs is over, and he who would speak about the "Majesty of the Law" would earn a belly-laugh. In spite of organized vice (which is also a family affair) the Italians are basically a sound people, much sounder than the Germans, who are a relatively sick people; observe Italian Fascism, an infinitely milder disease than National Socialism. By now Italian society has become acquisitive but the quality of life is still placed higher than just living standards. But what about the Italian Communists? They still exist but do not take their Communism too seriously. (Investigated more closely, it was as a rule an inverted anarchism. Communist parents usually saw to it that their children got a Catholic instruction in school.)

Most, but not all of it, is true of Spain. There the work ethics have increased by leaps and bounds. The Spaniards not only have found out that there are so many nice gadgets to buy and that the surest way to buy them is to make money, more money. They can be excellent workers of high skill. I have known German entrepreneurs who were inclined to fire German workers to hire Spaniards. The Lottery in Spain no longer plays the role it did in the past.

Yet even within Spain there are sizable differences in the *gana de trabajar*, the disposition for work. The Catalans work harder and are richer than the Castilians and look down on them as backward lazybones. The Castilians in turn think that the Catalans are not courageous warriors and are softies. These feelings even were represented in Cuba. There is a sad folksong among Cuban Blacks which expressed the longing not to be black but white even if one only be a Catalan. (Yet Catalonia has a wonderful cultural and artistic past, and is still an industrial leader.)

It is interesting to note that there is today a real shift in Europe. In the Seventeenth Century we have seen a turn of power and wealth from the South to the North. This was perfected in the Eighteenth Century. Today the North is starting visibly to lose ground. (The East loomed very large at the beginning of this century and still does militarily although economically socialism put the brakes on that evolution. The economic growth between 1890 and 1914 was in Russia greater than in the United States and frightened the heart of Europe.) Today, however, we witness the curious fact that the per capital GNP in France as well as in Austria is higher than in Britain. Even under the "Iron Lady," who is mainly mending fences and with a certain success trying to reverse the trend, Great Britain is today a relatively poor country where the trade unions within the frame of a provider state have ruined the nation more severely than Hitler ever dreamt to do.

The Continental countries, on the other hand, have become more materialistic. Still, the quality of life (as opposed to the living standards) in the South continues to be high and therefore the Scandinavian, British, Dutch and North-German tourists go to Italy, but the Italian tourists go mainly to Spain, France and Austria. The fine foods, the good wines, great art, animated conversation (even the pleasant climate) are more concentrated in the South where, significantly, there is also more mental health.

Two American firms have tried to make a tabulation of life quality in the world – not of living standards. Both of these companies placed Denmark on the top which is not so surprising because Denmark is precisely the country which offers what the average American expects to get – at home. For the second choice one company chose Italy, the other one Austria. The United States figured way below. (At the same time it must be admitted that if living standards are far down, life quality also will suffer. There is a certain interconnection.)

FAR EAST

High work ethics? We get it in a large part of Europe, in North-America, and also in the Far West where you have not Christian but Confucian ethics. These are based on CHU-KO loyalty and filial piety, two ideals close to each other. Yet the filial piety is directed not only towards your parents, your teacher, your emperor but also towards your boss, your employer. CHU-KO also implies work ethics. In Japan a man who changes his job more than once in his lifetime easily loses his friends because they think that one cannot be a friend of a person who has no loyalty to his firm. "He is a stranger to loyalty," they will say. "How can we trust him?"

In Japan the work ethics have also been beaten literally into the people. I once spent a whole afternoon with Prince Mikasa, the youngest brother of Emperor Showa (Hirohito), twenty years the junior of the Tenno. He is a world-wide known scholar, a specialist in the history of Asian religions. I spoke with him about a large variety of subjects, but my main subject was the work ethics of Japan.

He told me that after the arrival of the Europeans, who were primarily Catholic missionaries, the Japanese also saw their ships with guns and heavy ordnance, men with big black beards and muskets. They were afraid to be conquered and decided that the country must, therefore, be armed to the teeth.

At the same time also a great political change took place. The Emperor had become, to all practical purposes, a holy cow. He resided in Kyoto but was so sacred that, if he needed a haircut, he had to pretend to be asleep while the barber did his job. He could not have willingly given away a part of his body, and the barber, as a "thief," was punished symbolically.

All real power was now vested in the nobility – the daimyos with their samurais, yet headed by the Shogun who resided in Yedo (which today is Tokyo). They established a totalitarian regime with everything in the service of defense. Taxes were sometimes as high as 80 percent of the income (or the harvest) and he who did not pay was swiftly beheaded. The size of the houses for every estate was exactly prescribed. The population had to be fixed at 30 million people and farmers were permitted two children only. The third child had to be suffocated after birth which they called *mabiki*, that is, "thinning out." Thus in disciplining the Japanese and in making them such eager beavers at work, the Confucian principles alone were not responsible.

FINLAND

Take the case of the Finns. Their early medieval ancestors had no political unity, no rulers; they lived "fraternally" in small associations and borrowed things from each other without asking. The Swedish conquerors, however, had a very different notion of private property. They cut off a hand of whoever "expropriated" a useful object. The Finns thus became the most honest people in Europe. When travelling around Finland as a young man by rail, I just put my suitcase in some corner of the station and it was unthinkable that it would have been removed by the evening when I returned. Ethics can be beaten into people!

WORK ETHICS AND COMMERCIALISM

Work ethics and the gift for commercialism thus vary all over the globe. The nations and the races, the ethnic and the religious groups are decidedly not made of one piece. Race and ethnicity are not the same thing, but both play a role. The Germans are divided in tribes (with different accents) and they have different qualities, talents, tastes, and blind spots. The Austro-Bavarians live in Bavaria and Austria, the Alemannic Germans in Southwest Germany, Alsace, Switzerland, and westernmost Austria, in the little federal state of Vorarlberg. They are Germans. They are Catholics. They are Alpine. But they work harder, are more devout, are richer, have higher living standards, are more progressive. (Physically they do not look differently, though you can identify them if they open their mouths.)

Industrial and agrarian production on one hand and commercialism are not the same. This is also true of the Far East. The Chinese are more commercially minded than the Japanese; the Japanese jokes about the Chinese resemble very much the Continental jokes about the Hebrews. The Chinese are extremely sharp businessmen and very tough negotiators, but they are honest. I have known businessmen in Hong Kong who made their contracts by telephone. No written agreements were required. Business rests on credit and "credit" means "trust." I once asked a trader in Hong Kong: "Why are you all so honest? What you have in China is philosophy at the top and superstition, even gross superstition at the bottom. There is a very thin layer of religion between the two. We in Europe know that dishonesty is sinful."

The Chinese laughed. "Only honesty pays. A dishonest man in our eyes is just *stupid*. He might make a few killings but, finally, he lands in the poorhouse."

I never had anything to do with Hebrew diamond dealers in Antwerp or in the Netherlands. They are world-famous for their honesty. (I do not know how religious they are.) The Confucian philosophy is highly "practical." It rests on common sense. It is not a religion, except for simple, ignorant people who literally worship Confucius. Actually, you could be a Christian and a Confucianist at the same time, but certainly not a Hinduist.

EXPROPRIATION

Needless to say that poor work ethics and a lack of commercial know-how can work havoc in the political field. There are countries where the masses live in dire poverty while a few people are enormously rich. These are "perverts" who really want to work hard and they become rich because there are so few competitors. As a result you get social pyramids with a very broad basis, but it suddenly shrinks and goes up in a long, very thin needle. Envy and revolutionary stirrings are the result. The cry can be heard: "We have been exploited! We want social justice!" The Leftist revolutionary reformers want to establish "Social Justice" by breaking that needle, melting it, and pouring the contents over the indigent "exploited" masses.

The result of such an operation can well be calculated in advance. It just won't affect the living standards of the many but will destroy an intelligent, hard working top layer which, to find better conditions, will emigrate and leave their country to a Marxist *nomenklatura.*

As to an expropriation of the rich, they made such an estimate in Germany in 1958. Remember: in 1958, Germany at that time was already rather prosperous and an income-limit of 1,000 DM was proposed. Every *Pfennig* above that limit was to have gone into a jackpot from which every single German should get an equal share. The result? Each German would have received an additional nickel a day! A similar procedure in a country like Ecuador or Nicaragua might have meant a cent or less than a cent.

No way for the individual out of poverty in the Third World? I still remember a mestizo in a fur coat asking for an *apartment* in a three-star hotel in Bogota. He had to sign his name in the registration book which the room clerk offered to him. He made three x-es. Obviously he came from the lowest layers of the population but had brains, and energy. It is a grim fact that the

Third World has by now been living for decades from loans provided by the industrial West. Immense, not repayable sums have been given to them. Yet the solution to the problem of the Third World is to cease to live from handouts, not to talk about endlessly recutting a cake, but to bake a *bigger* cake!

LIBERATION THEOLOGY

Unforgettable to me is the encounter with a Bolivian priest who had fallen for the Liberation Theology. His main theme was "exploitation."

"When I listen to you, Father," I said to him, "I think that you see in your country something like a cell in a prison. Of its four inmates three are wretched, thin pick-pockets, whereas the fourth one is a muscular, brutal murderer who deprives his fellows in the cell of half their rations. He is getting stronger all the time, the others get weaker and weaker."

"Yes, exactly, that's the situation here!"

"My dear Father! There is no analogy to the situation in that cell and to a free economy in a free country. In that cell are four stomachs, four walls and a lavatory...in a free country there are labor unions and collective bargaining. That includes Bolivia."

"Yet the inequalities! Directors of our companies get enormous salaries...."

"Well, until or unless they bury their salaries, which I doubt they do, these monies will profit the entire economy. Big incomes either land in banks and these give credits to various enterprisers or they are used for purchasing goods...."

"Luxury goods!"

"What's wrong with that? They also have to be manufactured or they go into services and these have to be paid for. Through innumerable blood vessels the incomes of the rich go down to the poor!"

"They don't always. They are invested by banks in New York, London, Zurich or Amsterdam...."

"Precisely. But why? Because all 'dynamic' parties here have the word 'expropriation' written in large letters on their banners. Money is nowhere safe in Latin America. Last, but not least, it is precisely your Liberation Theology which is nothing but Marxism with a thin sauce of Bible citations torn out of their context, which frightens the local entrepreneur and terrifies the foreign investor – and if the latter ever has the temerity to trust the Latin American economy he is quickly denounced as an exploiter only interested in 'profits'! What your 'Liberation Theology' lacks is the knowledge of sound economics."

Yet there is something else lacking in Latin America and this is the teaching of the natural virtues by the Church. There is, at present, such an overabundance of political, sociological, psychological, and bad economical sermonizing in the Catholic churches in Latin America that a growing number of the faithful rather go to Evangelical churches to hear the word of God. In the older days emphasis was given to very marginal aspects of the faith: novenas, pilgrimages, wearing of medals, oddly assembled prayers – all very fine, but the preaching of the natural virtues was so very often neglected: "Save money," "Care for your family," "Do not commit fornication and adultery," "Do not get drunk," "Avoid all drugs," "Don't steal and don't lie," "Work regularly!"

A first rate scholar I know, Professor Fredrick B. Pike of Notre Dame University, took some years ago a sabbatical, visited Chile, wrote a book about it and filled it with the usual cliches. Today he is sorry that he ever wrote and published it. Six years later he took another sabbatical, went to Peru, but there, suddenly, the scales feel from his eyes. In a notable essay published in *The Review of Politics in 1964* under the title "The Modern Church in Peru" he berated the Church for her failings in the past and the Leftist idiocies she so often carries out at present, that is, embracing the "Liberation Theology". Guerilla-priests assassinating soldiers and policemen are often the consequence of this attitude. The Evangelical sects (U.S. financed) and even the Communists have in the past preached the natural virtues better than our Church did.

LACK OF ECONOMIC EDUCATION

What we see in Latin America is a "Liberation Theology" promulgated by clerics and laymen without a solid economic education. There was a Dominican, the late Father Joseph Lebret, an important co-author of Papal Encyclicals, who told the seminarians in Sao Paulo (I heard it from a most reliable witness): "If you ask me, young men, whether I believe that God backs the capitalists or the communists, I must tell you, that he is rather on the side of the communists. And if you ask me now if I am sad about this state of affairs, I tell you honestly that I am not!" Well, we had Cardinal Casaroli who told Castro in Havana "We too have read Marx and learned a lot from him?" (What I might ask? Antisemitism? Hatred of religion? Bad economics?) In Latin America, as a matter of fact, there are simple-minded Catholics who get sick and tired of hearing from the pulpit nothing but politics, sociology, economics and hardly the word of God. Thus they join Evangelical sects where, at least, they get messages from the Bible.

SOCIALISM

Socialism, of course, has one very great advantage. It can be explained within 12 to 15 minutes to a junior high school student whereas to explain the workings of the free market system would take a seminar of, at least, one month. I was aware of this in the Soviet Union where everybody, even the few convinced communists, know that we live infinitely better than they do. "Look here," they told me "how is that possible? Over here our economic life is organized along scientific lines. Everything is carefully calculated and planned. In your countries one enterprise is fighting all the other ones. There must be complete chaos. And yet your living standards are so much higher than ours."

Very difficult to give an answer in a nutshell.

Yet socialism is a temptation. It tempted, in a way, already the earliest Christians (read about it in the Acts of the Apostles) and it tempted also the Pilgrim Fathers who nearly perished in the first year after their landing. Simone Weil, this brilliant woman, who died at the very gates of the Church, told us that the preoccupation with "social" problems for the Christian easily accepts a Satanic character. It leads away from God. It is, I would add, in its final socialistic form a perversion of the monastic ideal.

In the USSR people asked me again and again what I thought about their country. I told them it was a godless monastery under a tyrannical atheistic abbot who imposed the monastic vows of poverty, obedience, and not exactly chastity, but certainly a puritanical life on hapless people born inside its walls. We all have a right to marry, to be free, to own property. Those Christians with a real vocation voluntarily renounce these God-given rights. But in the "Socialist Fatherland" neither the vocation nor the free assent is taken into consideration and when I told the people my views, they nodded in assent.

THE PROVIDER STATE

In our investigation we also have to look at the Provider State, wrongly called the Welfare State. The Provider State has almost always a negative influence on work ethics. The "exploitation" of the Provider State for personal benefits is everywhere considerable; if one gets something for nothing, then one is inclined to take it easy with work. Here the origins of the Provider State are not leftish. They came from the Right, from Europe's conservative parties which were profoundly influenced (and partly even financed) by the old, once rich nobility, historically a *landed* aristocracy. And these people always disliked the banker and the manufacturer. Then came the challenge of socialism and the "agrarians" argued that the worker in industry must be protected in old age and sickness just as in agriculture, the laborers in the fields, and the servants in the castle. Since the second and third sons of the aristocracy went either into the army or into the administration, there was also the personnel at hand to carry out a "social" policy which was basically patriarchal (and opposed by classic liberals). Joseph Schumpeter has well presented to us these origins, and it is worthwhile remembering that Bismarck and William II vied in their pro-labor policies. The break between these two was caused *partly* by the Kaiser's more radical view in this matter. He was more "pro-labor" than Bismarck. A similar situation prevailed in Austria. Edward Crankshaw insisted that at the beginning of this century Austria, under the Hapsburgs, was far more "advanced" than Britain in this respect.

Unfortunately this was an erroneous policy, and this for a variety of reasons. Not only because the Provider State weakened the work ethics, not only because it favored the cheating parasite, but also because it enfeebled the family; it reduced the family obligations and thereby decreased its importance. It took responsibilities from the parents to their children and equal responsibilities of the children to their parents. It became the royal road to state omnipotence, the road towards totalitarianism. From careful calculations made in Germany we know that the whole machine of "welfarism" could have easily been served by private "insuring" companies which would offer various forms of security to people working in the most different capacities. These companies would then compete commercially and not politically through parties in parliaments who, as a rule, have only one *real* interest: to get as many votes as possible. Just as one has to carry insurance when driving a car, one might make a law of obligatory insurance when engaging in work, but then it is up to the individual to choose the type of insurance desired. The live forces of society would come into play, not the ubiquitous state. And, finally, in emergencies, – please, don't be shocked! – even charity. (A "religious" motive? Indeed!)

CONCLUSION

In summing up let us have a final look at the "Third World." The Far East (with the exception of "liberated" Vietnam) is no problem. Japan, Korea, Taiwan, Hong Kong, Singapore are all very poor in raw materials; they all had a very late start in industrial development; they are all "overpopulated" (Taiwan, two thirds the size of Switzerland, has three times its population); but they emphatically do not belong to the "Third World." When China breaks with Communism, this huge, intelligent and industrious nation might become a world leader. Only Communism puts the brakes on it. Famous is the old joke: Castro asks Brezhnyev whether it is true that Communism wants to bolshevize the entire globe. "Of course," Brezhnyev replies. "This is symbolized by our coat of arms." "Fine," says Castro. "But where, then, will you buy your wheat?" Three percent of the Americans are feeding half the world, nearly 30 percent of the denizens of the Soviet Union are farming but cannot even feed their own country.

Yet how can we teach the Third World to become more prosperous? To work harder? To organize more efficiently? To make matters worse, the Third World always wants to be as modern as modern can be and thus they choose socialism combined with republican democracy quickly evolving into rank tyranny. (The most recent, the "youngest" republics are Iran, Afghanistan, and Ethiopia!)

And Latin America? Is it the task of the Catholic Church to teach there a "practical materialism"? The answer is not so easy. Is it not the primary duty of the Church to save souls and to be a spiritual leader – and not to engage in economics, sociology and, least of all, in politics? Nothing has been more tragic than the role of the Church in politics. Our Lord Himself had neatly divided the two spheres, Caesar's and God's. With this problem before our eyes, let us terminate the lecture.

DISCUSSION

Question: (From the floor): You said that the living standards in Spain and Italy have greatly increased and I'm wondering to what this could be at-

tributed? What has changed? And has religion
played a part in the change of work ethics in the
past decades?

Erik von Kuehnelt-Leddihn:

No, I would not say so. I have to admit, with regret, that
religion played no part in that change. It is rather the fact that the
material appetites had been whetted. All people are now literate,
they read the advertising in the papers and see goods they want
to buy on television. The southern societies have become acquisitive and the famous story about the railroad porter who was asked
to carry a load and replied: "No thanks," *ho mangiato*, "I have eaten
already" is no longer true.

Very interesting is the case of Spain. The country was in 1958
at the brink of total bankruptcy in a state-controlled economy.
Franco, a military man, cherished the idea of an economy central-
ly commanded like an army under a general staff. Yet economically the man stood with his back to the wall. Then a group of
Opus Dei members, among them Ullastres and Lopez Rodo, who
had listened to the lectures of Wilhelm Roepke in the summer
school of the University of Santander, proposed to save Spain
economically by free enterprise. They demanded, however, a
free hand and promised another hard year but then a spectacular
take-off. Franco reluctantly gave way but told the economists:
"Gentlemen, I warn you, you better succeed!" And they succeeded. So Spain, too, had her *milagro economico*.

This had been prepared by the many Spaniards going north, to
France, the Netherlands, Germany, even to Scandinavia where
they acquired skills and became used to disciplined labor. Financial aid also came from the large-scale development of tourism
which brought "hard" currencies to the country whereby expensive machinery could be bought. Today, no longer does the gold
from the Americas come to Spain. Now Spain is giving huge loans
to its former colonies and one can only hope that sometime and
somehow they will be paid back...to the *madre patria*, the mother-

land. (In the United States people never refer to Britain as the motherland.)

In Spain, the family also plays an important role while the near collapse of the family in Latin America is a grave moral handicap which affects the work ethics very strongly. In the Dominican Republic, for instance, 85 percent of the births are illegitimate. These women will have one sexual affair after the other. The result is a matrilineal civilization. The grandmother supervises the brood while the mother is working, but her authority is rather sketchy and frequently the grandchildren will not even go to school. Machismo plays a sad role in this state of affairs. I was shown a gentleman at a party in Santo Domingo who boasted about his dad — thanks to his father he had over a hundred brothers and sisters. In Peru the situation is better, but not much better. There is really no such thing as an "undisciplined family" — it would fall asunder.

Question: Professor, I'm a little bothered by your charac-
                 terization of the Japanese as workers. Maybe I
                 missed something in there or maybe there's a
                 point that you could expand a bit more. What
                 bothers me is your emphasizing that the
                 work ethic was beaten into the Japanese,
                 that it was a defense imperative against the
                 West, you make it sound as though much of
                 their industriousness is based upon a rather
                 passive slave psychology, which certainly
                 could not explain the expansion of the Japanese
                 economy today. Would you be able to expand
                 on any other qualities that you see charac-
                 terizing the Japanese that would carry us just
                 a little further than just a response to commands
                 from above? Robots certainly do not make crea-
                 tive workers.

Erik von Kuehnelt-Leddihn:
Yes, but you have not paid a hundred percent attention to what I have said.

From The Floor:
All right. But I am listening now.

Erik von Kuehnelt-Leddihn:
I mentioned the Confucian ethics, the CHU-KO and I said that "on top of this" the Japanese had the experience of the Bakufu, the "Rule of the Tent," the military dictatorship of the Shogunate. There has not been a *bakufu* in Korea or in China. In other words, I characterized the entire Far East in terms of the Confucian ethics and on top of it − as I have said "on top of it!" − the experience of the *bakufu*. In other words, there are *two* elements which contributed to Japanese work ethics and not one.

I have visited Japan seven times and lectured there extensively. Yet I want to mention one particular lecture with a most interesting aftermath. I spoke about economics in Europe and casually mentioned Max Weber's "Protestant Work Ethic." In the discussion the first, and last, question I was confronted with was: "Where does one get ethics from? From what can they be derived?" As you can imagine my answer did not make them too happy because it was a Christian answer. I insisted on God's revealed word as the only source of ethics *binding in conscience*. From the observation of nature, one cannot get very far: there dog eats dog. The "Natural Law" is a piece of human constructivism (however much beloved by many theologians). The discussion lasted over three hours.

The reason for this extraordinary interest can be found in the fact that responsible Japanese are deeply worried about a slow but certain decline of general ethics. This is being felt in the schools. The incredible atrocities committed by the Sekigunha, the "Red Army factions," a Marxist terrorist organization, was a real danger signal. Corruption in government circles also confirms this evil evolution. Young people start to say: "Confucius was an admirable, very nice and cultured Chinese gentleman who lived 2,500 years ago, but why – oh why? – should I be obliged to follow his moral propositions?" Ethics ought to be authoritative, but if one no longer honors the originator – what then?

The next day I received a visit from the Secretary of the *International Economic Association*, before which I had lectured. I received from him a long, thin envelope and in it a notable amount of Yen bills as a sign of gratitude. "This was the most important discussion we ever had in our group," my visitor said. Thus it was not my lecture, but the nature and content of the discussion which had moved the rather elitist public.

FORUM

SOURCES OF NEW WEALTH IN THE 21ST CENTURY

MODERATOR
Dr. Jerry D. Todd

Dr. Armand J. Guarino

Dr. Phyllis B. Siegel

Dr. John P. Walter

PANELISTS

MODERATOR
Dr. Jerry D. Todd

Dr. Todd received his Ph.D. from the University of Wisconsin in 1968, specializing in insurance and finance. He taught at the University of Wisconsin, the University of North Carolina-Chapel Hill, and the University of Texas at Austin, before coming to St. Mary's University in 1981. He is the author of over 40 books and articles on risk and insurance, has served as consultant to the federal government, the Texas State Board of Insurance, and various insurance industry trade associations regarding insurance economics and rates, and many businesses and public bodies on risk management. He was president of the American Risk and Insurance Association, whose membership consists of risk and insurance professors and insurance industry executives from around the world, in 1989-1990. He teaches risk management, insurance, employee benefits, and financial counseling courses at St. Mary's University.

Dr. Armand J. Guarino

Dr. Guarino received his B.S. from Harvard University and the Doctorate from Tufts University. His Post Doctoral Fellowship was served at Massachusetts Institute of Technology.In 1972 Dr. Guarino became Dean of the Graduate School of Biomedical Sciences at the University of Texas Health Science Center in San Antonio, Texas. During this time he was also Special Assistant to the President for Academic Services with UTHSC. From 1974 through 1988 Dr. Guarino served as Dean of the School of Allied Health Services.Dr. Guarino is currently Vice President of Research and Chief Scientist with the Biomedical Development Corporation in San Antonio, Texas.

Dr. Phyllis B. Siegel

Phyllis B. Siegel is the Chief Executive Officer of Biomedical Development Corporation. Under her management, Biomedical Development Corporation has received over $1,000,000 in SBIR funds and expanded from a single product company to a scientific incubator developing products in San Antonio, El Paso, Dallas, and Galveston. Dr. Siegel is a licensed attorney and certified public accountant. She graduated first in her class from St. Mary's School of Law and is listed in Who's Who in American Law and Who's Who in Emerging Leaders.

Dr. John P. Walter

Businessman and Scholar. Senior management executive in the Oil and Gas industry for over 20 years with top level management experience in decision making and problem solving. Extensive background in technology transfer both domestically and internationally. Foreign living experience with extensive foreign travel and business experience. Currently CEO of a Texas based high tech start up company in the area of avionics and consultant to leading U.S. and foreign private and public businesses. Received a Ph.D. in economics from the University of Notre Dame in 1970. Thereafter was a Fulbright Scholar at Universidad Catolica, Quito, Ecuador. Serves on the Board of Directors of a number of private for-profit and non-profit organizations. Is the author of a book and over 45 articles published in scholarly journals and business publications covering a broad range of planning problems and business issues in the U.S. and Latin America. Has been recognized by a number of Honor Societies, including the International Honor Society Delta Tau Kappa for his contributions to the development of social science theory.

SOURCES OF NEW WEALTH IN THE 21ST CENTURY

MODERATOR
Dr. Jerry D. Todd:

This panel discussion is on the sources of new wealth in the Twenty-First Century.

We have a distinguished and knowledgeable panel. I will introduce them one at a time prior to their comments. We will have a general discussion following all three comments.

Dr. Armand J. Guarino has had thirty years of academic and research experience. He is Professor Emeritus and former Dean of the Graduate School of the University of Texas Health Science Center. He was Chairman of the Department of Biochemistry and Special Assistant to the President for Academic Services. He is currently the Chief Scientist of the Biomedical Development Corporation.

Dr. Armand J. Guarino:

They call me the long-winded Italian at the University, so after a while, if you want to ring a bell, I will not be offended.

I'm afraid I don't have a concrete message that you might take back with you in terms of the great future in this or that field, and I am not even sure how you want to define "wealth." I want to define "wealth" in the broadest sense — opportunities, cultural opportunities, not just material or physical wealth.

I taught at medical schools in both of my academic careers, and I guess that anytime I get the pulpit, I have to kind of sound off on some of the things that have been bothering me that are going on in health profession education. It really relates to health care delivery; second, and closely tied to that, are the ethical aspects of health care delivery; and the third area that I would like to talk about I can call geriatric medicine for the increasing population of people in this country who seem to be taking over in terms of the older and older population versus the younger population who are paying for it.

HEALTH CARE DELIVERY

I am not an economist. I am a biochemist by training. But I am told the latest figure seems to be that health care delivery is occupying now about twelve percent of the gross national product. To me, that is a lot of money, big business, and it is business.

I see in the curriculum of the medical school and the health professional school both addressing the issue of the ethics of health care delivery. It is very easy to teach the scientific aspects of medicine, and yet we don't sensitize the students when they are with us to the potential costs of the decisions they will make. It is not a large part of the curriculum of this medical school or any other medical school to provide economics courses, but we should sensitize them to the issues of economics. It is going to cost somebody.

I am also concerned about the ethical aspects, and I think you know what I am talking about. Courts are making decisions today about when life starts and when life stops. Very little in formal education is addressed to how long you keep a patient alive, how literally we interpret the Hypocratic Oath. And these issues are not being addressed in most medical schools and in most health professional schools. But yet these two issues will be the two major problems that will face the health care professional person in the future.

The science of medicine is easy today. I suspect you could put dad in the corner with tubes and IVs in his arms and keep old dad alive forever. But is that living?And who is going to pay for that? Those issues bother me.What I want to talk about is really an industry that exists, namely, the health care delivery industry. It is a big industry in terms of dollars involved, lots of dollars. But I can tell you that it needs a major overhaul in terms of how we are going to proceed in the future. We were just talking during the coffee break about one of the things that bothers me most, and I played a role in this. We emphasize science to the incoming health professional. I said I don't want a physician holding my hand with great compassion and humanistic traits while I expire if I don't have to expire. So the first goal is clinical competency.

But what about the other aspects in terms of the ethical aspects? I think that in this industry in the future, right around the corner, I see great potential for economists, for instance, maybe beginning to play a role in the formal education of health professionals, and if not in the formal education, then certainly in the pre-professional education.

There is no question that the health care professions have to be sensitized to the costs of the decisions that they make. Maybe that means that in the near future we should encourage people to go into the field of economics. Maybe there is now a whole new era – medical economics – rather than having them go into banks or whatever else economists go into but certainly to be involved in the economics of health care.

It is big business. Uncle Sam obviously is going to pay a big part of the bill, and if Uncle Sam is going to pay the bill, then Uncle Sam is going to set the ground rules, and the ground rules are already being set. The medical profession will not set the ground rules. Terms are used as "socialized medicine," and you see terms like DRG, disease-related groups, and Uncle Sam is going to determine what the doctor is going to get, what the hospital is going to get. All of that is going to be dictated by people who make the decisions that an appendectomy is worth so much or a hysterectomy is worth so much and so forth and so on and not a penny more. There is going to be a whole new class of people who are going to have to monitor those decisions after they have been made by somebody.

The Federal Government has a great tendency to lay down ground rules but not develop an infrastructure to monitor the ground rules. I see the potential for bringing the humanists and the social scientists back into the hard science.

COLLECTIVELY-MADE DECISIONS

The courts are making decisions about life and death that should be made collectively by hard scientists, by the legal profession, by humanists, by people who are trained in ethics. These are decisions that should be collectively made and not made by one group where one group advocates it and then lets somebody else do it.

We need to turn out a health professional who is concerned with what it is going to cost for the delivery of health care. Finally, the decisions ought to be made in a way that all parties concerned have something to give – the housewife, the man in the street. I know a pediatrician who told me of three children with the same type of disease who have been treated three different ways:one, to die peacefully; another, to fight for the last breath of life; and the third one was somewhere in between – depending on the decision of all the people concerned with the life of that child and the child himself. That sort of thing I think has to be allowed in the curriculum of the medical school and also in the pre-professional school if we are going to address adequately these important issues.

GERIATRIC CARE

Geriatric care. People in my age bracket are taking over the world. I am proud my generation is turning out to have some political power. Nobody gets into office anymore who is not concerned about old people like me, and they don't get there if I perceive they plan to shut off my Social Security or my disposable income, but yet a younger population has to pay for us. I think right now only about five percent of the cost of health care is going into nursing homes. In the future that will swell. There is going to be a whole industry that is going to have to find ways to address these problems because the science of medicine perpetuates lots of old fogies like me at the age that I am, and it is going to continue that way. We have all those problems, and we have not developed an infrastructure for those problems, so I see great potential for whole industries to emerge to change the whole pattern of health care in the way it is delivered, especially in the problems of geriatric care. It is economic, and I can't give you a full picture of what those agencies are going to be, but I will tell you that they will have to be there, and the issues will have to be addressed.

RELIGION

One thing that I feel good about is I see in this country a re-emergence, a little bit, of religion. I think of the case of my own children, whom I thought we brought up religiously, but we must have missed the boat somewhere, but now there seems to be a re-emergence of interest on their part. That quality of life was late in coming. Then, too, I see more interest in the current generation and my generation toward the quality of life that embodies religion, and that is encouraging because it means that we have more compassion and feeling for the less fortunate of the world. That is a little bit of what the health profession needs right now, and I think that is healthy, instead of leaving the world to take care of itself.

I don't sleep well, so I turned the TV on at 2:00 o'clock in the morning, and what did I hear but a professor at the Harvard Divinity School saying that there ought to be more concern for the emotional care that students in medical school used to be taught to have. I think that is healthy. I think in my own family, my own children, I see more concern for the homeless, the arousal of the spirit of volunteerism. What can we do even on a volunteer basis to cultivate this attitude? It seems to me that something is beginning to happen in this country in terms of caring for the whole man.

Since I am not quite sure how it will happen, I can't define for you an industry that tomorrow, if you go into it, you will make big bucks, if you are talking about financial wealth, but I do see an industry that can use a lot of compassion, and which involves a lot of individuals who take pleasure in helping their fellowman. To me, that is a rich industry, and we should do all we can to advance it.

I wish I had a magic formula for how to do it, but I do hope that we will have a medical profession eventually down the line that is still clinically competent, that is sensitized to the cost of the decisions that they will have to make, and that, then, will make those decisions on broad ethical and humanistic considerations. Basically that is what I wanted to say, and I am grateful to have had the opportunity to say it.

Dr. Todd:
Thank you.

Dr. Todd:
Dr. Phyllis Siegel earned her B. A. in English at the University of Texas in Austin and her Doctorate at Saint Mary's University, where she graduated first in her class. She also studied Accounting. She worked for several years as an SEC accountant at Tesoro Petroleum Corporation. Today she is President of the Biomedical Development Corporation in San Antonio.

Dr. Phyllis B. Siegel:
I am going to take a little more limited view of the sources of new wealth and talk about one particular source and how it is evolving.

SMALL BUSINESSES

The management and development of small business and the resurgence of small business in the United States are developing new products and adding to the wealth of the nation. From 1974 to 1986, small businesses with less than fifteen employees generated 15.2 million jobs in the United States. They accounted for fifty percent of all the new innovations in the last thirty years.

Our company, Biomedical Development Corporation, is an example of one of those small businesses. I would like to give you a little background. We started in 1984, and since that time our company, as it has developed, and its affiliates have generated fourteen jobs for the San Antonio economy. Now, these jobs range from high school students and then high school graduates to Ph.D.s, who are also involved in our company.

Our goal is to develop science to improve the human condition. We only work with products or sciences with potential to improve our health. We are all the way from basic research or the use of the basic research to developing products. We are interested in commercializing some items, testing them, getting them through the regulatory authorities, and then introducing them into the marketplace.

We believe that transferring technology takes a variety of skills which are generally not held by scientists alone or businessmen alone. And because of this, we structured our company in a manner which allows the scientists to participate on a project-by-project basis as the science becomes applicable. And there is a great interplay between the small business entity and the developing of new products.

It is my personal opinion that small businesses are flourishing because people want more personal autonomy. Large institutions, including governmental institutions and educational institutions, do not allow the individual freedom for the entrepreneurs to do the things that they want to do every day and to develop in a more unstructured sort of way.

Secondly, technology is allowing those entrepreneurs to do this in small businesses, where years ago we would have to have so much more capital to start a new business. In a little company like ours, we not only envision a new product, develop the science on it, but we can take care of our own administration. Through the use of computers, we do our own accounting programs; we do our own tax returns; we answer to all the regulatory authorities with very few employees. Ten years ago you would have to have had an entire accounting department, maybe thirty people, to take care of thirty individual products that we are developing. Today, instead, we can concentrate this in a smaller number of people, and these people, through the use of computers and programming in telecommunications, are able to provide that service to the company. We not only take care of that but we even produce newsletters, where only a few years ago we would have had to have a print shop to do that type of work.

So between the two of them, we are able to accomplish a lot more, and, therefore, we can accomplish a lot more on less capital, and can take our capital and spend our time on things to expand the basic business, and can take our capital and think about things we never thought about ten years ago. We can think about exporting. We can worry about or think about or consider how we are going to get our products in countries that have little inventive industry, when we know the product is good but the infrastructure in that country is not in place to deliver the product. And these are the things that we are able to think about. I would like your interaction, after John speaks, on how you feel that small business and the emergence of small business as a creator of wealth will affect our nation and society. Thank you.

Dr. Todd:

Thank you.

Dr. John P. Walter earned his Ph.D. at the University of Notre Dame. In 1971 he was a Fulbright Scholar and was appointed Visiting Professor to the National University in Peru. He was also Guest Professor at the National University in Quito. Until the last few years, Dr. Walter was associated with Shell Oil Company on the corporate planning staff. He has also been a research economist in the Federal Reserve System. He is an Adjunct

Professor in our School of Business and Administration. Until recently he was Vice President of the Texas Research and Technology Foundation. Currently he is President of Radar Guidance Incorporated.

Dr. John P. Walter:

I do want to try to stick to the theme of the Conference, the sources of wealth and the causes of poverty. Interestingly enough, this isn't the first time this question has been raised. Along about 1776 a really interesting book, which, in my mind still remains as a classic, called "An Inquiry into the Wealth of Nations," written by Adam Smith, obviously raised the same question: What is the source of the wealth of nations? Therefore, what is the source of new jobs and income and enhanced material living? Those questions were asked in that book, the same questions that are asked within our program for today and the theme of the Conference.

THE SOURCES OF WEALTH

Adam Smith was a moral philosopher turned economist, and after surveying the world and doing an enormous amount of research in what was the world of his day, he concluded that it was — and pay close attention to this — the proper, underline "proper," organization, underline "organization," of goods and services that is the source of the wealth of a nation. So we already know that answer, and I would allege that it remains much the same today.

Smith allows, in conclusion, "And these resources are most productively organized if left to their own best interest," which meant Free Enterprise.

Now, while he wrote a classic, a classic in a School of Economics, Adam Smith, I think, had an inherent flaw in his thinking because of the environment in which he wrote, and I think that flaw is what I call the "fixed pie" theory. I think one of our problems today is that we still operate on the fixed pie theory, and it hurts us, and it hurts us a lot. I'll get back into that, but I want to talk first about "proper." Keep in mind, again, that Adam Smith was a moral philosopher, and I take that "proper" to mean "ethical." And I think that ethics, private business ethics, are extremely important, if not essentially important, to the proper functioning of the Free Enterprise system.

Let's take the word "organization" that I asked you to underline. Organization — what is that? That's knowledge; that's culture. The ability to organize stems from knowledge. That came back to haunt people later, and we still don't understand it today, and I would like to talk a little more about that, too.

But I think Smith was right that the wealth of a nation stems from these resources being organized properly in a Free Enterprise system because if you look at the world today, those countries that have generated the most wealth for their population are those countries that have the freest markets, and those countries that are by far the poorest are those that are still experimenting with Marxist and Socialist economic theories. That is a matter of statistical evidence.

LOSING COMPETIVENESS

Today what I see in the United States is that there are tremendous opportunities for new products and new companies and new income, but we are not, as a nation, taking advantage of that. No doubt, we are the fountain of new ideas for the world, but we are not drinking at our own fountain. Interesting faces are showing up at that fountain and drinking of our endeavors. They are called Japanese, the Taiwanese, the Koreans, and don't forget the Europeans are coming back to that fountain, and we are not doing such a good job. We are becoming totally uncompetitive. We are the largest debtor nation in the world.

We have serious problems that will impact on our lifestyle before we leave this world. The problems, I think, running through them very quickly, have their origin in the old "fixed pie" theory that is still with us.

How many times do you hear about income redistribution? Believe me, you don't have to redistribute incomes. Why should you take away from some man or woman who has spent a tremendous part of his/her life generating wealth and give it to somebody who hasn't spent a minute part of his/her life generating wealth?

Somewhere along the line we have to fully understand that the "pie is not fixed." It is infinitely expandable, and if we can properly organize our resources, we can make that pie grow infinitely, and we do not have to redistribute income or rob Peter to pay Paul.

Our government has an enormous redistribution of income program that has not worked, and it won't work. In fact, even under that program, the rich got richer and the poor, poorer, and that is not what it is destined for. Another problem is our culture and our institutions. In our culture our businessmen no longer take on the world. The U. S. businessmen – and I've been in that world for twenty-something years – now back away from the challenge. They are worried about this quarter's bottom line. You can't challenge the world and worry about this quarter's bottom line. That is cultural. That is all that is taught in the universities – worry about the bottom line. Our businessmen come out of the universities trained to worry about the bottom line and the short run. You cannot do that and compete in this world.

Our institutions, our government, have continuously frustrated the free market mechanism. I was talking to a very wealthy man here in the city the other day. I won't give you his name. He's an older gentleman now, but he made it big when he was young.

He said, "It's no longer fun to be rich in this nation."

He said, "When I was younger, you made the money, and then you went out and really enjoyed life, and now the minute you make money, you get a personal IRS man, and he sits there and tries to figure out how he can take that money away from you. "

BUSINESS ETHICS

Institutions take money away and kill the entrepreneurial spirit. We have had a complete breakdown in this country in business ethics, a complete breakdown. I am not so sure we are all aware of how complete that breakdown has been.

But let me ask — I was told to ask you this — is there a course in Business Ethics taught at Saint Mary's?

From The Floor:
Generally.

Dr. Walter:
But just Business Ethics? No. A Catholic institution, no Business Ethics. But it is not unusual because there are no universities teaching that. Oh, I should not say there aren't any, there are several, but there are very, very few. There has been a complete breakdown. You now do what you can get away with and have your attorney take care of it, and that is a very poor way to do business. It is true already that attorneys are running the business machinery of this nation, and that won't work, and it hasn't worked. It's an overhead cost.

KNOWLEDGE AS A RESOURCE

There is a lack of understanding about what our resources really are in this country. We are still thinking that resources are land, labor, and capital. They are not. There is only one resource, and that is "knowledge," and we haven't faced up to that fact yet. If I have coal and I have water, I can drink the water, and I can burn the coal, and you can deplete the coal, and you can deplete the water. But I can take knowledge and put the coal and water together properly and get nylon and rayon, and I can take dollars and continue to expand that coal and continue to expand that water.

But we have given the resource, knowledge, short shrift, particularly in this State, where the first thing to be cut anytime there is a budget cut is Education, and we pay our professors and our high school and grade school teachers slave wages, and yet we turn our children over to them.

The United States is still the fountain of ideas, but we are uncompetitive, and we have to learn anew how to get those ideas to market. We once knew; we have forgotten.

THE CAUSES OF POVERTY

What are the causes of poverty? The causes of poverty, I allege, are the "fixed pie" theories that say you have to take away from those who have and give to those who don't. That results in economic suppression, and that is all that occurs through those theories, the economic suppression of those who do have. It results in the wasting away of the resource, knowledge.

Because I am limited to eight minutes – and I know I'm touching on it, the solution that I see – and unfortunately I won't be able to discuss it with you – is more education. If the source of wealth is knowledge, let's get on with our educational system.

CONCLUSION

We have really gotten to the roots in this country. Let us raise the ethical code. I hope Dr. Guarino is right. I hope that people are showing a renewed interest in religion and ethics because it won't work without them. It won't work if you start a business built upon a what-can-I-get-out-of-it point of view, which is where we are starting today.

Let us offer medical care. I have often thought of, if I had my own island, what I would give the people. I would give them two things, free education and free medical care, and beyond that, I would give them nothing, and I think they would take real good care of themselves.

We need a really serious revision of our tax laws. Our tax laws are killing our business. The Reagan tax cut was nothing but a tax increase, and even some of the smarter people haven't figured that out yet, but that's all it was, and it allowed the IRS under the alias that they are rendering a service, to proceed as they have done before. They are strangling this country. Government regulations are killing the free market.

Let us give our children training in the international business arena in our universities and colleges because that is where we are – we are in an international world, and we are not competitive in it.

Thank you, and I look forward to the discussion with you.

Dr. Todd: We are now open for discussion. I can certainly start it here. I want to ask Dr. Walter about the kinds of education he would propose.

You spoke of education. What types of education would you provide? I heard references to international business and ethics.

I also wonder about how you propose to expand the knowledge base.

Where is there room for technology in your proposal?

Dr. Walter:

Well, I include technology in knowledge. To me, they are one and the same, almost. Knowledge may have a little bit more of a flare to it than technology, but technology springs from knowledge. It comes out of that body of knowledge. But the point is: How do you use that? Knowledge also includes how you use that technology. For example, atomic energy, how do we properly use that? That is knowledge. How do we properly use that technology? I don't think we have answered that question yet and don't show a lot of interest in answering it.

Question: In general, to be competitive, what kinds of education do you propose?

Dr. Walter:

I think you are going to have to increase that across the board and go right down to the grade school level and start getting more science and technology focused in our grade schools and our high schools as well. I don't want to overlook the technical trainings because they are so critical. So we need a good system of technical schools, technical support schools, and I think we have to go back and overhaul our grade school/high school educational system.

What is really interesting is that if you look at students in Asia and look at their enrollments in the universities, the vast majority of them are enrolled in scientific courses. When you look at the United States, you turn that over. The vast majority are enrolled in what I call cafeteria courses, at the risk of insulting some, psychology and stuff like that, which makes you almost a liability when you get out instead of an asset to that whole system of wealth generation.

I think we must either get to the point where we can command science and technology in the curriculum or we have lost our ability to generate wealth in a large degree in this country, and it is pathetic what we are turning out of our schools as students.

Dr. Guarino:

The important part of education, I think, is interest. If we don't love learning, if we don't love the truth, we are not going to bother to study. And, to me, a full sense of truth, the love of truth in all of its aspects, is very important.

We keep looking to Washington to make us interested, to solve our problems, to tell us how to do it, and somehow we try to have faith that they will work out the problems. If we have medical problems here, in the San Antonio area, I can't imagine how Washington could do better as opposed to the resources we have. If we don't know how to put them together, how could Washington do it any better? We have the best. Now, I give you that as one example.

If we are not going to bother to learn how to harmonize our potentials so as to produce an effect, which has to come with knowledge and also our common culture, our values, interest, the whole business of getting a group of people coordinated as a team; then, you know, we don't look at ourselves and take that responsibility upon ourselves, but we are looking for somebody else to do it for us.

Dr. von Kuehnelt-Leddihn:

I want to make just two remarks, as an outsider, as an alien.

As to what Father just said about the renewed interest in religion, I want to mention a book, which is an old book by Richard Hufstedler, entitled "Anti-intellectualism in America." As he points out, there are three sources of anti-intellectualism, but the biggest source is democracy, because learning means nothing of itself. You have a vote for a number of years because you are a citizen, and hopefully if you have a vote for a larger number of years, you may be elected. In other words, knowledge has no kingdom, which was not true in the pre-democratic period prior to, say, 1828; in other words prior to instruction in the French ideology of the revolution.

But the other great handicap I see in America is because, although the Constitution doesn't say so, it is a republic; a republic, as it has become, governed by law but not governed by men, with all of the emphasis on that. Therefore, the legalism, the rise of legalism in America is a serious problem.

Only think about the doctors' burdens of malpractice, which no European would understand for a second, until or unless somebody who has a mental problem who goes three times a week to a psychiatrist hangs himself, and then all the relatives sue the doctor, as an example.

When I came to America for the first time in 1927, I considered my own country in Europe far more legalistic and hidebound by laws than America. It is now the other way round. It is terrifying. In other words, it is this new legalistic approach, about which Robert Lisborne has written a very good book.

Dr. Todd:

Are there other comments?

Dr. Guarino:

Yes, we were talking at the break, and somebody made the point about the medical curriculum. When you say we need to get ethics and economics in the curriculum, the curriculum committee says that is the responsibility of the university at the premed level. We talk to them about what we want our students to know, and they say that is the responsibility of the high school level. What it comes down to − and doubtless to say, it's the truth − is we rely too much on a formalized education system to educate our children and don't do enough ourselves in our homes.

The family was mentioned this morning. I will say that in the thirty-five years I have been in the university system I can always pick out the ones who were brought up in the home where it was fun to read. You show me somebody who was brought up in a home where it was fun to read, and I'll show you an educated person, pretty much. Somehow we have to get back to that. I think in the old days, without the radio and without television, you didn't have anything else to do but to read. I don't care if it was mystery stories. Read whatever is available.

I was going through a trying time learning French, and my professor said to me, "You are terrible."

I said, "I find it very difficult."

He said, "Go to France and live with French people."

I said, "I can't afford it."

He said, "Then, if you don't care for good French books, read trash books, just as long as you read French."

Our students don't know how to read, and somehow we have to instill that. We cannot allow that not to happen. In our educational system, we look at that as someone else's responsibility, and I think one thing we must do down the road is to change that around. Then it will be time to talk about the curriculum because once somebody has learned how to read, then everything is exciting. I don't care if you read murders or the "Great Books" or whatever, everything is exciting, and you can't read enough. I think we cannot rely too much, as we have been, on the universities to teach that. Home is where it should start, in my opinion.

Dr. Todd: One of the books I read last year was Aldous Huxley's, written in July, 1920, I believe, in which he projects life twenty years hence.

Dr. Guarino, if you would project life thirty years hence in the area of health care, what would be the more important changes, in your opinion?

Dr. Guarino:

Well, I am worried about it because I think it is Uncle Sam who will call the shots, whether we like it or not. Nobody else can afford it. And the third party payers will follow suit. Once somebody has decided that it is going to cost $1,500 for an appendectomy, that is all the physician is going to get, and that is all the hospital is going to get.

The medical profession for a long time has abrogated its responsibility. It could have and should have taken a role in the economics of health care delivery; it should have taken a role in malpractice insurance. You cannot find a doctor who will testify against another doctor, but there are a few out there who make it bad for all. And, we ought to sit on those people. And the fact that we do not sit on them raises everybody's malpractice insurance bill. Who pays for this? I just spoke to a neurosurgeon whose malpractice insurance bill was over $100,000 last year. Now, he is not going to pay that. He is going to pass it along to me.

So I think the medical profession particularly needs to get involved. I do not think it is going to happen in my generation, but thirty years down the road they will get involved in it because they will not allow somebody else to call the shots. But they have allowed it to happen, and I am not sure they can get it back.

Let's talk about hospital administration. There is a whole future in hospital administration. We are not talking about physicians anymore. This is on a higher level, janitors and plumbers and the like. Hospitals are bulging. This is a booming big business.

I am very much concerned about the technology. I am a biochemist, and I had a good idea about using magnetic resonance in diagnosing cancer long before somebody else did. I was just too lazy to do it. But the fact of the matter is that not every hospital should have an MRI machine. I mean, it costs $5 million, $10 million, and to keep it going, you have to put patients in it, and you must not put patients in it who don't need it because somebody has to pay the bill for that. We cannot continue to be irresponsible because somebody has to pay for that, and somebody has to start making these decisions.

Now, I can tell you one thing: When Uncle Sam is paying the money, Uncle Sam will call the shots. Now, I am worried about that.

Comment:

I would like to mention one thing. We talked about education. I notice the emphasis on the ground level, the grade school, the primary section. I understand that many teachers now are complaining because we have people like H. Ross Perot telling them how they are supposed to educate. These are businessmen who have never had anything to do with education, and it worries me that they are giving these teachers so much paperwork that they can't do their teaching. They are complaining about that. I wish people would take notice of that.

Comment:

Getting back to Dr. Guarino's remark about the cost of health care in the future. If it winds up in the hands of the United States government, we can look three thousand miles across the Atlantic Ocean and see what happened to our English-speaking cousins in Great Britain, who have had National Health Care for a long,

long time. We know now that there are large waves developing in that scheme. It has contributed certainly to the economic down-fall of Great Britain because of the high cost. But there now is private health care which is moving in the Free Enterprise system and which is quite different and quite unique and quite surprising.

But to lay that aside, since that is another issue, I would like to ask a question. We have heard blame put on government; we have heard blame put on equipment; we have heard blame put on education. But I think our problem is far more fundamental because no nation enjoys any strength without a strong nuclear family, and we have seen the erosion of the nuclear family in these United States for at least two decades and maybe the last three.

I would say that a program that would reinstitute the value of the nuclear family, which is really the cradle for developing standards of behavior, developing love of learning, is badly needed. We should generate an enormous program with business contributing and government contributing. What greater leader could there be than the Church to try to start this wave of a return to values that have their genesis in the nuclear family.

I would hope that some member of the panel would address that problem.

Dr. Todd: Are there any comments from the panel?

I will make one, that overall there are some changes that have been made in the welfare system recently that seem to give some encouragement there in the nuclear family by stopping, denying, benefits based upon the absence of a father, and am sure we could get into some discussions about that if we had the time. But this is an aspect in the development of the nuclear family that we need to consider.

Father Langlinais:

The previous speaker has stolen my thunder about the role of the Church.

It seems to me that the panelists made an effort in their areas of expertise to emphasize moral values and education, which is quite interesting. I think that especially Dr. Phyllis Siegel spoke of the success of small business in generating so many jobs. She spoke in terms of the GNP. I would hope we have the imagination here to look at the law and the hazards of government intervention. An example is a small business that uses imagination to do things on a small scale while big companies buy each other out, which seems to me a futile exercise.

The medical profession, as Dr. Guarino has said, really should take hold of things and clean up its own house because if it doesn't, the government will do it. Here in Texas we talk about Bill 72, by which Mr. Perot and the State Legislature sought to fix education. But why did the professional educators so mess up their world that we turned to the State Legislature to fix it?

You do not know how much trouble you are in until the government attempts to fix your problems. When you talk about the hazards of professional practice, instead of talking about professional standards, you talk about allowing the government to decide how much an appendectomy should cost. The medical profession had better put its act together, or the government will do it as only Washington will do.

The second speaker talked about business ethics. I think we can learn from foreign countries, the way they emphasize science as exact knowledge and differentiate between hard and soft science. It is not a compliment to be considered a soft scientist. Yet we know that other countries – West Germany, Korea, and Japan – are running circles around us by taking our own technologies – and technology, I believe, is the tying together of technical things and knowledge – and we are not putting together with good results what our pioneers in these fields taught us fifty years ago.

We are lazy and concerned with today's bottom line, when we should be putting money in development and teaching people to save. We have a $2.7 trillion debt, which costs us $150 billion a year in interest. We, as a people, seem bent on self-destruction. We are not teaching wealth creation.

Dr. Walter:

Let me make a few comments to pick up on a previous gentleman's statement earlier and yours.

I mentioned in my brief discussion that I thought that technology alone does not exist in a vacuum but is reinforced by culture and institutions, and history is full of cultures destroyed by their technology, and I would hypothesize that the United States is in one of those cultural modes right now where culture is, indeed, in a state of destroying technology. And I haven't yet arrived at the answer as to why we are doing that. I just see that we are doing that with our culture.

But, then, on the other hand, technology has a very interesting way of destroying cultures too, and I want to touch on that.

But I want to drop back and say I don't think it is possible to have a good technological base without discipline. Where you start is discipline in the family unit and by extension of the family unit. For example, when I was in grade school, my mother picked me up every evening after school, and once a week my parents visited with my teacher, and if I had a spanking at school, I got another one at home. Now if you are spanked in school, the teacher is fired. That is a result of an institutional breakdown. And if you have lost basic discipline, then you are going to start destroying your technology.

Now, let's look at that from a different point of view, that sometimes technology destroys cultures. Look at all the women in the work force today. They have, they believe, a right to be there. I know there's a lady up here, and she may hit me before this is over. But why are there so many women in the work force? Because technology literally threw them out of the kitchen. They used to open cans and all that, and they had to go through

all the enormous meal preparation, and they had to have babies.
Now they have birth control pills, electric kitchens, and you can
buy whatever you need in terms of a meal in the supermarket.
There is now no need for them anymore in the kitchen. The whole
thing can be done by pushing a button. Okay. So they were
thrown into the labor market.

But, curiously enough, that may be good because records show
that the two-wage-earner family now is just about as well off as
the one-wage-earner family was in the Fifties because of government interference and the pattern of taxation that has taken hold
in this country. The enormous overhead it now takes to make a
living in this country is tremendous.

Now, I think we have to work our way through this, the fact
that culture does destroy technology and technology does destroy
culture, and come to a final balance to that trade-off and realize
that none of this works outside of a system of discipline. That is
Joseph Schumpeter's disciplined environment. It has to be disciplined enough but not too disciplined. Now, we have, as a
nation, not thought through that problem and have shown no real
interest in doing so.

Dr. Siegel:
I don't think a small business has a real opportunity to do it.
When you have less than fifty employees, most of these rules and
regulations that you have been talking about don't matter because
they don't apply to that small a business. I do think you can set a
tone in a small business and have enthusiasm and produce high
quality.

But the main problem I find in our small business on my part
is that I have to retrain every high school graduate in basic English
and punctuation in my office. I have had to get college graduates
to get my word processing out immediately. If I give that
secretarial job to a bright college graduate, she is underemployed
and is not satisfied with that job. So I hire high school students or
graduates to do it, but I know I am going to have to train them.
We have to get the work out and want to do it fast, so I have to

pick the person for the level with which she is happy in order to get stability in the work force so that I can work in my office rather than on the mechanics of the word processing.

This has been my experience since 1981.

I think that these people should have achieved a basic level of education when they come in my office.

Dr. Todd: Our topic is the creation or sources of new wealth in the Twenty-First Century. Why don't you give us some examples in your corporation of the technologies that will create this new wealth.

Dr. Siegel:

We have talked about the Japanese. In Japan you can bring a product to the marketplace in three years, a process that takes us from eight to thirteen years in the United States. It is part of our endeavor to try to shorten that process by bringing in the new product and working with it from the early stages of technological development and following it through the regulatory procedures at an earlier stage to try to get the product out sooner. For instance, many dental products, including a diagnostic test for periodontal disease and another way to treat cavities are being worked on now. We hope that our scientific approach to enhance this production process will generate new industry in those applications, as well as others.

Comment:

I notice that very few people have much of an understanding of the physical laws in our environment. Don't you think there should be a general science course given even in grade school to orient people to that sort of thing? Most people do not understand what goes on.

Dr. Todd: Are you just thinking about basic science?

From The Floor:

That's right. How can we achieve any real new wealth if you do not understand something about science or technology?

Dr. Todd: I do not know how early they start basic science, but my wife teaches sixth grade, and there is a basic science course; and I think perhaps it starts even earlier.

If there are no other questions, we will adjourn.

ERIK RITTER VON
KUEHNELT-LEDDIHN

ECONOMICS, WAR, AND REVOLUTIONS

Economics must, of course, always be seen in the right perspective, and there is always the danger of under- or over-rating it. Economics is such a complicated matter that, compared with it, theology seems an exact science, last but not least because in economics the schools differ far more widely from each other than those of theology within one and the same Church. In addition, economics arouse even greater fanaticism than theology – the *odium economicum* is greater than the *odium theologicum*. There is a certain basic theological consensus among the various schools within our Church which often represent mere differences of emphasis, whereas in economics the various schools are more or less contradictory.

THE EMPHASIS ON ECONOMICS

When I first came to this country I was struck by the fact that economics were often overevaluated. I once had to give a lecture for a Catholic association in Detroit about the many European wars into which the United States were dragged – by their leaders, we must remember. Even during the lecture I could see that the sponsor was very dissatisfied with my thesis and afterwards he took me to task. "I will tell you what history is," he said sternly, "history is nothing but economics." I thereupon asked, whether he was a Catholic. "Of course," he replied, "I am a daily communicant."

"What a pity," I ventured, "otherwise you would have been an ideal research professor in Moscow's Marx-Engels Institute."

You see, here lies the problem. Most of the evils of our time go back to World War I. This is not only my view but that of outstanding American historians, among them George F. Kennan. And Sidney Fay, another eminent scholar (in spite of the fact that he was a Harvard professor!), wrote in his *The Origins of the Great War*: "For ten years I have consulted all the archives and looked through them, but practically never did I find a hint about economics." A teacher in a non-denominational women's college who also insisted that history was nothing but economics, admitted that, in the past, people were indeed motivated by religion, honor and glory, but she added: "Since then we have progressed and we now go to war over economic issues." "Well," I replied, "like dogs fighting over a bone. How progressive." She did not like this at all.

ECONOMICS AND THE HUMANITIES

And as for the econometric school, despised by my friends of the Austrian School, you ought to realize that economics must not be studied in a void but always in coordination with the other sciences, above all with the humanities. In other words, economics must be seen in reference to races and nations, their psychologies, their historic backgrounds and, as I pointed out in my first lecture, their religions. Only thus can we understand the interplay of economics and humanities which forms the true pattern of human thought and actions.

LIBERATION THEOLOGY

If, for example, we take the social and economic structure of Latin America, we understand the motives of Liberation theology in the light of the frightful poverty of both laity and clergy. I cannot forget a Monsignor in his middle thirties, a Mestizo, a very intelligent and pious man who kept fit by using dumbbells. He had a bed, but his two chaplains slept on the ground and each had only one dark suit. Then it rained and they got wet they had to wait in their underwear until the suits were dry. They had a few books. From the Sunday collection they got altogether between eight and fourteen dollars a week (as of 1960). Their meals consisted of beans, *frijoles*. When I told the Monsignor that I would like to visit the seminary he replied sadly: "Look here, you are a friend of our nation, I don't want you to see that pigsty."

These are the realities and that, under these circumstances, the clergy succumbs to the nonsense of Liberation Theology is not surprising. And another thing pushes the priests and monks of Latin America in that direction: the age-old accusation that the Church always sides with the rich. (Each time I hear this, I take pencil and paper and ask for details which, of course, are never forthcoming.)

Now, if we want to investigate the impact of Marx on the social and political scene, we must try to understand his personality and his mind. Nobody who writes about Marx should fail to read his poetry, for there one finds the real man. His poems, needless-to-say, have never been translated, but in them we find a hate-swollen megalomaniac whose dream was the annihilation of our world in an inferno. One of the poems ends with the words "...We, the apes of a cold god." I thought of this when I saw in Moscow's Lenin Museum the desk of the red dictator and on it the statuette of a pensive ape, in its hands a human skull.

SOCIALISM

In Marx we have the founder of a dynamic movement mobilizing mankind's strongest passion: envy. As I said in my previous lecture, Marx was very competent in philosophy, a little, a very little, in theology, certainly in social sciences, in geography, history, and languages, but he had one weak spot, an area where he knew very little, and that was economics. Yet, Marxism is basically economics. But remember: the falser and the more primitive a theory, the better its chances for a near global victory in a short time. We saw the swift success of socialism: only 20 years after *Das Kapital* was published, "Social Democratic" and "Socialist" parties sprang up all over Europe. From the moment socialism was founded until it was organized and spread over large parts of Europe, only a few decades elapsed and the same is true of other false ideas, of Islam, for instance, which swept three Continents in less than a hundred years, whereas Christianity took three hundred years to "surface." Socialism encountered opposition and restrictive measures in some countries, but early Christianity suffered persecution and suppression — witness its many martyrs.

Socialism always had one great advantage over a free market economy: being a false, but clear idea, it can be explained to any high school kid in about fifteen minutes, whereas the workings of free enterprise require a four-week seminar. (Islam has the same advantage over Christianity.)

THE UNIMPORTANCE OF ECONOMICS

The topic of this lecture is "economics, war, and revolutions." Now, where do we find pure economics resulting in wars? It was the case in a few colonial wars, like the one waged by a western European power against China, the so-called Opium War, although opium was only a minor issue. The colonies rarely brought the expected profits, and major European statesmen like Disraeli and Bismarck were not at all happy with the colonial system. Of all the German colonies only little Togo was in the black, all the others were entirely in the red. "India," so many Britishers said, "we could lose anytime and it wouldn't hurt us; Argentina, on the other hand, would be a real loss, because there are our major investments." To establish the economic basic structures in one of the (mostly tropical) colonies was extremely costly. The Belgian Congo, for example, was in the black only from 1940 to 1954.

We have to bear in mind that the phenomenon of Colonialism merely follows an old law, I would even call it a natural law; that is, that nature does not tolerate a vacuum and neither does the political map; wherever it shows a vacuum, one or the other power is going to move in.

As for revolutions, I want to remind you of the title of a book by Richard Weaver, the great American author, *Ideas Have Consequences*. Having studied the French Revolution for years, I discovered that its outbreak was not due to any economic cause, only at a late date did the Jacobins start to agitate against the rich. In spite of a bad harvest, the revolution broke out at a time of general prosperity. The state was bankrupt, yes, but that did not bother the people because they had what they needed. And the state was bankrupt because it could not collect taxes, a problem it shared with other countries. Remember Charles I of England and the problems he had with the parliament about taxation, which finally led to his tragic death. The very idea of having to write out a confession of one's financial situation for a whole year was considered preposterous. If you felt like making a general confession you went to a priest, not to the collector of internal revenue. The powers of a king, even in an absolute monarchy, were very limited. If he wanted to wage a war, he had to look into his coffers to see if he had enough money, and I mean real money, gold and silver, not just printed paper. And he couldn't conscript anybody, he had to hire mercenaries. (The word "soldier" derives from *solidus*, a Roman coin.) Prior to the French Revolution this was the situation in most countries. Nor could a monarch issue a law affecting the dinner table of his subjects, as it was done in your country through prohibition. Such impudence can be expected only in a parliamentary system claiming that its representatives stand for the people.

THE RUSSIAN REVOLUTION

And here we enter an area where economics do matter. "Plenus venter non studet libenter" — a full stomach is not inclined to study. That is as true of nations as it is of students. Nations which are badly off materially are more likely than others to reflect, to think and thus to argue, to aim for improvements, whether wise or unwise. At a certain level of poverty and hunger, a revolutionary ambiance can develop or be created – not only materially, but intellectually or even religiously, if there is really a desperate desire for change at any price. Such a situation arose in the big cities of Russia in 1917 when two revolutions took place, the democratic revolution in March and the social democratic one in the Fall. Remember, it was the Russian Social Democratic Party which, on November 7, 1917, staged the "Red October" – October according to the old Julian calendar – the Orthodox Russians having rejected (and still reject) the Gregorian calendar as "Popery." (And so did the British and Americans, for the same reasons, until 1752.)

THE GERMAN REVOLUTION

We had something similar in Germany in what Carl Schmitt called "the legal revolution" because it was made through the ballot. In 1923 Hitler attempted a violent take-over in Munich. He could hardly have chosen a worse place: besides being very Catholic, Munich is basically also rather conservative. The *Reichswehr* fired at the marching National Socialists and thus Hitler failed, was arrested and imprisoned in the Fortress of Landsberg, which gave him the opportunity to write *Mein Kampf*. He had learned his lesson and understood the usefulness of legal means for a takeover. As Plato said: "From no other form of government does tyranny usually arise but out of democracy." Of course, a tyranny can be established through a revolution which has weakened authority, but it can also be brought about through the ballot and then we see a "man of the people," a "common man" acting as protector of the people against unpopular minorities. The "wicked minorities" he then presents as aliens, as impostors, exploiters, or traitors.

In the case of Hitler we might imagine him taking paper and pencil and making a list of unpopular and "suspect" people as likely targets in an election campaign. And this is how his list might have looked:

No. 1, the Jews

No. 2, the aristocracy, they and the Jews are rich

No. 3, the rich generally, the plutocrats, bankers, and manufacturers

No. 4, the modern artists who cannot paint but make a lot of money

No. 5, the insane who are useless and bothersome

No. 6, the Gypsies who steal

"Only the simple, common people are decent and to them we must appeal."

Here a historic force comes into play which some authors, myself included, have characterized as one of the strongest in history: *envy*. Now, the situation is somewhat different in America where, compared to Europe — and especially to my own Austria — there is very little envy. This may have partly to do with the fact that we live relatively crowded in small countries whereas you still have wide open spaces. Anyhow, Europeans are envious and to mobilize this vice is a sure means to success in a democracy. It is how Hitler proceeded and succeeded. Even Bertrand Russell, whom nobody could call a man of the right, told us that "envy is the most potent element in democracy."

One of the basic tenets of democracy is that we are all equal, no man is better than any other. But what if some people are unequal or otherwise different? Most of the Jews were wealthy and in the popular mind "rich" was synonymous with "Jewish." But why were the Jews rich? Not because they exploited anybody, but because they were intelligent, ambitious, and hardworking. If the child from a Gentile family brought home mediocre marks, this was shrugged off by the parents, but a Jewish boy would have been punished severely. In mixed populations it always happens that one group is better off than another, think of the Christians in Lebanon, the Copts in Egypt, the

Chinese in Malaysia, the Parsees in India, the Spaniards in Mexico, or the Indians in Black Africa. You see how German anti-Semitism could be organized, creating a vast potential of voters.

And Hitler had another asset: he looked like an average man. He might have been a waiter in a coffee house or a salesman in a department store, a type easy to relate with for the average person who could never imagine himself as a Metternich, a Bismarck, or a Franz Joseph because these were "uncommon" men.

Other than the German Revolution, the Russian Revolution was a coup, a rash action done with the help of a mutinous, because beaten, army and navy. In world history mutinous navies have often played an important part. Navies require stricter discipline than armies, but if that discipline breaks, it breaks thoroughly. So the Social Democratic extremists, the Bolsheviks, took over very suddenly. But then, in 1918, came the counterattack in the form of the civil war which was won by the Red Armies primarily for economic reasons. The peasant-soldiers deserted from the White Armies and went over to the Social Democrats who now called themselves Communists and told the peasants that all large and medium landowners were going to be expropriated and the land given to the peasants.

RUSSIAN AGRICULTURE

Now, what was the economic situation in the Russian farmlands? In order to understand this, we must realize that Russia had been developing by leaps and bounds ever since 1890. Its economic growth was, in fact, bigger than that of the United States. Russia is basically a very wealthy country, it was, in a way, an "Eastern America." Unskilled European workers emigrated to the United States, but the highly skilled ones went to Russia where they earned fabulous wages, and so did intellectuals, doctors, scholars, chemists, engineers, and physicists. Do not forget that Russia is two and a half times the size of the United States, an enormous country with all sorts of raw materials. And

as for Russian industry, it constructed the biggest aeroplanes in
War I.

But now let us return to agriculture. Russia had serfdom until
1861, you had slavery until 1863. Only 45 percent of the Russian
farmers were serfs, the others were free farmers. And serfs
existed only in central, western and southwest Russia, but none
in the southeast, the East, the North, and Siberia. But the situation
of the serfs was radically different from that of the American
slaves because the serf was merely tied to the land. Some serfs
became very rich indeed. I am thinking of an extreme case at the
time of Catherine the Great; the man was worth, in present-day
purchasing power, between 15 and 18 million dollars. But in spite
of this he hesitated for years before he decided to buy his freedom
(from Count Sheremetyev), which cost him between $150,000
and $200,000 at the present rate. However, he now had to pay
taxes, whereas before he only paid the head tax, the obrok, of
about $2.50 a year for himself and each male member of his
family. There were doctors and lawyers who never sought
freedom from their overlords and went on paying the small head
tax. This was so because serfdom had been only introduced by
the Czars in the 16th Century as a means of taxation; the landlord
had to hand over part of the obrok to the government. When I
was in Moscow, I lived in the Austrian Embassy, a palace built
for his mistress by a sugar king who had been born a serf.

In pre-revolutionary Russia anybody who worked hard and
was intelligent could make a meteoric career. But the Russians
are not hard workers by nature and now they are gravely handicapped by the socialist system. In 1861 the former serfs were
given land which they had to maintain collectively, which means
that the land belonged to the entire village and was assigned in
rotation from family to family. One can imagine, that they did not
take good care of the soil which had to be passed on after a few
years. It was a very bad system. In 1905 the first Russian Revolution took place, Russia was liberalized, it became a constitutional
monarchy and in what amounted to an agrarian revolution the

former collective farms became the real property of the peasants and, in addition, the large landowners had to cede a sizeable part of their land to the small farmers. As you can imagine, there were lazy farmers, drunkards who sold their property to others who worked hard and prospered. Now there were wealthy peasants envied by the less industrious or unfortunate ones and rural inequalities increased steadily.

LAND OWNERSHIP

Then a great change took place. Not only did the land become private property, but the big landowners had to yield more and more land to the farmers and it was planned that by 1930 only eleven per cent of the agrarian surface of Russia should be in the hands of the big landowners. Such were the realistic calculations of Pyotr Stolypin, Russia's great Minister of Agriculture and agrarian reformer, who was murdered by an anarchist. (The leftists were all for the Mir, because it was collectivist!) In 1917, the year of the Revolution, already only 23 percent of the arable land and pastures were in the hands of the still big landowners. In other words, 77 percent belonged to the farmers who had infinitely more animals, more cows, horses, sheep, and goats than the big landowners, which means that they farmed far more intensively.

Now, for the Russian farmer – and the same is true of European farmers in general – the size of his land is immensely important. Thus the remaining 23 (and, finally, 13) percent still belonging to the big landowners were a most tempting bait. The Russian historian Michael Florenski said, that in order to avert Communism, Kerenski should have done two things: make peace with the Central Powers, and distribute the last square inch to the farmers. One must remember that in England, Scotland, and Ireland at that time (1917) the big landowners had 55 percent of the land. But nobody wrote lachrymose books and articles about this situation: England was democratic, liberal and progressive; Russia reactionary, medieval and wicked!

As I said, the farmers and sons of farmers deserted in droves from the White Armies and joined the Red Army because for them the victory of Communism meant "all the land." But then, as we all know, came the terrible punishment. Under Lenin the farmers had prospered in a minor way, but when Stalin came into power, he declared: "Now we are going to be real Communists. Until now we have not lived up to our program, we merely mouthed Marxist theories. In order to be orthodox Communists we shall collectivize everything under the NEP" (New Economic Policy). In Lenin's time only the big industrial enterprises had been socialized, now it was the turn of the naive Russian and Ukranian farmers. To begin with, the *Kulaki* ("fists"), the larger farmers were expropriated, but soon came the turn of the little ones. We must realize that, until five or six years ago, a farmer could not get a passport (for inland travel, that is) and thus was actually no better off than the old-time serf who was tied to the land. And one can say that, in a way, it served him right since he had naively and greedily fought for Communism. And now his life is dismal, he is brutally transferred from one collective farm to another, families are torn asunder, and poverty has turned into misery. The situation of the farmers was infinitely worse than that of the working class in the big cities. Andrey Amalrik gave a most depressing account of rural life in the USSR which remains a closed book for tourists as well as foreign correspondents who have not the slightest chance to experience it.

INFLATION

As you see, economics are important for an understanding of history. In this connection we must mention another decisive factor, the enormous inflation that hit the heart of Europe after World War I, largely as a result of the imposed reparations. It caused the end of the German middle class who lost their savings, their investments, and in many cases, even their real estate property. The money was devaluated to the extent that 4.2 trillion Marks became the equivalent of one dollar. The agrarian class survived financially, but statistically it forms today a very small sector. And thus another reason to envy the German Jews was found: They usually had relatives or friends abroad from whom they got help and support. But help was also given to others, especially to children. In 1920 I spent, like many other children, several weeks in Denmark with a kind family to recover from the indescribable starvation of the postwar years. We children often cried from hunger and our survival is partly due to an American, a wise man and a blessing for many: Herbert Hoover. Through him we school children got pork and beans, lots of beans but always with a piece of bacon and that saved our lives.

In Denmark I had also met an American, a little boy from Newton, Massachusetts. When in 1922 he read in the papers about our inflation he sent me one dollar through the American legation in Vienna. You can imagine our excitement. The dollar was converted into 780 Austrian Crowns and for this sum my parents bought me a new suit, twenty(!) supplementary mathematic lessons (math was my weakest point in school), and a book on world history – all that for a single dollar amounting to about $525 in present-day purchasing power. Imagine what a German Jew could buy if he got 100 dollars from a relative or friend in America – and the envy it aroused!

The reparations were based on Article 231 of the Versailles Treaty, attributing the war guilt entirely and one-sidely on Germany. In the case of Hitler his guilt in starting, together with Uncle Joe, World War II cannot be questioned. But World War I was different, in a way accidental, and the various European powers, so to say, drifted into it. Nobody really wanted it, but once it had started the enthusiasm was enormous. Not so in 1939. I experienced the outbreak of both wars and I can tell you that in September 1939 the Germans were a people in tears and crushed by a sense of guilt.

ECONOMICS AND WARS

And now back to economics. In what respect are they responsible for the outbreak of wars? What of the big international combines and cartels, the wicked "multinationals"? Of course, there are always some people who make money through wars in remote countries, but I can assure that: a) due to the totality of modern wars, and b) to conscription which sends the sons of tycoons, industrialists, and bankers to the battle fields like any other men, their lust for armed conflicts does not exist. Big business is, on the whole, more interested in peace than in war. Take the Krupp family, for instance, makers of military hardware. Accused, in the second Nuremberg Trial, of having used slave labor, the oldest son had to stand for his desperately ill father (a procedure utterly in contradiction to the legal tradition of a civilized country). He was given seven years of hard labor but was prematurely released. Two other sons had been killed in the war, one gravely wounded, and one spent ten years in a Russian prisoners camp, mostly in strict isolation. Now, can you imagine the Krupp family saying: "We want war in order to make more money." What for? Another house? Another car? Another steak for dinner? And this at the cost of the lives of their children?

J. R. Hobson, an educator and teacher in England, said: "There will never be a European war unless permitted by the House of Rothschild." This, of course, is utter nonsense, but it was believed by Lenin who got his theory of "imperialism" straight from Hobson. Let us look once more at World War I. Does anybody believe that William II, Nicolas II, Franz Joseph, Sir Edward Grey, Asquith, or Clemenceau thought in economic terms? There is apparently a temptation to explain world history in terms that can be understood by any greengrocer, but in world politics quite different passions are decisive. We must, of course, take economics seriously. Human beings, consisting of bodies and souls, have economic interests but we also have infinitely more valuable interests. Marxism tries to explain history entirely through economics and that, of course, is simply not true. But we do, indeed, need sound economics, we need economic health just as we need bodily health. That is natural. And healthy economics are free economics. Austria produced Adolf Hitler, that is unfortunately true, but it also produced the well-known Austrian School of Economics and its outstanding theorists. On our 100 Schilling bill you can see the portrait of one of these, Eugen von Böhm-Bawerk, despite the fact that we have a semi-socialist government and Socialism violently opposes the Austrian School of Economics.

Let us repeat: we must see the role of economics in the right context. Economics alone do not explain the outbreak or non-outbreak of revolutions or wars. On the other hand, a healthy economic situation can well create a climate unfavorable to tensions which favor wars and revolutions. Very hungry people normally do not have the energy to revolt, they might vote for extremist parties, but they are unlikely to erect barricades. For that you need energies.

DISCUSSION

Question: Relative to what you have just spoken, would you venture a word of forecast with respect to Russia under Gorbachev and his Glasnost?

Erik von Kuehnelt-Leddihn:

What Gorbachev is trying to do is very different from what Stalin did. Gorbachev wants Communism to work, so he – apparently – tries to "democratize" a state capitalism, but this is like trying to offer a glass of dehydrated water. It amounts to trying to square the circle. State capitalism, called socialism, simply cannot be democratized because, after all, this system is unavoidably bureaucratic and technocratic. Admittedly people in Russia today are speaking their minds far more openly than they ever dared before, except within the family or with very close friends. On the other hand, what worries me is the awakening of nationalism in the Baltic States, in the Caucasus, and in

Central Asia. We must not forget that the Great Russians constitute only about 50 percent of the population, the rest being other Slavs, Ukrainians, Tartars, Lithuanians, Georgians, and Armenians. Many Great Russians are now asking themselves, whether they are going to lose all these outlying areas they have dominated for so many generations.

There is a movement called *Pamyat* ("Memory") which encounters a surprising toleration from the Communist Party. Is it directed toward a Russian national socialism? Some people might feel that, international socialism having so obviously failed, national socialism might be a possibility to be considered. I was amazed to see on our TV the demonstrations in Moscow sporting Imperial Russia flags as well as a red flag with the Russian colors added, and even a flag of the Imperial Navy, a blue St. Andrew's Cross on white. None of our silly commentators saw the significance of all this!

Let us not forget that the economy of the Third Reich was really socialistic. This reminds one somewhat of conditions in China and its "patriotic capitalists" who became the stewards of their enterprises and produced for the "national economy." Also, in Mao's time there was the short period of the "thousand flowers" when free speech was permitted. But when this interlude was over, those who had spoken freely were executed and the same could happen in Russia. I do not say that it will happen, but it could. Russia is not China, nor are the Chinese Russians. That something is afoot is evident, but what direction it is going to take I dare not prophesy in spite of my knowledge of Russia and my several friends there.

Question: I have heard that Gorbachev has to do what he has to do within two years or else he will have to move aside according to a timetable that has been preset.

Erik von Kuehnelt-Leddihn:

As for the future timetable I want you to consider this: if one knows the facts, it is quite easy to foretell the future, but for heaven's sake beware of making a timetable! When de Tocqueville wrote the second volume of his *Democracy in America* he gave a precise and detailed description of the provider state to come. But then his book was forgotten for a hundred years and only in our time have people become interested in it and recognized the genius he was. He also foretold the crisis between America and Russia, but it took much longer for this particular tension to develop. (At that time Alaska was still in Russian hands.) Plato foretold us that democracy eventually becomes tyranny – in Russia it took seven months, in Germany fourteen years. Timetables vary. I stick to my forecasts but am always careful not to speak of years or even generations.

Question: If you ignore the timetable, then, isn't it likely that the inevitable conclusion of this openess and freedom can only result in more revolution?

Erik von Kuehnelt-leddihn:

The openess and freedom in communist countries might, of course, lead to revolutions. For Russia I believe this to be likely. Evolution is dear to the English and the American mind but in other cultures, such as the Russian, things are more often broken than bent. In 1962 a local revolt in Novocherkassk developed into open revolution and had to be brutally quenched. But some day the "fire brigade" might come too late and the fire will spread....

FORUM

BUSINESS AND THE ALLEVIATION OF MATERIAL AND CULTURAL POVERTY

MODERATOR
Rev. J. Willis Langlinais

Paul W. Myers

Charles W. Sapp

PANELISTS

MODERATOR
Rev. J. Willis Langlinais, S.M.,St.D.

Father Langlinais is a native of San Antonio, earned a degree in Education from the University of Dayton, Ohio, and the Doctorate in Theology from the University of Fribourg, Switzerland. He has done advanced studies in Theology at Notre Dame and in college management at Carnegie-Mellon University. Father is Professor of Theology at St. Mary's specializing in contemporary ethics, professional ethics – especially bio-medical ethics, and religious spirituality. He has been Dean of Arts and Sciences and Academic Vice-President of St. Mary's University and is currently President at Central Catholic Marianist College Prep High School.

Paul W. Myers, M.D.

Dr. Myers did his residency at Ellis Hospital in Schenectady, New York and Albany Medical Center in Albany, New York. He is certified by the National Board of Medical Examiners and the American Board of Neurological Surgery. Dr. Myers is a Fellow of the American College of Surgeons and the American College of Legal Medicine. He is a member of the American Medical Association, Society of Air Force Clinical Surgeons, Congress of Neurological Surgeons, Military Neurological Surgeons, and the Society of University Neurosurgeons. Dr. Myers has held medical positions as Commander of Wilford Hall USAF Medical Center, Lackland Air Force Base, San Antonio, Texas, Surgeon General of the United States Air Force, and as an On-Site Researcher with the Vietnam Head Injury Study Group, Walter Reed Army Medical Center, Washington, D.C. His honors include the Legion of Merit, Distinguished Service Medal, and the Distinguished Service Medal with Cluster. He is currently Clinical Professor in Neurological Surgery at the University of Texas

Health Science Center, San Antonio, Texas. Dr. Myers serves on the Board of the Southwest Foundation for Medical Research as well as the Board of United Services Automobile Association, both in San Antonio, Texas. He is the author of numerous presentations and publications.

Charles W. Sapp

Mr. Charles Sapp earned degrees from South Dakota State, where he got his Baccalaureate, and his Master's from Michigan State. From 1958 to 1966 he was with the American Stores in Salt Lake City, and from 1966 to 1981 he was with Alpha Beta, a subsidiary of American Stores. He is now Group Vice President of HEB Foods-Drug Stores, responsible for manufacturing, distribution, and construction.

BUSINESS AND THE ALLEVIATION OF MATERIAL AND CULTURAL POVERTY

Rev. J. Willis Langlinais:

I am going to introduce each of our panelists individually before each one speaks, and, then, of course, we will open the floor for discussion at the end.

Our first panelist is General Paul W. Myers. He is a former Surgeon General of the United States Air Force and was Commander at Wilford Hall Medical Center from 1971 to 1978. He is presently the Medical Consultant at USAA, here in San Antonio.

Please welcome General Paul Myers, M.D.

CORPORATE PHILANTROPHY

General Paul W. Myers, M.D.:

Thank you, Father Langlinais. Ladies and gentlemen, perhaps you are wondering why a neurosurgeon is involved in corporate philanthropy. I can only tell you that following my military career, I became very active in the business world, the entrepreneurial world, and I have likened myself to a biomedical politician, so I feel reasonably qualified to speak to you on this subject.

In a publication that comes from the Institute I picked up this morning, I could not help but see the quote from Henry Ford when he addressed corporate giving.

He said, "It is good to give alms. It is better to work to make the giving of alms unnecessary."

And that is a beautiful lead-in to the historical perspective of corporate philanthropy, written in 1908-1909 by John D. Rockefeller, a series of some seven interviews; that book has been re-published. I would just like to quote passages from that book because Mr. Rockefeller very clearly defined corporate philanthropy, and identified his own difficulties with philanthropic efforts.

The interviewer noted that as Mr. Rockefeller's fortune increased, requests for assistance proliferated; he was willing to give, but could not bear to give blindly.

He said, and I quote: "About the year 1890 I was still following the haphazard fashion of giving here and there as appeals presented themselves, investigated as I could, and worked myself almost into a nervous breakdown, while groping my way without sufficient guide or chart through this ever-winding field of philanthropic endeavor."

And what he needed, he felt, was to rationalize this philanthropy, to develop an organized plan based upon some underlying principles of giving, and that the philanthropy that mattered most, he concluded, was philanthropy that struck at the root of fundamental problems.

Again to quote Mr. Rockefeller: "To help the sick and distressed appeals to the kindhearted always; but to help the investigator who is striving successfully to attack the causes which bring about sickness and distress does not so strongly attract the giver of money."

The best philanthropy is constantly in search of the modalities, the search for cause, in an attempt to cure evils at their source. And as a guide for giving, the principle of attempting to cure evils at their source is as relevant today as it was when Rockefeller articulated it.

For example, Rockefeller wrote: "It is interesting to follow the mental processes that some excellent souls go through to cloud their consciences when they consider what they are doing. For instance, one man says, 'I do not believe in giving money to street beggars.' I agree with him, but that is not a reason why one should be exempt from doing something to help the situation represented by the street beggars."

THE PHILOSOPHY OF CORPORATE GIVING

With that bit of historical introduction I am going to take some time and review with you philanthropy, as we view it today, and bring you up-to-date on what the philosophy is behind corporate giving. Then, in the middle of the slide presentation, I am going to tell you of some experiences that I have had in interviewing personally several chief executive officers from large, medium, and small corporations here in the San Antonio area, and relate to you some of their thoughts, obviously tempered with the current Texas economy.

If one looks at the growth of giving here in the United States, corporate giving, in 1936 the amount given was $30 million; and, as you see, with each ten-year increment in time, the giving was increased enormously. Between 1976 and 1986 the amount of corporate dollars given almost tripled. Now, it is interesting to note that during the Reagan years, backing up from 1988 eight years, the largest growth was during the Reagan years, which followed President Reagan's direct appeal to corporate America to increase their contributions in the various fields of that particular kind of endeavor. So in 1986 $4 billion, 500 thousand was given by corporate America in the five areas that I will identify.

If we look at the growth of giving as a percentage increase each year, we see something very, very interesting. From 1981 to 1982 there was a sixteen percent increase in giving; twenty-five percent, the high-water mark, from 1982 to 1983. This is the amount of increase from one year to the next. Then the leveling off began in 1983 to 1984 and then in 1986 it was three percent, which was a reflection of the downturn in our economy, and in 1987 the estimate is that it will be about the same or perhaps even a little bit less. So the track record is a very encouraging one. There has been reasonably steady growth up until the last year.

CATEGORIES OF CORPORATE GIVING

Corporate giving is measured in five major categories: health and human services, including donations to local medical institutions, for instance; education; culture and the arts; civil and community endeavor; and others, – I have put here a couple of examples, the CARE program, administered through the United Nations, and special fundings that we have been asked to give to our Olympic teams.

For a long time, health and human service giving was somewhat depressed, but it is now re-surging, and I think probably a lot of that has to do with the graying of America and the increased concern that we have with health care, particularly long-term health care, as was pointed out this morning.

NON-CASH GIVING

Now, it is very interesting to look at non-cash giving. You might imagine that a large corporation that has a very useful product will give its product, and that amounts to about one-fifth of our contributions when you talk about how much that given product costs. Fifty-six percent of the corporations do provide product gifts in addition to cash grants. You can take, for example, Colgate Palmolive products. They could very easily make product gifts. We have a small manufacturer here in San Antonio that makes plaques. He could provide plaques to various organizations, memorial plaques to hospitals that are being built, or awards to employees in those areas – all could be included; that is a major part of corporate giving.

If you try to determine the philosophy that is behind corporate giving, I could draw an Air Force analogy because you will find the philosophy is somewhat akin to flying, where the donating corporate decisions will range all of the way from "seat-of-the-pants" to full instrumentation. And by that, I mean that one CEO will give from his heart and give emotionally; while another organization calls in an outside consultant to advice on a program that has to be approved by the Board of Directors, and they have a given sum that they budget for every year. So it varies, and, of course, I think you would draw the immediate conclusion that the more structured the corporation and the bigger it is, the more structured would be the process of corporate giving, and that turns out to be very, very true.

A LOCAL SURVEY OF VIEWS ON CORPORATE GIVING

I told you a moment ago that I had the opportunity to talk personally with executive officers of a large financial insurance corporation, a banking institution, a small manufacturing concern, and a privately-held construction company, and then I had a telephone interview with an executive of a building construction company. Those interviews were enormously interesting and they gave me a lot of insight.

The medium-large construction company was a highway construction firm, and the CEO of this privately-owned corporation would be labelled a typical Texas redneck, I think. He said that his decisions to commit any dollars from the company were very personal; that he always gave directly, and he had a real hang-up about organizations that would come in and take off the top dollars, professional money-raisers, and he avoided them like the plague and would not give them a nickel. He concluded by telling me that he felt that although we look sometimes to our neighbor to the South as having a plethora of those on the streets with their hands held out for money, he thought that certainly the United States was the biggest beggar nation in the world.

He went on to say that it was impossible to honor all appeals, and that theme ran through all the interviews.

He had one major allocation. His largest commitment was to the United Way.

And he went on to say that he makes no corporate religious contributions. And, believe it or not, that was true throughout.

There are no corporate religious contributions. That does not mean that there have not been contributions to religious education efforts but not to a parish or a building project, for instance, of a given church.

Financial banking institutions are far more structured. The moneys come from a set-aside cash contributions sum. The Board of Directors dictates that the amount cannot be more than one percent of net income before taxes. The philosophical goal is to improve the quality of life in communities where they are operating, and approval will have to be by the Chief Executive Officer, and the contributions are in support of the five areas that I mentioned.

For a while, a large communications corporation was committed to long-range contributions, that is, they would pledge a given number of dollars over a period of three to five years, but they have stopped that. There is no one that I am aware of in the San Antonio area that now engages in that kind of giving, and the reason is that the economy is so cyclical, with periodic downturns, that you just cannot make long-range commitments of any magnitude. They believe in making large donations where the program is well managed and the money will have a broad impact. I find that seems to the trend in the various organizations as one begins to look at those policies in detail.

I am not going to go into more detail because I do not want to take up too much time, but I would tell you that the San Antonio community is dedicated toward pledging moneys to the education of the minority groups, and they go into that in a big way.

I would repeat again that the more structured the company, the larger the company, the more the contributions. But all are feeling the pinch, and all have cut back their giving rigorously; they cannot meet the obligations that they would like to, or made pledges as they did in the previous years.

One man, who runs a relatively small company, has a pretty straightforward philosophy. He says that he believes that there is a gross amount of skullduggery in what he calls boiler-room operations.

If you have been called about dinner time the number of times that I have been called about dinner time, I think you may agree with those who are voicing pleas for different kinds of approaches to cope with the skullduggery in boiler-room operations. The same people are making the telephone calls, but they are asking for money for different kinds of groups. My interviewee goes on to conclude that the more you say "yes," the more calls you get. Also, the "product" that you give is never counted in the tabulation of corporate giving, that is not on any chart I have seen, nor is the contribution of corporate personnel time.

For example, United Services Automobile Association has a number of people involved in civic activities which require them to be away from work. That time away from work is obviously company money that is being spent for civic activities; it is not included in the totals.

To wind up the result of these interviews: it was quite obvious that you can't do everything for everybody. Most of the corporations are involved in between seventy-five and one hundred obligations of one kind or another, and they may range from some local activity to something very big, where a company contributes from 80 dollars to 100 thousand dollars to a particular cause.

Contributions should not be widely diversified; monies need to go to projects which are quite specific.

The major contributions made by any one of the organizations that I had the opportunity to interview go to the United Way; up to forty percent of the total money given is to the United Way.

To conclude these remarks, I will just share with you some more information that is of general interest. There are some interesting trends.

TRENDS IN CORPORATE GIVING

There is a corporate group in New York that tracks corporate giving. In 1986 cutbacks were made by thirty-six percent of the corporations, and those cutbacks ranged anywhere from two to seventy percent. The cutbacks in corporate giving were made because of our economic downturn.

There has been an upward trend in the giving to the health and human services needs, after a ten-year downtrend.

The basic manufacturing industries have all declined considerably in giving this year. Service industries, such as insurance, are also down severely. While retail/wholesale trade, finance, banking, and transportation in San Antonio, have increased their corporate giving. One of the large banking institutions in San Antonio has increased its corporate giving in the last two years by more than fifty percent. It is one of the stronger banking institutions. Obviously that kind of community responsiveness speaks very well for that particular institution. One of the reasons it has responded so generously is because it is one of the oldest banking institutions in its field, and it feels that it truly has a role to play in this community, and it wants to make certain that that role is well-known.

The major donors are of interest because the corporate contributions are concentrated across the United States among a relatively small number of firms. While the survey that is conducted is done every year, seventeen percent of the people who were active philanthropically in the survey and provided information were giving seventy percent of the money. And if you look across San Antonio, the same thing is true, that the same small group keep giving and those who never give never give. And it is very hard to overcome that. You keep going back to those who have given before and continue to hope that they will give again, although the shoe is beginning to pinch rather severely.

One of the people I interviewed said: "The hardest thing for me now to do is to turn down the personal appeal from a friend who has a special cause and I have to tell him I cannot help him."

A little additional data. I noted that the smaller contributors gave more to health and human services, and since 1978 more dollars have been given to education; and the data reflect that twenty-nine percent of all giving is given to education now. The manufacturing concerns give more than service-oriented companies.

And we have a distribution that is geographical, and probably demographic as well, that the New England and Southwest match up, giving more to education, forty-seven percent, versus thirty-seven percent for health and human services; while the bread-basket states, such as Minnesota and Kansas and Iowa, give more to health and human services.

SOURCES OF INFORMATION

Among the important sources of information, if you ever have a requirement to know where you can get information about corporate philanthropy in the United States, one is the National Charities Information Bureau. They have an eight-point investigative program. They will go in, at your request, and look at something. If somebody comes to you and says, "I want money," you can ask the bureau to assay that particular group that is making the request, and they will investigate eight separate areas to see whether or not that would be a worthwhile giving exercise for you.

The Conference Board, Incorporated works out of New York City. They publish a very, very complete and statistical summation of corporate giving in their yearly corporate report, which is due out early or in the first part of the next year.

That, in summary, is corporate philanthropy, a brief glimpse at what we are looking at across the nation at the present time.

We could say, I think, with some degree of honesty that a corporation that is highly structured is giving one-half to one percent of its net income before taxes or one-half percent of gross income. Some like to do it one way, and some like to do it the other, but it comes out about the same.

There has been some steady growth in this arena, and corporations do make a significant impact when you consider four and a half billion dollars that is being given in the five areas that I have presented to you.

Rev. Langlinais:

If you have not yet noticed, we have only two panelists rather than the three on your program. Mr. Mike Hopkins was not able to be here today, so we have allowed our panelists more time than we could have if we had a third one.

Mr. Charles Sapp is here, with degrees from South Dakota State, where he got his first, and his Master's from Michigan State. From 1958 to 1966 he was with the American Stores in Salt Lake City, and from 1966 to 1981 he was with Alpha Beta, a subsidiary of American Stores. He is now Group Vice President of HEB Foods-Drug Stores, responsible for manufacturing, distribution, and construction.

Please welcome to the rostrum Mr. Charles Sapp.

Mr. Charles W. Sapp:

Thank you very much for the opportunity to be a part of this very important Symposium.

I would like to think today, and direct our thoughts, in two directions relative to wealth and poverty and to corporate giving.

THE USES OF WEALTH

First of all, as Dr. Goelz so correctly identified in his invitational comments about the impact of wealth, there are gross misunderstandings in this day and age. I think we are missing the understanding that it is the use of wealth that is the driving force rather than somehow a concept that seems to pervade society that wealth is, in fact, the dirty coin waiting for the Master's return.

As we think about wealth and the use of wealth and its impact in its relationship to relieving poverty, clearly it is the creation of jobs and the things that are associated with jobs that become that driving force.

I will give you a simplistic idea from our own company. Take an eighteen-wheeler going down the road. Obviously ownership, legalistic ownership, of that resides some place. But I would not ask you to think in any other terms but that the driver of that vehicle considers that truck to be his.

It is not where the wealth resides that is so important; it is how wealth is used, and it is the use of wealth that creates jobs that begins the cycle that is, in fact, the driving force for the reduction of poverty.

But what I would like to spend most of my time discussing with you today is the other side of the company, or the giving, that is a little more abstract, and that is this area of contributions, corporate contributions.

A CASE STUDY IN CORPORATE GIVING

I work for what I consider to be an unusual company in this area. It is a company that likes to keep its giving quiet. It reserves public recognition for its activities, in fact, tries not to have a lot of publicity around the giving, it gives quietly. A value of the company, upon which the company was based. I can certainly speak to this. I have been with the company eight years, and I have some awareness of the giving that the company has done.

For over fifty years the HEB Company has given in excess of five percent of its pre-tax earnings to charitable causes. Those have been primarily in the areas of health, education, recreational, arts, and cultural activities.

Several years ago, as recession hit our State, areas along the border primarily, were hit; first of all, by the devaluation of the peso, then the oil crunch; and then the agricultural depression significantly impacted many of our border communities, and unemployment began to rise. There certainly was a need, a great need, of recovery. And so HEB became very involved in the development of food-bank work. We helped, first of all, to begin to develop the food banks themselves, to assist in structuring them.

There was a national organization called Second Harvest. Second Harvest tended to be an organization that concentrated in large cities. While certainly there was a need in our large Texas cities, there was a larger need among our border communities. So we began to develop food banks, supported them and got them structured, and then began the giving of food.

We adopted a policy that no food that was edible and nutritious would go to waste in our corporation. And so any food product that is safe, edible, nutritious but, for some reason, unsaleable through our normal marketing channels is, in fact, distributed to food banks. We centralize all of that by returning the merchandise to San Antonio and then distributing it to the various food banks. In total last year our giving of food exceeded ten million pounds of food to these communities. That giving of food brought the corporate contribution of value to ten percent of pre-tax earnings.

HEB, I think, is a unique company. I am delighted to be a part of it. But I think that its value system, extending well over fifty years of continuous contribution, is built on solid principles. Believing deeply in the freedom of the economic values of this country, believing in having a value system under which we operate, we have a mission statement, and our mission statement defines our purpose for existence, and it is to serve our customer, our partners, our community, and our stockholders last.

I use the word "partner," and you may think in the context of ownership. We have kind of a unique culture in HEB in that we refer to all our employees as partners. We refer to each other as partners because collectively we make up the company. Collectively our value system directs our attention toward our customer, toward the needs of those partners, towards the needs of our community, and, then, finally to the need of the stockholders.

That is a thumbnail sketch of the activities of the particular corporation with which I am involved. I will leave it at that point, and as we begin the panel discussion, any questions you have I will be happy to address: about our value system, about the basis for our giving, about our philosophy.

Thank you.

Rev. Langlinais:

Thank you very much, Mr. Sapp and Dr. Myers. I think we have had two interesting, complimentary presentations. One, an across-the-board view of how corporations give, the recipients of their gifts, what kinds of corporations give, and, then, an example of a local firm and how that particular firm helps various groups in our State and our area.

I would hope that we could now have a discussion, questions to ask the panelists, exchanges among the audience, such as we had this morning because there are more than just two people who are resource persons here. You are that, as well as they.

First of all, are there any questions from any of you that you would like to address to either one of the panelists?

DISCUSSION

From The Floor: General Myers, do you attribute any of the decrease in contributions to the Tax Reform Act?

General Myers:

I didn't get that from the people I interviewed. The reason was very clear and very simple; their profit margins were too thin and they necessarily had to cut back.

One man, a Chief Executive Officer of a small manufacturing concern, said: "I want to take what excess monies I have and put them back for my employees' direct benefit. I don't like any middle man involved."

He made that very clear.

I heard no one refer to the difference in the tax base as a cause.

The same gentleman went on to say that it is increasingly difficult in this community to get sufficient funds to support the very worthy efforts because eighty percent of the small businesses in the San Antonio environment are marginal or losing money and only twenty percent are showing profitability. So that gives you some idea of the magnitude of the economic impact that we have locally.

Rev. Langlinais:

I was at a symposium recently where it was indicated that when you try to persuade people to give to your cause, the idea of deductibility, that dimension, is not why they give. They give because they think it is a good cause, just as HEB helps the cities along the Rio Grande. That is the "why," rather than the tax benefit.

Paul Goelz: General Myers, you from a national point of view, and Mr. Sapp in your corporation, to what extent do the stockholders have a voice in the policy and the procedures for giving?

General Myers:

Two examples of stockholder counselors were in very large companies, one a mutual organization and the other, a stock company. The Board of Directors must approve the budget or set the amount that will be given, one-half of one percent, one percent, one-and-a-half percent, whatever it is. That is where the stockholder has an input, through the Board of Directors.

Mr. Sapp:

In the case of HEB, it is a private corporation, and it is a family-held corporation, and through the Board of Directors the philanthropy does come out of the original value system of the foundation of the Company.

It has happened that various speakers in this symposium have talked about entrepreneurial enterprise. HEB – and remember the size company that it is today – was a company that started with $60 in a rented store in Kerrville, Texas, and that same family is the continuing ownership of that corporation, so that is probably not an appropriate analogy to other corporations.

Comment
from The Floor: I am curious to what extent these donations are
publicized.

General Myers:

You heard my fellow panelist, from HEB, say that they would like to have their corporate philanthropy at a very low noise level. I have found that to be true more often than not.

There was only one company, a very large company, that said: "Yes, we look at corporate giving with an eye to what impact that has on the general public."

And that same corporation has been struggling for some time with its corporate image, and in behalf of whatever it can do to reverse the negativity of that image, they would like to reap that reward.

But, in general, it is done very quietly.

I would just like to make this statement, so that none of you leaves without this knowledge: that corporate America has an incredibly fine conscience, that there are Chief Executive Officers who are terribly concerned about adequate monies to support the five categories that I mentioned. Culture and the arts certainly play a major role, and they feel that they must, that it is an obligation, almost to the point that some have religious fervor, that they must make those contributions if we are to survive as the cultured nation that we are. I applaud them for that kind of effort, and I don't say that because I am necessarily a friend of big business.

Rev. Langlinais:

Any other questions? Yes.

From The Floor: Mr. Sapp, when you spoke of HEB's offering
structural assistance to the food bank system,
did you mean building a structural organization
inside HEB, or what?

Mr. Sapp:

The structure of the food-bank system is that major supplies contribute to the food bank operated by the HEB Company. That gets into the context of major truck loads, in the neighborhood of several hundred a year, that go out to the various food banks. Once that food is received by that food bank, the food bank becomes only a distributor to agencies. The food banks that we support and to which we supply food are basically Waco, Austin, San Antonio, Victoria, Corpus Christi, Brownsville, McAllen, Del Rio, Laredo — we ship to those food banks. They become a funnel to agencies, and among those food banks there are in excess of 650 individual agencies that receive food from the food banks. That is the way in which the system works. It is a massive organization.

Once the food is out there for the needy, it goes, for instance, to church feeding organizations, under-the-bridge type of assistance, and there are just all kinds of volunteer activity going on of a major nature to get food into the hands of the needy.

So among those 650 agencies that receive food from the food banks, I would not venture to guess how many volunteers in South and Central Texas are actually involved in that work.

From The Floor: When HEB gives this food to these centers, does it have any control over how they distribute it? Do they manage the centers?

Mr. Sapp:

No, we do not manage the centers.

And not to get into too much detail, the Second Harvest organization is a national organization that controls the food banks that are members of Second Harvest from the safety standpoint, for the assurance that their 503C is in proper order, that the giving is done, and that the accounting is done properly.

Of the food banks with which we are dealing, seven of the ten are not Second Harvest, and so HEB provides a person full-time to get together with these food banks to make sure that they are operating legally, that they are operating with absolute safety of product. The fact that the product is given rather than sold doesn't allow you to be any less conscientious about the safety of that product that goes into feeding people.

We provide the supervision only to the extent that we want assurance that it is being given to authorized agencies who have their legal requirements under which they are, in form, non-profit organizations. Obviously we do not want any of this product to be given to profit-oriented operations. To that extent, we provide control and super vision, and I identify that primarily as safety and secondarily from the legality standpoint.

Erik von Kuehnelt-Leddihn:

> Are all the donations tax deductible? I mean, whatever a company gives will not be taxed. Is that correct?

General Myers:

The monies that are given are measured from income pre-tax.

Erik von Kuehnelt-Leddihn:

> I ask because in Austria it is a unique situation. Nothing at all – educational or artistic or philanthropic or otherwise – is tax exempt. In Germany they are, but in Austria they are not.
>
> Now, the question is: If you would be taxed also for your donations, how much would they decrease?
>
> I ask because this is a piece of news that I can take home to Austria.

From The Floor: He is asking really: would the contributions be reduced if they were not tax deductible, and I would venture that one answer to that would be to look back to the experience prior to our Income Tax Act, when we were still laying the foundation for doing a lot of giving.

Mr. Sapp:

I can address it from our company's standpoint. I really do not think that tax considerations enter into the basis under which our giving occurs. Giving occurs because of a value system that exists within the company, and it is not a tax consideration, because while it is not taxed, it is tax exempt, it is still money out of the pocket that would have been there had you not given it. So I think that – I don't want to say "I think" – I'm very, very comfortable that because of the value system of our company, the contributions would be there.

General Myers:

I think, if you will recall, that one of the first charts I showed conveyed that corporate giving had increased dollarwise threefold in spite of the change in taxation and that the growth had been steady and constant over the years. That would be true in the last eight years. So there has been a continued support and continues to be heavy support, and it is all done, I think, as Charles pointed out, because of corporate conscience.

ERIK RITTER VON
KUEHNELT-LEDDIHN

IDEOLOGIES AND UTOPIAS: YES OR NO?

Dr. Erik von Kuehnelt-Leddihn
Austria

THE NATURE OF "RIGHT" AND "LEFT"

Today I am going to talk about ideologies and utopias. Being a rightist I move largely in America's conservative camp where both are constantly attacked and vilified, partly due to the widespread belief that ideologies and utopias belong to the Left. But even the American Left does not like to admit that it stands for these concepts. I know one outstanding exception, the so-called neo-conservative Irving Kristol. In "The Wall Street Journal" of October 1981 he said of the Republicans, that their weak spot is the fact that they have no ideology. "You cannot fight an ideology (such as Marxism or Leftism) with no ideology." Kristol, of course, admits that bad ideologies have created untold harm and suffering.

If we think of Communism and National Socialism, of Democracy in connection with the French Revolution, we cannot deny that the sufferings caused by ideologies were enormous. But so were the sufferings brought on by religion. There are right and good, as well as bad and negative ideologies and religions. For me personally, as a Catholic, my faith is the right one and I do not regard other religions as equally good, though they might have more or less valuable components. We can certainly not say that

the Quakers, for instance, have caused much harm; they certainly have not.

Sharia, the Moslem law, on the other hand has evidently
created a great deal of suffering and continues to do so. Or take
the Thuggees and what they did in India. From them stems the
American word "thug." They believed that they did good when
they waylaid travellers and choked them to death before a statue
of Kali; or certain religions of Haiti, or New Guinea where a
mother had to bash out the brain of her first child in the jungle
(so as not to defile her hut) and feed it to a sow whose piglet she
then had to adopt and nurse in order to establish her reputation
as a good mother! Of course, she suffered agonies. Or think of the
millions of Hindu widows burned alive.

However, these monstrous religions do not prove that
religion is wicked intrinsically, it can be either constructive or
destructive.

Now, what is really "right"? I have called myself a rightist and
I always insist that right is right and left is wrong, because in all
languages right has a positive, left a negative, meaning. In English
we say "this is right," and the seat of honor is at the right, and the
same is true in German. In Italian *la sinistra* is the left and *il sinistro*
is the calamity. In Japanese *hidarimae*, "In front of the left" is evil,
and in Sanscrit *de kshinah* "right" and *vamah* "left" have the same
implications. I could continue this list with Hungarian, Russian,
Spanish, and so forth. One is also reminded of the Bible where,
in Ecclesiastes 10,2 it says against any anatomy: "The heart of the
wise man beats on his right, the heart of the fool on his left side."
From this one deduces the number of fools....

And finally, on the Day of Judgment, as represented in so
many works of art, one sees on the right those who are saved
and on the left the damned, with Popes, kings, monks, and
nuns on both sides.

In all great civilizations "right" is, as we said, something positive, but how are we to apply this to the political scene? Let us
begin our analysis by stating that we all have two basic tenden-

cies. One we share with the animal kingdom, it is the desire to seek the company of persons of our own age, class, race, ethnicity, our own sex. We enjoy the harmony of feelings, opinions, tastes, and so forth. But since we are human beings we also have a contrary tendency: we enjoy variety, we like to meet quite different people, to see strange countries, to hear exotic music, to learn foreign languages, to be with persons of the other sex. Putting it in a nutshell, otherness is exciting and stimulating for us. One might say that sameness gives us a sense of security and calm, while otherness promises adventure. Nature produces variety, diversity, and inequalities: tall and small trees, wide and narrow rivers, enormous and tiny animals.

EQUALITY

As we just said, we sometimes enjoy sameness and identity, both closely related to equality. Ten dimes equal one dollar, but a dollar bill, except for the serial number, is identical with any other dollar bill. Whatever is identical is also equal. But both, identity and equality, are artificial. They are not natural and have to be established by force. Take a hedge, in order to give it an even surface, one has to clip it. In order to achieve an even surface one has to level mountains and fill up valleys. Equality and identity do not exist in nature, nor are they compatible with freedom. Freedom and equality are opposites, *we are either free or equal.*

Human beings are unequal in every respect: physically, intellectually, morally and, last but not least, we are unequal in the eyes of God. If Judas Iscariot is equal to John the Baptist, Christianity can close shop. God does not love us equally. Jesus preferred Saint John to Saint Peter, as we know from the Gospels. God does not give us equality, but He gives each one of us sufficient Grace to save ourselves. There is no equality on earth, nor in Purgatory, nor in Heaven. But there might be equality in Hell because that is exactly where it belongs.

FREEDOM

Freedom (*eleutheria*) is mentioned in the New Testament, whereas *isotes* is mentioned only in the sense of equity, never of equality. Goethe told us, that revolutionaries and law givers who promise both, equality and liberty, are either frauds or scoundrels. Therefore, the democratic and the liberal principle are incompatible. And what do these two principles stand for? Democracy answers the question who should rule, namely the majority of politically equal citizens, either in person or through representatives. Here we have the principle of majority rule and political equality. *True* liberalism, on the other hand, is not concerned with the origin of power but with the question how government should be exercised: every citizen should have the greatest amount of liberty still compatible with the common good.

IDEOLOGY

Now, surveying our globe, we find that ideologically the various forms of Marxism have a monopoly. American liberalism, on the other hand, is a sponge without profile. Ideologically we are naked to our enemies. We have no ideology. All we have nowadays is a tendency toward relativism and fake liberalism plus a plurality of incoherent views. But in the battle against Marxism (as, in the past against National Socialism) we have no ideology to oppose these forms of tyranny. We have religion, but religion as such is not an ideology and, as a rule, does not stand for a specific form of government, society, economy, and so on. Ideologies do. They can, don't forget, be anti-religious, even atheistic. On the other hand, they might have a religious foundation.

Early 19th-Century conservatism had a distinctly Christian basis and in this century the Christian conservatives were the ones who fought ideologically and religiously against leftist totalitarianism. We have clearly seen this in the resistance against

National Socialism, a leftist, nationalistic, racist and socialistic ideology. Who were the people who really resisted them? They were of two kinds: On the one side were the competitors, the Socialists and, even more so, the Communists. (One must always distinguish between competitors and enemies. One beer brewer is the competitor of another beer brewer, but his enemy is a prohibitionist.) The true enemies of National Socialism were the men and women of the right, people with strong religious convictions who tried to slaughter the beast and perished in the process, the heroes and martyrs of July 20, 1944 and thousands of Catholic priests, nuns, and friars who died in concentration camps or were brutally tortured and executed.

In Russia we had the same situation. Who fought in the White Armies during the Civil War of 1918-1920? The anarchists, because they stood for absolute freedom, but mainly the monarchists and the Christians of the Eastern Orthodox Church – but obviously not the liberal democrats. We do not see Marxists effectively opposed by liberal democrats because their attitude is this: "I think that I am right in my own way and you are right in yours; we both are right and wrong, so let's make it fifty-fifty." One might fight and die for an exclamation mark, but who would die for a question mark?

In our struggle for freedom it is, therefore, important to have an ideology, an ideology of the right to oppose those of the left. Both, Marxism, which is International Socialism, and National Socialism belong to the left because both are "identitarian." And a leftist, because he is an identitarian and egalitarian, visualizes a country of one race, one language, one class, one level of income, one type of school, one party and one leader. One, one, one and no variety.

The right does stand for variety, but it must be coherent, there must be a uniting bond. In a country like old Austria-Hungary this was the dynasty. At present we have in the western world democracy, though luckily not in the form of a closed ideology as in the French Revolution where all opponents were immediately slaughtered in the presence of the applauding populace. Democracy is nowadays liberal, it is but a frame into which free elections can fit all sorts of pictures. Certain pictures, however, can destroy the frame: totalitarian parties can win elections and put an end to all elections. This was the tragedy we saw in Germany when the National Socialists became by far the largest party. For years they had been kept out of the government by "emergency laws," a most "undemocratic" procedure. Finally they were "democratically" invited to join a coalition with other parties – in the hope that, in view of the country's great economic difficulties, they would fail and then be defeated in a later election. It is the everlasting shame of the German army that, as late as 1932, it did not establish a military dictatorship, the only means that could have prevented the National Socialist takeover. Admittedly, the army would have needed the support of the trade unions in this venture. General Kurt von Schleicher negotiated with them, but the Social Democrats forbade them to support an "aristocratic general."

There are, of course, situations – in Latin America, for instance – where the army has to step in because otherwise either the extreme left or complete anarchy would overtake the country. This was clearly the case in Chile.

The French Revolution is, of course, hailed in the "Age of the G," of guillotines, gallows, gas chambers, genocides, and Gulags. And what is going to happen if and when democracy comes to an end? What sort of vision, what kind of plan do we have? A keen observer will already notice the Hippocratic traits on the face of democracy. But are we prepared? Do we have an alternative, a "utopia" to replace democracy? The answer is no. And yet we can hear the desperate outcry of conservatives in this country: "No, no, no ideology!"

But man is an ideological creature. The average man in this, or any European country, who is not a Marxist, has already some vague, though immature and incomplete ideology. Take anybody from the next street corner and cross-question him methodically and I am sure that very soon the dim outlines of an ideology will surface. It may be a jumble of contradictory tenets, it may lack profile and be subject to dispute, but it is there.

THE END OF DEMOCRACY

You will now want to know why I believe that democracy will come to an end. Apart from the fact, that everything has an end, (only the sausage has two), I am going to mention only two or three pertinent factors. One is the ever growing abyss between *scienta* and *scienda*, between the actual knowledge of voters and their delegates and the knowledge necessary to judge today's minor and major problems facing the various countries. In a Swiss Canton like Glarus or Appenzell-Ausserbaden we find direct democracy and there it makes sense. Glarus, the largest of these Cantons, has 36,000 inhabitants. If, for instance, the question arises whether a chocolate factory should be licensed, the men (standing in line to facilitate the count) discuss the pros and cons of the problem. Would a chocolate factory mean more jobs? Would the cream from local farms no longer have to be transported to Winterthur because it could be used locally? The votes are indicated by three fingers of the raised hand, as in an oath. If the count shows a majority for the factory, it will be licensed. This still makes sense. I now think of another example. I was in Vietnam five times during the war which I thus saw in all its phases, three times at the risk of my life. I also studied the situation there with the help of books and reports. When, later, I lectured on the subject in the United States, I can tell you from the discussions that my audiences never had the right to utter an opinion on the Vietnam War. They could merely judge sentimentally – which is what you do if you cannot judge rationally.

Now, if somebody took me to the railroad depot and asked for my opinion about a locomotive, I would be stuck; I write novels and learned essays, I paint pictures and deliver lectures but, being a technological idiot, how could I judge a locomotive? I could make it the subject of a poem or a short story without having the slightest idea of its functioning value in the railroad system. Similarly, people can no longer evaluate the social and political problems of their countries. The inhabitants of San Marino, Monaco or Andorra might, but not those of large countries and certainly not those of world powers. Unarmed they are exposed to the barrage of half-truths, lies and oversimplifications showered upon them by the mass media.

Another reason why I believe that democracy will come to an end is the approaching bankruptcy of so many countries. This is due to the usually left-of-center Santa Claus parties on the one hand, and the right-of-center tighten-your-belt parties on the other. One doesn't shoot Santa Claus whose parties therefore automatically win elections, until or unless they are revealed to be so corrupt and stupid that even their supporters unwillingly cease to vote for them. Thus the tighten-your-belt parties get a break and can form a government, but they rarely have the courage to undo the evil and stupid work of the Santa Claus parties, because if they were even to attempt to wipe out the whole machinery of mass corruption, they would never be re-elected. One can see this all over Europe where the financial evolution usually consists of two steps forward and one step back. The provider state and its enormous deficits ·might be clipped here and there, but it will never be abolished. And in the long run technocracy beckons, because people will gradually become aware of their ignorance, and because technology requires an efficient bureaucracy.

Technocracy, however, could be a grave menace to individual freedom and what we must do is bring technocracy and personal freedom under a common denominator. This is not easy, but possible and we will discuss this later on.

AGAIN: IDEOLOGY

Now let us return to ideology. A young person must have a vision of his or her future. These expectations will hardly ever be fulfilled, yet they are necessary. A Portuguese proverb says that "he who has no hope will not work." A man (or woman) must be aware of his gifts *and* his ensuing obligations, must set himself a goal. And this is also true of a nation. WHAT DOES IT REPRE-SENT? What has it to offer to the rest of the world? Between messianism and self-centered isolationism there is a third way.

As professor in Georgetown University, I once asked a post-graduate class of 37 in a secret ballot what they wanted to become later in life. Twenty-one of them wanted to become President of the United States. This may have been a jejune or infantile ambition, but the White House does act as a sort of magnet, a vision, a goal, a program. To reach for the stars is not ignoble. If one asks the conservatives in this country what sort of vision, what sort of blueprint or program they give to the young Americans the reply is verbose and indistinct. During a five-day CCA symposium in Hillsdale College, about eleven years ago, the problem came up in full force. A great friend of mine – it was *not* Bill Buckley – objected to what I had said in my lecture about the necessity for a vision of the shape of things to come. A utopia? Why not? Some utopias are impossible, others can be achieved only through too many unwarranted sacrifices, but some can become true. Remember: the United States of America in 1770, too, was nothing but a utopia!

Summing up my lecture, a great conservative leader – again it was not Bill Buckley – said: "Our dear friend Erik cannot really have proposed an ideology, there must have been a misunderstanding. Ideologies are unconservative and must be rejected!" "No," I replied, "there was no misunderstanding. I live in the hope that an ideology and also a utopia be born." (A few years later this actually happened.) And I added "What have you conservatives given to young Americans to live for, to work for, to strive and, if necessary, to die for? What kind of picture of the future could they expect? You have given them absolutely noth-ing concrete. You were very clever in your critique of leftism, you gave them a brilliant critique of socialism and a first-rate critique of what, in this country, is called liberalism but in the rest of the world would be called socialism. Lots of excellent critique, but where is the blueprint for tomorrow? Your books are well written and some are even bestsellers, yet they only are what the French call de la *litterature*." Well, I got a standing ovation which as you can imagine, surprised the other speaker no end.

You must ask yourselves, what is the alternative to an ideology, to a concrete vision of the future? The alternative could be the method of trial and error so dear to the English-speaking world. But it is not a very human method and rather resembles what goes on in an animal psychology lab where a chimpanzee tries to catch a banana hanging from the ceiling. When he has found and then stacked enough boxes he finally, finally succeeds. We, however, do not have the time for experiments and it is a human trait to be Promethean in the Greek sense of the term, which means "thinking ahead, planning, reflecting on the future." The legendary Prometheus had a brother called Epimetheus (which means "thinking afterwards") who married Pandora, the lady with the fatal box containing all evils, and they had a daughter Pyrrha who, according to Greek mythology, is the mother of mankind. Thus one should not be surprised to see mankind behaving like the inmates of a hospital for the criminally insane, the totally irrational world we live in. But outstanding Americans have always known this.

I am thinking here of two men I knew personally. One was Crane Brinton of Harvard, the other Ralph Henry Gabriel of Yale. Both wrote, independently of each other, that "Since not a single tenet of democracy can be rationally or scientifically proved, democracy has only one chance in the future:to become a secular religion, which you can achieve only by an act of faith." In other words, you close your eyes, put your hand on your heart and say: "I believe – in the goodness and intelligence of the people, in human equality and in the wisdom of majorities." The only trouble is that, as Brinton also said, a secular religion has to deliver the goods right here on earth and this it usually cannot.

THE NECESSITY FOR AN IDEOLOGY

The necessity for an ideology was brought home to me very clearly when I heard of an event I mentioned yesterday and which I want to analyze now, namely the revolt in Novorossiysk, a Russian city very near the Black Sea, with about one-hundred-thousand inhabitants. In 1962 a riot developed in the market place because there was no food to buy. The riot became a revolt, the revolt a rebellion, and the rebellion became a revolution. Locally the Soviet system broke down completely. The city was in the hands of a seething, furious populace. The Russian Army was sent for and advanced into the very heart of the city where the people barred its way. The officer who was to command them to fire turned to his soldiers and said: "Don't fire. These are your brothers and sisters"; took out his pistol and shot himself. The soldiers retreated but soon the KGB arrived in large planes, killed 300 to 400 people and deported thousands. Thus ended the resistance. These people had no ideology to replace Marxism. They were against Marxism, against the Soviet system, but they had no alternative ideology. Convinced Marxists are extremely rare in Russia. When I was there the last time, I met only two convinced male Communists. Everybody I met had, in his heart, a different alternative, some vague, some more concrete, but since there was no free speech, no free exchange of ideas an alternative picture had not yet crystallized – not yet!

The alternative could definitely not be democracy. Among Russians it is all but impossible, because there simply is no common denominator and no readiness to compromise among the Russians. When Solzhenitsyn gave his famous Harvard lecture, he was furiously criticized by the American Left because he said, that there is no future for democracy in Russia and that religion must again become a leading moral force. And what do we have to do? What we must do is to establish governments in which knowledge, experience, principles, especially ethical principles which ultimately derive from the Bible, can come to the fore. There are undoubtedly areas where the government has to be supreme on the basis of expertise, in foreign affairs, military affairs, and security, for instance.

What we all need – and this is a weighty problem – is minimal government of maximal quality. What we have, on the other hand, is maximal government of the lowest, most amateurish order. There are domains which our governments have invaded and from which they must be made to retreat. But where the government must be supreme, as in military and foreign affairs, there can be no democracy whatsoever. There can be popular representation, an honest lobby enabling a representative to say, for example, "I represent the teachers of the Southwest," or "I represent the miners of Virginia," or "I represent the dentists of the Deep South." With these men or women the government then ought to maintain a real dialogue.

THE IDEAL GOVERNMENT

In other words, the ideal government some of us visualize is minimal and elitist in quality and leaves to the live forces of society (and to small, local self-governing bodies) the many tasks which modern, centralized government has appropriated. What we are envisaging is, obviously, a non-democratic rule. It was the French Revolution which foisted democracy on the rest of the world and I hope that you are aware of the fact, that the Founding Fathers despised democracy. Charles Beard said that they loathed democracy more than Original Sin. This is the reason why the word "democracy" appears neither in the Declaration or in the Constitution and the same is true of the noun "republic." Even Jefferson, the most leftist of the Founding Fathers, called George III merely "a prince not fit to rule a free people." A free people can accept a ruler who understands freedom, who has a sense of the freedom of his subjects. Most Americans today can no longer envisage a crowned ruler over a truly free people. But there had been a sort of conspiracy between Nathan Gorham, President of the old Congress, and General von Steuben who tried to persuade Prince Henry of Prussia to become hereditary Stadholder of the United States. All great European thinkers were men of the right and so were the great American thinkers, beginning with the Founding Fathers, above all John Adams and Alexander Hamilton. And remember Henry Adams, William Graham Sumner, Henry L. Mencken, the great genius Orestes Brownson, or Herman Melville who, in his Clarel sounded his fears for this country:

> "An Anglo-Saxon China, see, May on your vast plains shame the race in the Dark Ages of Democracy."

The watershed is 1828, as Henry Adams saw very clearly. From then on an *alien*, French ideology called democracy invaded America, a thoroughly aristocratic country, a Whig country. The Whigs represented the genuine aristocratic spirit and that is why the European nobility, fired with enthusiasm, came over here: Steuben, Kosciusko, Pulaski, Lafayette, Rouerie, St. Simon, Segur, Rochambeau, et. al. Only in 1828 a man who calls himself a democrat, enters the White House. America then becomes the executor of the ideas of the French Revolution and later led several crusades in Europe "to make the world safe for democracy." What they actually did was pave the way for Adolf Hitler first, and then for Joseph Vissarionovitch Stalin.

PREPARING FOR THE END OF DEMOCRACY

So you see what we need, for the end of democracy is approaching. As I said before, even if we know all the facts and the development is obvious, we never know how long it might take, we must not set a time-table for historic events. The end of democracy might come tomorrow or after another generation. But come it will and so we must be armed with an ideology and with a religion. For a concrete alternative, have a look at the *Portland Declaration*. It was born in the United States and has been translated into Spanish and German. Several small groups are already studying it and last year I was asked to lecture about it to the seniors of a prep school. How had they heard about it? Not from the *National Review* where it had first appeared, but from a *Reader for Christian Schools!* This, naturally, pleased me very much. This is the direction we have to work toward. We must have an ideological alternative to Marxism and something to replace democracy after its demise and the ensuing, dangerous vacuum. There never has been a political institution that lasted forever. Democracy is not immortal and we must plan for something better to succeed it. In the first half of this century we saw it replaced by something much, much worse – so let us be prepared.

DISCUSSION

Question: You said that your audience had no right to an opinion about the war because they had not seen it firsthand. That would seem to imply an awful quietism or muteness for most people. If they have no right to opinions on matters they haven't experienced firsthand, that would leave us wide open to professional opinion makers who would fill such a vacuum. You are not suggesting that kind of quietism for most people, are you?

Erik von Kuehnelt-Leddihn:

It is quite impossible for the vast majority anywhere to have a grasp of world politics because they have not been prepared, nor had the time to prepare themselves. Think of a hard-working industrialist or physician. How much time has he left to study the international situation, the necessary languages? As for the quality of Congressmen, I refer you to a shattering article by William E. Simon, giving his opinion about politicians. Simon, former Secretary of the Treasury, expressed himself in terms of abuse positively inviting libel suits. But none came, needless to say. He calls the Congressmen lily-livered, bloodsucking, simple-witted, ignorant men. The American people should crucify them. And our European parliaments are not better. Thus it is not surprising that politicians are generally despised. *Espece de depute* is a term of abuse used by Parisian taxi drivers. It is surprising that on the European Continent people still vote in large numbers (80 to 90 per cent to American's 55, as an average). But this contemptuous attitude resembles that of the very religious Middle Ages toward their priests which, nevertheless, did not affect their religious sentiments. But then, one nice day, Luther and Calvin appeared on the scene and the greatest catastrophe of all times hit the Church practically overnight. Something analogous might happen on the political scene.

In our day of television the voters, though unable to fathom the problems of the day, can and do judge appearance, the language of a campaigning politician. As a result, a man who is cross-eyed or stammers will have no chance, even if he were a brilliant, gifted man. I remember how, in October 1960, I watched the famous debate between Nixon and Kennedy, together with a group of Ivy-League University professors. They had, of course, already decided to vote for Kennedy, but then the candidates' wives appeared on the screen. Pat Nixon was considered nice-looking, but when Jackie came on there was an uproar: "Look at those legs! We've got to get that babe into the White House!" Well, how many votes were due to Jackie's legs? After all, Kennedy's majority amounted to only 160,000 votes. In Europe things are not very different. Majorities may be right or wrong.

The German majorities in 1932 and 1933 were dead wrong. Mussolini had the vast majority of Italians behind him in the 1930's. Even in Russia people cried when they heard about the death of Stalin, that singular monster. Take an international body like the United Nations. Who represents Cambodia? It is still the regime of Pol Pot. And while Rhodesia was in the doghouse, Uganda under Idi Amin Dada was welcome. Idi Amin had once asked his Minister of Health whether he had ever tasted human flesh. When the Minister denied this, Idi Amin exclaimed: "You must try it, it has a lovely, salty flavor!" Such monsters can be found in many places.

We really must return to knowledge, reason, and experience. Of course, I don't demand that every American should have been in Vietnam. But if I had had a son in that war, I would have known that the likelihood of his being killed there was infinitely smaller than the likelihood of his being killed on the American highways. For every soldier who died in Vietnam, eight Americans died on the roads in the United States. Remember, the American Army in Vietnam was never permitted to fight – to fight and to win. The political background of that war is unbelievable. I am prepared to countersign every page of General Westmoreland's book on that subject. Most American correspondents in Vietnam knew no French, the only means of communication with the local population. As for their readers and audiences, they were so ignorant about distant regions of the globe, that it was easy to bamboozle them and that is exactly what the mass media did.

But the mass-media people, too, have an ideology, a leftist one. In his book *The Irony of Vietnam – The System Worked*, Mr. Leslie Gelb states that the victory of Communism was a victory of democracy. The system worked indeed! The American people forced the President, the Pentagon, and the Congress to withdraw an undefeated army. The American people had been successfully "re-educated" by the mass media. What a disagreeable surprise were the Boat People! Even Jane Fonda finally recanted.

Question: Must we despair that any of our major political
                   parties will ever define an ideology?

Erik von Kuehnelt-Leddihn:

I do not think that it can be reasonably expected, but something has happened that seems to indicate a polarization. When I first came to America in 1937, Democrats and Republicans were not nearly as distinct, there was a very big block of Southern Democrats who, for lack of a better term, were called conservative, and there were many very liberal Republicans. Now the two main parties are more definitely right and left and the polarization seems to continue.

I believe, that some sort of movement to capture the imagination of the Republican Party should be started. A concrete vision of the shape of things to come could thus become a real factor. The conservative movement is an important element, but one cannot say that it has captured the Republican Party, certainly not with its present candidates. This is a country of the Reformation and the term "conservative" has become almost a good word. It used to be a bad one, whereas the term "liberal," once a very good word, has slightly changed for the worse. I say this because there is no Catholic or even predominantly Catholic country in Europe with a party calling itself conservative. All conservative parties in Europe are in the countries of the Reformation. The Catholic Church is *not* conservative, whereas the Reformation was indeed a conservative movement, it was a medieval reaction against the spirit of the Renaissance, as I have said before. Luther and Calvin were conservatives and would have strongly objected to being called "Protestants." The psychological beginning of the Reformation was the winter of 1510 to 1511, when Luther came to Rome and suddenly encountered the Renaissance and Humanism. To him this meant a revival of paganism. He did not understand the Catholic tendency to absorb everything and "baptize" it − everything that is beautiful. Luther was convinced that Socrates, Plato, and Aristotle, because they were not baptized, were in Hell. He was an extreme conservative, radically anti-Jewish, and rabidly against the common man. To him the princes were gods and Herr Omnes, "Mr. Everyman," condemned to humble servitude.

Certain Black people call their sons Martin Luther, unaware that Luther was a furious racist. The average person knows little about Luther and Calvin, or about many other things. Mark Twain once said: "I am not afraid about the ignorance of people. The people to fear are those who know a lot − a lot of things which just ain't so."

Question: Speaking of racism, does that not, in practice, insist on characterizing people the way that a botanist characterizes flowers so that if you have a brown skin you are a slug, and you can never be a noble?

Erik von Kuehnelt-Leddihn:

Of course not. There is no connection between the two. Ideology is never ever necessarily racist, but it can be so as it was in the case of National Socialism. The foundation of racism is to be found in Darwinism. One must not forget that freedom can and must play a fundamental role in an ideology. There can be an "ideology of freedom." An ideology can have many components, but it cannot embrace both freedom and racism. That the different races have different gifts is obvious. The south European has a much clearer complexion than the north European. A south European has quicker reactions than one from the North. He is also less likely to become an alcoholic. Jews very rarely become alcoholics because they belong to the Mediterranean race. Whereas even a small amount of alcohol has devastating effects on a Red Indian or on an Oriental. Spanish workers are highly valued in Germany for their quick minds and their dexterity; the Spanish worker is highly motivated, he works better than the German worker and overcomes him.

In other words, one should not talk about superior and inferior races. God created the entire human race to which we all belong with a great variety of gifts and talents. Thank God that we are not all of the same mold.

FORUM

INDIVIDUAL FREEDOM, ECONOMIC SECURITY, AND PERSONAL DIGNITY

MODERATOR
Dr. Charles L. Cotrell

Rabbi David Jacobson

Rev. Charles H. Miller

Rev. W. Francis Schorp

PANELISTS

MODERATOR

Dr. Charles L. Cotrell

Dr. Charles L. Cotrell, Vice President of Academic Affairs of St. Mary's University since 1986, received his B.A. and M.A. degrees from St. Mary's in 1962 and 1964, respectively, and his Doctorate in Political Science from the University of Arizona in 1969. Cotrell began his teaching career at St. Mary's University in 1966 as Assistant Professor of Political Science, was tenured in 1976, and became a full Professor in 1977. He has also taught at Texas A&I University, and was a Fellow in the Center for Behavioral and Social Research at Wesleyan University, Connecticut during 1969-1970. Dr. Cotrell has served as Department Chair of Political Science, as Dean of the School of Humanities and Social Sciences, and as Assistant to the President for Planning and Institutional Research at St. Mary's University. In 1985, he was the recipient of the Marianist Heritage Award. He has been a consultant to the U.S. Department of Justice on elections systems and political participation, was guest editor of PUBLIUS: Journal of Federalism, Special Issue on the Voting Rights Act, November, 1986 and is the author of numerous articles in professional journals. Cotrell is married and the father of four sons.

Rabbi David Jacobson

David Jacobson is a native of Cincinnati, Ohio. His college and seminary education was received at the University of Cincinnati and at Hebrew Union College where he was ordained in 1934, the 14th generation of rabbis in the paternal line. He pursued his post-graduate studies in sociology and biblical history at the University of Cambridge, England, and received his Ph.D. from St. Catherine's College. He has been active in health, education, welfare programs, and criminal justice. He has received a number of awards and honors including an LL.D. from Our Lady of the Lake University. Rabbi Jacobson is the author of *Social Background of the Old Testament* and a contributor to the Universal Jewish Encyclopedia. He is listed in Who's Who in America, Who's Who in the World, and Who's Who in Religion.

Rev. Charles H. Miller

Father Charles Miller is a native of Parsons, Kansas. He entered the Society of Mary in 1951 and was ordained a priest in 1964. He holds the Bachelor of Arts from St. Mary's University, the Licentiate in Theology from the University of Fribourg, Switzerland, the Licentiate in Sacred Scripture from the Pontifical Biblical Institute in Rome, Italy, and his Doctorate in Theology from San Anselmo College in Rome. Father Miller has been a faculty member of Saint Louis University, the International Marian Research Institute of the University of Dayton, and of St. Mary's University, where he has served as Dean of the School of Humanities and Social Sciences since 1987. He has numerous publications, is a Fulbright Scholar, and has conducted some thirty study tours to Middle Eastern and Mediterranean countries since 1972. He is a member of the Texas Committee for the Humanities and of the Board of Trustees of the American Center of Oriental Research in Amman, Jordan.

Rev. W. Francis Schorp

Father Schorp was born in Pearsall, Texas in 1931 where he grew up on a ranch. Franz, as his friends all know him, had an education focused on mathematics turning to philosophy. His first degrees were earned in Philosophy and Mathematics from St. Mary's University and Theology from the University of Fribourg in Switzerland. Father Schorp is presently working as a candidate for a Ph.D. in Philosophy of Law at Washington University. His interests include machining metal, casting, wood-working, working in the Emergency Room at Medical Center Hopsital and in Hospital Ethics policy formation at Santa Rosa Hospital. A knowledge of languages has helped provide further bases for grasping and interpreting meanings.

INDIVIDUAL FREEDOM, ECONOMIC SECURITY, AND PERSONAL DIGNITY

Dr. Charles L. Cotrell:

Good morning. I am Charles Cotrell. I am a Vice President of St. Mary's University, and I would like to welcome all of you to this particular panel, a part of the Seventh Symposium, addressing "The Sources of Wealth and the Causes of Poverty."

I would like to pay recognition to someone whose energy is ceaseless, whose efforts to bring about these important discussions have been and are ongoing for decades, and that is Brother Paul Goelz.

Will you applaud him?

This morning's panel will discuss "Individual Freedom, Economic Security, and Personal Dignity."

We have three distinguished guests on the panel. Our format today is that each guest will be asked, upon introduction, to speak for eight or ten minutes; then we want to engage the audience in a discussion with the panelists.

Our first guest, whom it gives me great pleasure to introduce and welcome to Saint Mary's again, Rabbi David Jacobson, who is Rabbi Emeritus of Temple Beth-El in San Antonio. He earned his Doctorate in Philosophy from Saint Catherine's College at the University of Cambridge. He is a fourteenth generation in a paternal line of Rabbis. For those of us who are San Antonians and generally aware, his name is literally a household name in the finest sense. He has been very, very active and has been recognized numerous times, including various awards. I have visited with him on a number of occasions. I don't know with how many boards and civic opportunities he has been associated. And most importantly, as those of you who read the paper last evening or this morning know, he will celebrate his fiftieth year of association with Temple Beth-El this Friday and also the fiftieth year of being married to a lovely person, who is not able to be with us this morning, Helen Jacobson.

Join me in welcoming to Saint Mary's University Rabbi David Jacobson.

Rabbi David Jacobson:
Thank you very, very much indeed.

Dr. Cotrell said that my name is a household word. Indeed, it is. In our house I'm the one who takes out the garbage.

INNOVATION AND FREEDOM

I must agree with the premise that a shining achievement of this country's purpose and beginnings has been its amazing opportunities for personal growth and success. This chance to become a star is really not a remote possibility. It happens all the time. Prime examples are young persons, barely out of college, who obtain wealth and leadership in businesses with which they start or are affiliated, such as those who have created an innovative microchip and computer enterprise. Now, this phenomenon springs directly from the American penchant to invent and improve devices that work. For instance, the Smithsonian Institute in Washington. There is an opportunity to gape and exclaim over the multitude of machines and items that were built by Americans, to our great pleasure and gratification, with any number of smaller and larger fabrications to enhance people's welfare and pleasure. In the American Pantheon are such names as Benjamin Franklin, Thomas Alva Edison, Henry Ford, and Samuel Morse.

In the short space of time so much has been developed to provide people with more freedom, more well-being, than ever before in civilization. The rate of technical expansion in our country and in the western world is without precedent. Moreover, the increment seems to be exponential, for what is a "gee-whiz" accomplishment today becomes "old hat" tomorrow. Scientific discoveries and applications based upon research and development, augmented by attaching one stream of new products or new knowledge to other such chains of ideas and improvements, keep growing and evolving. Inevitably people live longer with more and more things to sustain and delight them. It would be a mistake to think that such results can so amplify our way of life that these are confined within the boundaries of this country or even in the western world, although we are the principal beneficiaries. The world is, of course, one village. We are assured through exchanges with other groups within this world that there are many factors which account for the divergencies, including the history and traditions of the country, the political and ethnic attitudes, which help make up the culture of all the segments of the world.

Natural resources are not equally distributed, and governments vary immensely in the ways they relate to their own people or those outside their borders. And there is some variation of the intelligence of human groups of various peoples, but the astounding fact is that these differences are not as great as many mistakenly believe, for the IQs of individuals of every race and country tend to be relatively the same within the expected ranges of individual variation.

DETERRENTS TO FREEDOM, SECURITY, AND DIGNITY

Since freedom, security, and dignity are our objectives, what are the deterrents?

The major handicap is inadequate training and education. While knowledge accumulates at a prodigious rate, with books, discs, and journals of all kinds shelved into libraries and memorialized in many forms, ignorance abounds. Good teachers are rare, and even mediocre ones are at a premium.

Functional illiteracy drags down the hopes of students who stay in school right through the college years, and remediation efforts are never quite good enough. This is a staggering problem, which must be directly faced and solved or alleviated. Going to school and really learning, stimulated by good teachers and by good books, should be part of every person's birthright, to be expected for taking part in the accelerated adventure of growing up in this land of promise and fulfillment.

And this dream has been the magnet that drew millions of the disenfranchised to this part of the world, which, for so many, became paradise. We are a nation of immigrants, who could and should exhaust ourselves in thanksgiving. Many who came worked so hard and effectively that they sometimes evoked the jealousy of others who had been here for a longer period.

Yet these latecomers from Asia and central Europe and from Russia added their strength to the might and wisdom of all the others who responded to the call, which was: "Give me your tired, your poor, your huddled masses yearning to be free, the wretched refuse of your teeming shores."

These words, inscribed on the base of the Statue of Liberty, as enticing as they are, were far less significant than the nucleus of the Declaration of Independence and the Constitution of the United States, the broad proclamation, "All men are created free and equal," which became the model of all the other declarations and constitutions throughout our continent and others.

We are still very much in the process of attempting to bring individual freedom, economic security, and personal dignity to all who live here. We have become sensitized through realizing that "all men" means "all men and women," shoulder to shoulder, as we strengthen ourselves. We are moving ahead.

Religious restraints and restrictions have also had a very long history in this country, but, again, whether we are Catholics or Jews or Jehovah Witnesses or any other sect or denomination, the barriers and walls have changed, prompted, I believe, by our common experience in the wars of the Twentieth Century, where we have learned to know each other, and where the military leadership has become more advisable and economic and effective to make provision for each and every group to be as equals.

Much more difficult had been the burdens borne by people of different colors, particularly the black and the brown, although the yellow and the red have had their experiences of privation and suffering.

POVERTY

Everyone in this land must be aware of a growing concern for the American dream, which is becoming less attainable for an increasing number of Americans who suffer from poverty, from, as I mentioned earlier, functional illiteracy, handicaps, weakness or disability, mental illness, and crime.

Today twenty percent of all children are living in poverty. The poverty rates for blacks rose to over thirty-three percent. Twenty-four percent of all children live with a single parent. For blacks, the rate is forty-one percent. Forty-six percent of all single-mother families are below the poverty line. For Hispanic and black single-mother families, the percentage is approximately sixty percent. Although median family income rose in 1987, black and Hispanic incomes dropped. Fifty-four percent of first marriages by women aged twenty-five to twenty-nine will end in divorce. Of the seventy percent who remarry, about half will divorce again. About half of all the children who live with a single parent drop out of school at some time before they reach sixteen. For black children, the number is nearly nine out of ten. There are more black men in prison or jail than attending college full-time. These statistics show a greater gap between the haves and the have-nots and a growing lack of attention to our children.

THE COSTS OF CRIME

In the future, we, as a nation, will suffer from such neglect with more crime, which, in turn, will increase taxes to pay for more police, prisons, and jails or other important state services, such as education, health, and job-training. We must recognize that the escalating crime rates are not the product of failure by criminal justice agencies.

If we simply attempt to solve the crime problem by more severe forms of punishment, we will fail to achieve the primary goal of creating a more healthy and productive society.

A CAUSE FOR OPTIMISM

A candid approach to our situation does not imply a pessimistic forecast. None of our problems is out of control. Together, however, they demand the best thought and inventiveness as well as application of research into rational and compassionate answers to the problems. As in a chess game, the first move determines the outcome. So we all are handicapped by early flaws in planning, but we can capture our original stability if we devote ourselves towards scrubbing the uneven jointures.

We in America, particularly the oldest segment of this slice of history, have experienced unprecedented prosperity. We have seen this civilization slowly drained by devastating wars, and we have studied crises of various sorts and kinds, many types, but the evils have reinforced many truths, such as human equality and the persistence of individual brotherhood, of justice and liberty. With God's help, we shall overcome.

Thank you.

Dr. Cotrell:

Thank you, Rabbi Jacobson, for that analysis of the challenges facing our people.

Our next panelist is the Reverend Charles H. Miller, of the Society of Mary. He is currently our Dean of the School of Humanities and Social sciences here. He received his Bachelor of

Arts degree here at St. Mary's University, his Bachelor of Sacred
Theology and his Licentiate at the University of Freiburg, and his
Doctorate in Sacred Theology at the Sacred Seminary in Rome. I
would hesitate to give his background in terms of his breadth of
interests, but he has a deep and abiding interest in Scripture, in
Biblical archeology, in field trips, in leading our students and
guests on such trips throughout the world. He is a student of wide
issues. I know that you will benefit from, and enjoy the breadth
of, this individual's intelligence, and I also know that you will
enjoy, as I do, his wit and his humor.

Father Charles Miller.

Rev. Charles H. Miller:

Thank you.

Actually, as a Biblical scholar and an archaeologist, I feel much
more at home in a hole in the Middle East, a hole in the ground
that has been excavated to enlighten our concern with the things
of three thousand years ago; but I will have on my secondary hat,
as a theologian, this morning.

As a theologian, I propose to address the topic, "Individual
Freedom, Economic Security, and Personal Dignity," from the
ground of a Roman Catholic theological perspective. The recent
developments in human rights theories among Catholics,
Lutherans, and Reformed Protestants, however, have shown
signs of an increasing convergence, so that much of what I say
may well be held in common among mainstream theologians.

THE CONCEPT OF PERSON

Let me begin by saying that an idea of a human person that
denies the possibility of authentic and radical freedom and dignity, such as, for example, in the picture given by B. F. Skinner
in his "Beyond Human Dignity,"would appear to me to be incompatible with a Roman Catholic perspective. Political, religious, or
spiritual freedom of a programmable machine is simply meaning-

less, although one could more easily make, I suppose, a case for assuring the economic security for such a machine.

Before I proceed, however, let me rearrange the title, if I may, to "Personal Dignity, Individual Freedom, Economic Security."

I would hold that our personal dignity as human beings is simply a given and that upon it rest our rights to freedom as individuals and in political, religious, social, and other matters as well as a right to economic security. Personal dignity itself is based upon our creation in the image and likeness of God, taken to mean that we are like God in our intelligence and freedom of will and that we are called, by virtue of our origin, to communion with God, as Vatican II has expressed it. Now, each of us has, therefore, a non-instrumental value such that none of us should be simply subordinated to the group.

On the other side, the Gospels, quoting from Deuteronomy and Leviticus, on the essential ethical content of the Jewish Torah and of the Christian tradition, the Gospels join together love of God and love of one's neighbor as one's self. In short, the dignity of the individual human person is radically linked to that of the common good of society.

HUMAN RIGHTS

Human rights are, therefore, especially important and inalienable moral rights belonging to all of us, to all persons, simply by virtue of being human. Now, these rights are moral rights, whether or not they happen to be recognized or protected by law, whether or not they are legal rights. The term "human rights" automatically refers to those that are essential to one's being treated as a human being with this kind of dignity, to those common to all human persons as such. In our American Constitution, these are summed up in the expression "life, liberty, and the pursuit of happiness."

In a 1984 article in the "Review," Stanislov Chalwajak, a philosopher at the Catholic University of Lublin, Poland, argues that the different views of human rights to be found in Marxism and in Christianity result from their conflicting conceptions of the person and society. Human rights are not derived from social structures but from the peculiar character of human beings, according to the Catholic view. Such human rights are in themselves inherently unchangeable since they adhere in human nature as such. On the other hand, our perceptions, our ideas, our theories of those rights change over time, as in the movement from monarchy to democracy, as in a more concrete expression of political freedom, or as in this country, development of the idea of freedom of religion. Rabbi Jacobson has just briefly detailed some of the development in this country alone.

But our human rights are not necessarily absolute, since one human right may well conflict with another or even other people's claims to the same human right. What may have begun, for example, as an infringement upon the rights of others, as in the westward expansion of the United States at the expense of the native Americans, can later become such a given that reversing the evil done to some could well infringe upon the rights of others. It would be profoundly unjust to simplistically give the country back to the Indians today. However, the same principle of the recognition of the right to own property that we in this country hold so dear would appear to demand an equitable recognition of the rights of native Americans who were tramped upon about a century ago by our ancestors. This is simply an example of the conflict of rights.

Or in the medical decisions about the allocation of expensive resources or transplants of available organs, who shall live and who shall die.

Individual freedom and economic security require certain distinctions among our human rights. Most theologians would probably distinguish between civil political rights, such as freedom of religion, assembly, participation in government, civil political rights, *and* social economic rights – food, shelter, basic health care, education. Some writers in the classical liberal tradition, not the "L" word but the classical liberal tradition, deny that social economic needs are human rights at all. Marxists, on the other hand, would appear to reject claims to individual civil and political freedoms. The Catholic and Protestant theologians in our midst would take a more inclusive approach, as did Pope John XXIII in his "Pacem in Terris."

LEVELS OF RIGHTS

A more recent Catholic writer is David Hollenbach, a Jesuit. Hollenbach differentiates among three levels of rights – first of all, personal rights, which belong to the person as such; secondly, social rights, by which he understands conditions for the preservation of the well-being of the individual person but specifying positive obligations of society towards all its members; and, thirdly, instrumental rights, that is, essential institutional conditions in larger institutions if human dignity is to be preserved.

Now, perhaps the most important rights conflicts are not so much between personal rights, for example, personal liberty versus economic well-being. The loss of political liberty tends to undermine economic well-being, as we can see in some Marxist countries. An economic crisis, on the other hand, may well impact on political freedom, as in the oft-expressed concern over the situation in Mexico and some of the other Latin American countries. Hollenbach sees the critical conflict between social rights for the society and support for human dignity and, in the other extreme, unrestrained exercise of personal rights. In the Nineteenth Century Industrial Revolution there was a time when children went to work at no later than thirteen years of age. On the other side, institutional dominance undermines human dignity, that is, proletarian government of either the right or the left. Think of the *desaparecedos* ("the missing persons") in Chile and Argentina.

PERSONAL LIBERTY VERSUS INSTITUTIONS

How should institutions act? Should they restrain personal liberty in behalf of the dignity of all? That is the question. Should

pornography, for example, be forbidden? Should there be legislation to control the kind of Wall Street takeovers that appear to
be nonproductive, terribly expensive, costing the jobs of many,
and benefiting only a few? How should the institutions act to
assure personal liberty while restraining personal liberty in order
to assure the dignity of all? Lists of human rights such as those
found in "Pacem in Terris" and the "Universal Declaration of
Human Rights," include the rights to food, clothing, shelter,
education, and medical care, rights to political participation and
migration, rights of assembly and association, rights to adequate
working conditions and a just wage, the right to have a family,
rights to freedom of religion, expression, education – these concern basic human needs, personal freedoms, and binding
relationships among persons.

PRINCIPLES FOR THE FORMULATION OF POLICY

So from all of these human rights Hollenbach proposes three
cardinal principles as one of the ethical standards for the formation of policy. First of all, the needs of the poor must take priority
over the wants of the rich, that is, there should be some kind of
guarantee of a minimum standard of living for all. Second, the
freedom of the dominated takes priority over the liberty and
privileges of the powerful. Basic freedom must be at the heart of
an adequate human rights policy. Thirdly, the participation of
marginalized groups takes priority over the preservation of an
order which excludes them.

These priorities are reflected in much other recent Catholic
thought on human rights, including the 1986 "Pastoral Letter of
the United States Bishops on the Economy," and also Pope Paul
VI's "Populorum Progressio," which considers the economic well-
being, for example, as critical and essential to other standards of
value, such as human dignity. In short, then, Catholic theology
grounds human dignity in our condition as children of God.
Respect for that dignity in others means that I must afford them

personal freedom and such economic security as is essential to their enjoyment of that dignity.

Thank you.

Dr. Cotrell:

Thank you, Father Miller, for that insightful and challenging exposition on the ethical guides to policy and also the very comprehensive and intelligent discussion of human rights.

Our third panelist is Rev. Franz Schorp, Society of Mary, who is an instructor in Philosophy here at Saint Mary's. He graduated with a Bachelor of Arts degree in political science from Saint Mary's University, took a Bachelor of Theology at the University of Freiburg, and he is currently a Doctoral Candidate for the Ph.D. degree at Washington University in Saint Louis. Father Schorp teaches courses ranging from general ethics to medical ethics, from a survey of western philosophy to Christian values, one at a time; but mainly those who hang around the campus and watch him will see him as his avid interest is being displayed in numerous conversations with students that range far beyond the field of philosophy and ethics, such as maybe looking at new developments in the field of physics. His intellectual interests are broad and wide-ranging.

Please help me welcome Father Schorp.

Rev. Franz Schorp:

Thank you.

One should not get the idea that philosophy offers a set of axiomatic general principles by which one could formally deduce specific acts here and now to be done. Rather, it deals with principles.

Reform thinking, which reformed high civilizations around 500 BC, was the beginning of philosophy. This mode of thinking enabled culture and civilization to survive and progress.

PHILOSOPHY IN AN ECONOMIC STRUCTURE

To relate philosophy to the practical and pragmatic,I shall begin by distinguishing expertise used inside a structure from that used outside and then use this to illustrate or to point out the role which philosophy has in an economic structure.

Let us take an automobile as a structure, designed as wheels to transport. When one adjusts this auto according to this design, one uses expertise within that structure or design. If marshy conditions require that the wheel must be given up, expertise from within, like knowing how to adjust the shock absorbers, will not suffice as the expertise needed to make a new structural design. Such expertise comes from outside the structure. As you may suspect, now, as a devotee of philosophy, I am preparing to carve out a place for philosophy in dealing with the real world. Those schooled in the technical structures are the ones best able to improve them from within. One should not call in a philosopher to test a machine part. This requires technical expertise. But to know whether the machine should be built or not requires a very different expertise, even though views of the experts are an essential element in reaching this judgment.

Philosophy or reflective thinking has to do with the analysis of the very operations of the mind by which we set up any rational structure. To think about thinking and the other acts by which humans exist as humans, there tend to be fundamental principles that form the goals and meaning of all technology. Philosophy, then, deals with designing, maintaining, and improving those basic rational structures from which all other structures arise with rational meaning and order.

To illustrate how philosophy can help in dealing with our economy today, I am going to set up an over-simplistic production/distribution structure. Its design is based on: First, profit as structure-motivation, getting its members to make products of quality with efficiency and to distribute these products widely; second, private ownership, to bring about efficiency by developing responsibility in each individual; thirdly, profit, to elicit support from individuals for the corporate structure by investments and corporate legislation; fourth, supply and demand, to regulate production and distribution. Success will be measured in the form of growth and/or wealth. Now, suppose that poverty and unemployment, i.e., the failure or non-success of the system, is ten percent. A plan to fix the problem is set up where all the impoverished are to be equipped with the training equivalent to a Harvard degree, and they enter the structure with enthusiasm and energy. Unemployment drops, inflation rises, interest rates rise, and, then, enterprises, unable to pay such rates and show enough profit, fail. As they fail, the unemployment rises back to where it was before.

VALUES OUTSIDE THE STRUCTURE

When everybody is trying and the system still fails, we have evidence that there is a basic flaw in the system itself, like the wheel in marshlands. What can be done? It seems to me that what is called for is the willingness to look outside the system. What reasons do humans have to exist? What enables this existence? What makes this world rational and meaningful? What justifies the existence of any production/distribution structure?

But sometimes we get so caught up in a structure that we are reluctant to consider anything outside its limits. If we go back to our automobile example, we can imagine somebody so taken up with making perfect wheel structures that he will not let anybody use the automobiles for fear that these machines will be knocked out of adjustment. The expert has made the auto's structure the sole, ultimate reason for doing anything and forgotten any other superior reason for the autos. In a similar way, one might get so caught up in adjusting the production/distribution structure according to design plan that he forgets that this plan is rationally meaningful only in the light of other purposes.

MATERIAL GOALS VERSUS SPIRITUAL GOALS

Grisez and Finnis, two philosophers, suggest that basic human goals or life purposes center about material goods, enabling physical functioning, involving food, protection, health care, and so forth for self and family; and, secondly, spiritual goals, enabling rational functioning, including one's ability to know the universe, one's capacity to create or develop this universe, and one's potential for appreciating the universe. These principles might be used to design another production/distribution structure, where the individual is motivated to corporate effort by, first, the material resources to assure nurture for self and family, which now include profit but from a conditioned point of view, that is, not just wealth for wealth's sake; second, the satisfaction of a greater understanding of the universe; third, the success in getting something to exist or work; and, fourth, valuing and appreciating the universe. The balance between production and distribution would be regulated not only by supply and demand but also insofar as it facilitates the development of individuals and the common good. Pooling of resources would be not only on the basis of the returns from one's investment in the form of what we now call money but also in terms of how successfully this support has brought forth new talent and capacities. The security of talent and expertise, so to say, is in the bank.

Surely all of this is simplistic and does not really happen in such a naive manner. The presentation is intended to show only how philosophy has a role in bringing about reform much in the same fashion as it has from its very beginning at the axis of history.

Probably the greatest danger which might arise from using philosophy in isolation from other expertise is naivete. Expertise from specialists is needed to build new structures in order to prevent so much disruption that more harm results than is cured. What are the values and meanings which are to shape our production/distribution structure and be the basis on which one is able to trust, communicate, and extend credit to another? Clarifying what the whole person is, what brings persons to perfection, are areas of expertise which reflective thinking attempts to develop.

If we conserve and develop the talents of our people, we have wealth in its most basic form, and without this wealth, all other wealth becomes meaningless.

Dr. Cotrell:

Thank you, Father Schorp, for those insightful views on the role of philosophy and discussions of the precepts and values underlying a system of supply and demand.

DISCUSSION

Erik von Kuehnelt-Leddihn:

I very much enjoyed Rabbi Jacobson's analysis of the situation in this country, and I think that he showed very clearly the problem between the destruction of the family, the single-parent children, and the increase in various social problems and crime, and this connection I see very clearly.

I am citing now the statistics of 1967, which show something very interesting. Not all countries were enumerated. The smallest rate for manslaughter and murder in the world was in Spain, with roughly one in a million; the next lowest was the Republic of Ireland, with three in a million; then England, ten in a million; Austria, twelve in a million; and Germany, twelve in a million.

Then the maximum were three countries, and the three countries are Columbia, Nicaragua, and the highest, the highest, would be El Salvador, with 319 times the number of murders and manslaughters as Spain.

The interesting thing is these two countries are both Catholic and these two countries are both Hispanic.

You know, you can say, "Oh, well, there is a large Indian element in El Salvador."

But the question is: How big is the rate of illegitimacy in these three last-mentioned countries? It is simply enormous. In the Dominican Republic the illegitimacy is eighty-seven percent. In other words, the really organized family hardly exists. The key is to have sound and healthy families.

Now, how we change that in this country here with the Hispanic and the blacks, of course, is another problem and one that I don't want to touch on. I think the only solution is religious, but how do we go about it I just don't know.

But I think here is the key. In a healthy family the rate of crime would be much smaller. Statistics bear that out clearly.

Dr. Cotrell:
Thank you.
Would any panelist like to comment?

Rabbi Jacobson:
Well, one has to comment. The observations require comment of some kind. One can simplify an issue which is so bristly with problems and get an answer.

However, the other day I was very much impressed with the presentation by a man who himself has been a very successful entrepreneur. He is a scientist, and he is also a person who has tried very hard to concern himself with the possibilities of human effort. He spoke at a meeting of a group of people who were concerned about the young and older individuals, mostly Hispanics, to find a way in which their lives would be fuller. He said that he had been asked some years ago to address the graduating class at a high school, and he had prepared in his mind, perhaps even written it out, what he felt were very clear directions for improvement. When he looked at them, he was ready to present them, he suddenly realized that what he was saying was a series of asininities, totally irrelevant to the situation of these young people. They would listen but would not hear, no matter how true were the individual pieces of his carefully prepared program. They would not have an application at all to the interests and lives of these individuals.

And so he discarded his prepared address, and he launched into a very bold and basically rather dangerous suggestion, which emanated from a sudden insight that he felt was the only answer to some problems.

He said, "You know, what you people here need more than anything, and not only you but those behind you in classes, is the opportunity to continue your schooling. I know there are any number of pitfalls to prevent you from reaching that goal. However, I guarantee that you will be provided from now on until your graduation from college or a university with an adequate amount of funding to provide for all your needs. I will pay for it."

And afterwards he was struck with horror at the boldness of his approach. How in the world could he possibly meet this challenge that he had set for himself?

But, indeed, it was not overwhelming, and he undertook it and was so successful that he urged anybody, any business, any industry, any combination of businesses, to serve as similar foster parents of schools – they would take over a school and guarantee to all the students this kind of offer of continuous education with some provision for other money to meet the students' financial needs also. I think that was really important because there are employed here many, many things.

Prevention is the key – prevention of problems, utilization of the family as a unit to get these things done, and the realization, as was suggested earlier, that you have to have a high motivation in order to keep this thing going – money, reward, whatever. And it can work; it can work. There is no doubt. It has been proved successful empirically.

So your question elicits a whole set of observations that the powers that be and the constraints of time will not permit us to go into now.

Dr. Cotrell:

We might continue this for those of you who will be continuing with us at the luncheon or shortly after our panel disperses. I know there are questions, and I know that we have more to say on this topic. However, I am going to conclude and bring our session of the panel to an official close in the light of our time limits.

I want to thank the members of the audience for being here.

I also want to thank again Brother Paul Goelz and our panelists for their contributions this morning. I hope our discussions of these issues are not over.

I want especially to thank Brother Goelz for bringing to the Catholic and Marianist campus a forum for the discussion of the issues involved in the sources of wealth and the causes of poverty. Those are the issues which campuses like this one can ill afford not to discuss and to reflect upon and to engage in enduring conversations in these times.

Dr. Goelz:

Charles, in addition to expressing appreciation to those who have participated in these last two days, to all of our panelists, I want to express a word of appreciation and also to all the people who, for the next years, will read the cloth-bound proceedings of this symposium.

!ANUNCIO!
This Symposium is being continued in
Mexico City
on Friday, November the Fourth
sponsored by
El Centro De Estudios En Economia Y Education
under the direction of
Dr. J. Rolando Espinosa R.

Dr. Cotrell:

Thank you. This session is officially adjourned.

EDITOR

About the Editor

Paul C. Goelz, SM is a member of the Society of Mary (Marianists), a Catholic religious Order of Priests and Brothers who conduct schools and universities throughout the world.

He is the Director of the Algur H. Meadows Center for Entrepreneurial Studies at St. Mary's University. Previously he established the Myra Stafford Pryor Chair of Free Enterprise. He was the Dean of the School of Business and Administration from 1962 to 1977.

He earned a Bachelor's degree in Business Administration and a Master of Arts degree from the University of Dayton, and a Master of Business Administration and a Doctor of Philosophy from Northwestern University.

He is the author of articles, books, and research monographs on: industry structures, administrative policy, budgetary control, marketing management, public housing, and higher education.

His experience in business has been in banking, shoe, oil equipment, and automotive industries. Before entering the educational profession he was associated with the International Shoe Company and General Motors Corporation.

A principal academic interest is conducting seminars and institutes for teachers of Free Enterprise.

In addition to his university duties Dr. Goelz serves as a consultant to corporations and government agencies and is on the boards of regional and national associations. He has addressed executive development programs of the U.S. Department of Defense, the U. S. Agency for International Development in Mexico, and professional associations.

He is a member of the Academy of Management, the American Marketing Association, the American Institute of Industrial Engineers, the National Association of Business Economists, and is a member of the Board of Directors of Junior Achievement of South Texas, and of the World Affairs Council of San Antonio.

For ten years he was a member of the Board of Directors of the American Assembly of Collegiate Schools of Business. He was President of the Southwestern Business Administration Association (Deans) and for twelve years was a member of the Executive Committee.

He is a co-founder of the Association of Private Enterprise Education and former President of the Association.

He is the Editor of the *Entrepreneurial Commentary*, a publication devoted to economic thought and innovation.

Dr. Goelz is a Founder and Chairman of the FORUM ON ENTREPRENEURSHIP. He is listed in Who's Who in America, the Blue Book: Leaders of the English-Speaking World, American Men of Science, and Who's Who in American Education.

In February, 1979 the Freedoms Foundation at Valley Forge conferred on Dr. Goelz the Leavey Award for Excellence in Private Enterprise Education; this carried a stipend of $5,000. Four additional Certificates and George Washington Honor Medals were received.

In May, 1982 the San Antonio Young Lawyers Association conferred on him The Liberty Bell Award in public recognition of outstanding community service in the fields of education, business, religion, and youth organizations.

In November, 1988 he was inducted into the National Enterpreneur Hall of Fame at the University of North Carolina at Chapel Hill.

The philosophical and theological interests of Professor Goelz focus on the Freedom of the Individual in the pursuit of economic objectives.

Contents

✊✊ There is a fascination in watching a figment of the imagination emerge through the aid of science to a plan on paper. Then it moves to realization in stone or metal or energy. Then it brings jobs and homes to men. Then it elevates the standards of living and adds to the comforts of life. That is the engineer's high privilege.

The great liability of the engineer compared to men of other professions is that his works are out in the open where all can see them. His acts, step by step, are in hard substance. He cannot bury his mistakes in the grave like doctors. He cannot argue them into thin air or blame the judge like the lawyers. He cannot, like the architects, cover his failures with trees and vines. He cannot, like the politicians, screen his shortcomings by blaming his opponents and hope that the people will forget. The engineer simply cannot deny that he did it. If his works do not work, he is damned. 🙊🙊

—HERBERT HOOVER

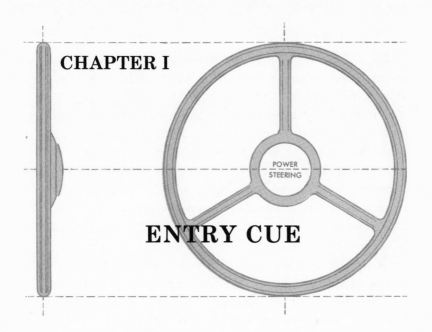

CHAPTER I

ENTRY CUE

Today 50 million drivers cut closer corners because Francis W. Davis invented power steering.

Yet, many people feel that Francis Davis has much more than that to answer for.

For instance, males, whose blood pressures rise at the sight of a woman behind a steering wheel, largely blame his invention for putting her there. Because a bulldozer now can practically spin on a dime, others indict power steering for the scarred hills and rubble-filled ravines that deface what was once a pleasing land. And almost everyone who has been nauseated by the fumes of the giant trucks that choke the tunnel and bridge approaches to our great urban centers, or has been sideswept by the gust waves of huge semi-trailers barreling along our superhighways, wonders if freight hauling shouldn't have been left to the railroads.

On the other hand, the late General George W. Patton stated that the high maneuverability of a few American-designed military vehicles was the margin that made possible the "break out" from the Normandy hedge rows, enabling his armored columns to slice through the might of the Third Reich and bring World War II to a quicker conclusion.

Every May a peaceful breakout starts in Texas and ends months later in Canada. Long columns of self-propelled combine harvesters cut a giant haircut across the Great Plains. They may have air conditioning for comfort, but power steering is a necessity for these machines; a single machine, in one day with one man, can harvest enough wheat for 260,000 loaves of bread. And anyone who seeks weekend escape to the mountains, desert or shore will agree that Davis' extra hand on the wheel has made travelling to pleasure, a pleasure.

Whenever a man succeeds with an important invention and manages to control his brainchild we ask, "How did he do it?" In the case of Francis W. Davis many elements must be considered; among the least of these is that Davis perceived an obvious need and had the technical experience and vision to develop a practical servo-mechanism that would fill the need.

To men who are his peers and who know the whole story (a few fellow members of the Society of Automotive Engineers), Fran Davis is the coolest poker player around. He is the man who took on a whole industry; who stood on a "pat hand" in what they consider the longest deal in the history of the game. The 72-hour round-the-clock sessions of legendary gamblers like Nick the Greek seem child's play to these men when compared to the cool surety with which Davis played his single hand in a game of feint, bluff, squeeze and freeze-out, with more than jokers wild. While the pot climbed to millions, Davis hung in for a quarter of a century. From the start it was a "no-limit" game, and each opponent knew it.

One Davis crony, an innovator in his own right, had this to say, "Our hair used to stand on end as

Fran stood pat. We knew what these fellows were capable of and what they would try to do. Fran did too, but if they ever scared him he didn't show it. They were pros. But one thing none of us realized— and they didn't either—Fran knew the deck better than they did."

Since then Davis himself has often said, "I knew I held a pat hand; it was only a question of living long enough to cash it in."

Let's stop all this talk of poker and take a look at that "pat hand." *A forty-year domination of the patent rights to power steering* is proof of Davis' originality and continuous imaginative improvement. However, the significance of power steering is not its originality but its utility. According to Frank Donovan in WHEELS FOR A NATION, Chrysler Corporation lists fifty-nine "automotive firsts" between 1929 and 1960. Typical items on the list are such things as exhaust-valve seat inserts, built-in defroster vents, rotor-type oil pump, powdered-metal filter in fuel tank, power-operated convertible top.[1]

There is nothing on the list that is not desirable, but the only one of the fifty-nine engineering advances that stands out in itself as being important, is "full-time power steering."

What Chrysler doesn't tell is that the gear they introduced and that didn't work well was built around expired Davis patents. They were endeavoring to avoid paying royalties but when they had trouble with their system they had to incorporate improvements Davis had patented. In other words, while the industry improved their hands with his discards and tried to patent around him, Davis had to constantly keep improving his hand or be washed out of the game.

From the start Davis knew he had the inventive ability to win. He thought his biggest problem would be getting into the game with the world's largest and most ruthless industrial power, the American automotive industry. To Davis, this story begins the day that he felt certain he had entry stakes. It was a minor incident entirely lost on other witnesses, but he remembers it just as you might remember the first time you saw your wife although she was half a car away on the Eighth Avenue D train at 5 o'clock in the evening.

Davis had come out of a hardware store in Waltham, Massachusetts, when he noticed a leading citizen's wife struggling to maneuver Waltham's longest, shiniest, most expensive, and most admired motor vehicle—a 1926 Packard Twin-Six touring car—out of a parking space. She obviously felt hemmed in even though she had a clearance of nine feet between two other vehicles. As the ruffled young matron descended and crossed the street to demand that a brickyard owner move his truck that blocked her way, passers-by stopped to admire the heavy unwieldy car.

Davis listened to their admiring comments for a minute or two and then, stirred by an inner excitement greater than any he had ever felt before, took off as fast as his long legs would carry him. He headed for a one-story frame building that was located quite a few blocks from the main business section. Opening the door revealed a well-stocked machine shop, though most of the machine tools were used and secondhand. The shop was dead quiet and seemed empty, but Davis was sure that it wasn't. And he was quite right, for over in the far corner a small man was silently studying a heavy lathe that apparently had seen several decades of rather rough service before it had been installed in this little shop. Francis Davis knew the quietly intent man was working out some novel adjustment which would make this antique tool perform a task for which it had never been designed. Ordinarily Davis would have

16

tiptoed across the shop and stood silently behind the concentrating man until the other became aware of him. But that was too much to ask of Davis this day.

"Mr. Jessup," he called out, "We're getting packed." The man addressed as Mr. Jessup looked up, then nodded, showing neither surprise nor excitement. The reason, perhaps, was that he had been meticulously packed for three weeks.

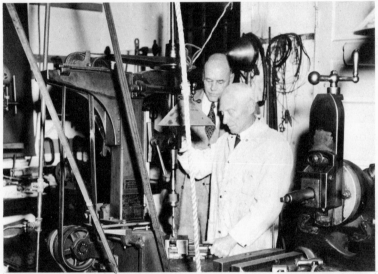

In their shop at Waltham, Massachusetts, the skill of George W. Jessup translated Davis' ideas to working machinery.

George W. Jessup was what, in poker parlance, could be called Davis' "hole card." Although Davis was familiar with machine tools, he was not a master machinist. After he acquired a shop and tools, Davis had carefully searched for an assistant. His search ended when he met Mr. Jessup. As a bachelor Jessup had used his freedom to methodically gain experience. He had moved from shop to shop and job to job until he had all the skills associated with a master craftsman. His experience included machine tool design, machine tool construction, drafting, and machine shop practices.

These two men were a perfect match; what Davis' brain conceived, Jessup's hands could build and tool into working metal. And because of Jessup's handicraft, no one was ever able to dismiss Davis' steering innovation with "that's a fine idea but will it work?"

Months before Davis received what might be called his entry cue, Jessup had machined and helped install a working power steering unit in Davis' Pierce-Arrow sport roadster. Without saying a word to anyone, the two men had tested it on Waltham streets and suburban roads, bringing it back into the shop for adjustments until they had ironed out every bug. Recalling his jaunt to the shop Davis has said, "I didn't run or even trot but I may have hurried a little, because with everybody gawking at that big heavy Packard I was now positive that what the American public wanted in transportation was something big, heavy, and showy. And if that was the trend, the first manufacturer who built greater maneuverability into his car would drive off with all the marbles."

"And in that case you were ready?" a Detroit newspaper interviewer was to ask many years later.

"Yes," Francis Davis replied, "I had been getting ready for some time."

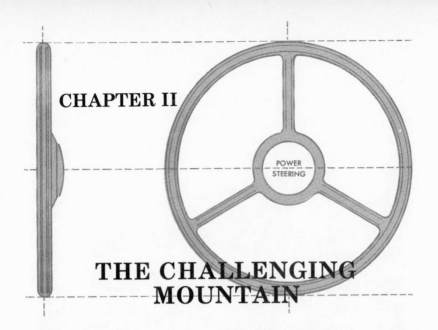

CHAPTER II

THE CHALLENGING MOUNTAIN

The future inventor of power steering was born on August 19, 1887 in Germantown, Pennsylvania, in a pre-Revolutionary house which, considering the later lifetime association with wheeled vehicles, certainly bore an appropriate name—"Roadside." However, the inventor's very practical mother always denied that either the house or its location near the old York Post Road played any part in shaping her son's destiny. Instead she stoutly and sometimes tartly maintained that if any influences were at work they must have been prenatal rather than environmental for the Davis family left the historic mansion before Francis Wright Davis was two months old. As Davis himself observed, "It's quite obvious I started moving early."

But, before he was nine, invention was determining his direction. His grandfather had invented the charcoal process for precipitating gold from a chlorine solution and, since Davis' father had practical experience with the process, when gold started rolling down from Cripple Creek, Henry K. B. Davis moved his family to Colorado. Mrs. Davis consented to the move only if they would be able to live in Colorado Springs. In her diary, she describes her decision and her family:

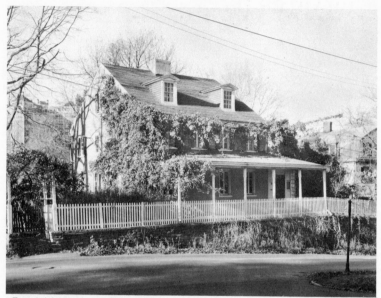

"Roadside", Germantown, Pennsylvania.

"Mr. Davis was obliged to be in Cripple Creek and other mining towns, but I positively refused to take our five children into any mining town, so, after remaining at the Antlers Hotel for six months, we rented a house for a year, and then bought a home and remained in it for seventeen years. While at the Antlers, Governor Thomas was there and one day he went to the proprietor of the hotel and said, 'See here, Mr. Barnett, if you don't put me at another table where I cannot see those Davis children, I will *starve;* I can't take my eyes off of them from the moment they enter single file until they leave in the same way.'"

Davis, in his later years after reading his mother's diary, was to consider this one of the great triumphs of his childhood. "We tried to look angelic when we filed into that dining room but I never knew we succeeded to the point of giving anyone nausea."

As the century turned, Colorado Springs provided a fascinating environment for a boy. The town was a focal point not only for the Rocky Mountains and the "rough and ready" life of mining centers, but a miniature stage on which the world broke in both new and old acts. The forces that were to shape the twentieth century, communism and capitalism, staged their first skirmishes there while the town's first citizens dressed, moved, and hoped they thought and talked like British aristocracy in the Royal Enclosure at Ascot.

The geography of Colorado Springs is symbolic of Davis' later achievements. The town was built at the base of Pike's Peak with the straight front wall of the first range of the Rockies blocking the western horizon. The peak dominated the town and no one who lived there was able to ignore its presence. The first thing a waking little boy saw as he rubbed the sleep out of his eyes was its summit bathed in glittering golden light. This, when the gas street light in front of his home still had another hour to burn. Then far too early in the afternoon, its long shadow would creep over the town— a signal for the sun devils out on the Great Plains to start flashing blinding spears of light into young eyes.

Young Fran never accepted the legend that these light spears were departed Pawnees doing a ghost dance on their way to the red man's paradise, the Garden of the Gods at Manitou five miles up the road. He had early discovered that these momentarily blinding miniature search lights were empty beer bottles out in the baked sagebrush reflecting the rays of a lowering sun which, because of the peak, skipped over the shadowed town.

The Plains stretched to the east of the town as far as the eye could see. On them, aside from empty beer bottles, a boy could sometimes find arrowheads and rabbits. And from them, he could also study the mountain and devise plans to conquer its granite wall by stages: if a boy began such a planned expedition by saying, "I can climb to *there*," he gained enough confidence to do it, and, having reached that level, he could continue on to a higher one.

In that mountain range, he might discover anything. At least in his mind he did. Maybe, like the Boys' Explorer Association of the First Congregational Church, he'd wriggle into a hole and come across another Cave of the Winds, or, better yet, his cave would have galleries encrusted with diamonds instead of humdrum carbonate crystals.

As an inventor Davis would learn to stand back from a problem and regard it as the small boy had once viewed that mountain wall from the plains. He would reduce the problem to a series of smaller problems, then solve each by stages. Often the confidence he gained by working gradually would sustain him until his imagination would create a solution where there wasn't supposed to be any. Apparently, he never quite gave up that boyish idea of finding a rich cave.

Colorado Springs started out as a railroad town. The site was originally purchased by General William J. Palmer, builder of the Denver and Rio Grande Railroad, and a sanctimonious pirate whose goons fought a pitched battle with Bat Masterson when the rival Santa Fe imported that gun-handler from Dodge City.

The Cripple Creek gold boom attracted the extremes of human behavior and occupation and everything in between. But Colorado Springs discouraged bunco men, prostitutes, and gamblers. They passed the town by on their way to richer pickings. Or they were segregated into Colorado City by the temperance and anti-gambling laws of General William Palmer. This nearby town was "wet" and, therefore, better equipped to cater to the less respectable, if not less human, inclinations of early Colorado society.

General Palmer saw to it that life in Colorado Springs was as far removed from the violence of running a railroad or mining camp as he could make it.

The General was an eastern aristocrat, married to Queen Mellen, daughter of New York lawyer William Procter Mellen. Together, the Palmers created a social spa rivaling Saratoga Springs in spite of its distance from the urbane centers of the East. Almost before the first false-fronted stores were up, the town had a Shakespeare Society. Within five years it had an opera house attracting the best European singers. Oscar Wilde, wearing velveteen breeches, lectured to an attentive audience on the art of decoration. The editor of the *Gazette* was imported from England and the town got the nickname "Little London" because the paper carried more foreign than local news. Rose Kingsley, daughter of English novelist and churchman Charles Kingsley, wrote glowingly of the new city. To her call, and the efforts of the Palmers, European aristocracy—mostly those empty of purse—responded. Youngest sons, who could inherit neither title nor land in England, came because here they could live as they had been reared to live. Among them were sons of Lord Chesterfield and Count James Pourtales.

The town prospered by building a reputation as a genteel vacation spot. At one time, with the completion of a casino sponsored by blue-blooded Count Pourtales, Colorado Springs attempted to become an American Monte Carlo. The casino was built outside the city limits so that liquor and gambling would be legal, but it had the blessing of General Palmer because in his eyes the style of this "sinning" differed from that in the Cripple Creek saloons.

23

The character of Colorado Springs explains Davis' courtly Edwardian mien and manners still evident after these many years. The background of his attitudes had its family roots in the East but, because of Colorado Springs, those roots were not broken when he was transplanted into this enclave of culture in the middle of a raucous mining region.

Mrs. Davis grew up at "Hazelbrook," the ten-acre estate of her father, James A. Wright, head of Peter Wright and Sons, merchants of Philadelphia. She was educated at Swarthmore and had one term at a Boston finishing school. In her memoirs, Mrs. Davis recalls that going to Boston was considered the proper thing to do, just as proper children should always enter a hotel dining room in single file.

When the founder of the I.W.W., Big Bill Haywood, led his miners into a series of violent strikes in Colorado in 1903, the Davis household was not as alarmed by Haywood's Communism as they were by his "improper" methods. "It's not what a man believes, but how he deports himself," was Mrs. Davis' dictum. This background enabled her son to regard this nation's most famous Communist, John S. Reed, with whom Davis later roomed at Harvard, as a most agreeable, sociable companion, and not as a radical.

Even the most shattering personal experiences appear not to have affected the Davis sense of propriety one iota. Imply that the automotive industry had a public responsibility to adopt the safety of power steering three decades before it did, and Davis reacts today as if such ideas would tear the social fabric of the nation.

The Davis household may have been proper but it was not stuffy. Mr. Davis would come home from the mining camps with stories about the new mining millionaires so different in their habits from General Palmer's aristocracy.

First among them and the most unconventional was Winfield Scott Stratton. Davis knew about him without his father's stories; how Stratton gave a bicycle to every laundry maid in Colorado Springs because trolley fares were too high. The town knew they took in laundry, but were they all maidens? In this reaction to Stratton the town showed the thinness of its veneer. The energy of Colorado Springs was the lusty vitality of a mining and railroad community. No matter how pious and lofty the aims of General Palmer, or how polite his created society, he could not change this fundamental earthiness with all the wicker pony carts, cricket clubs, and visiting English nobility in the world.

The energy of the mining camps was raw and it had a way of dissipating itself in drunken brawls. Francis W. Davis still shows this energy but with an important difference: his energy has always been controlled and channeled. The fact that it is channeled is largely due to his mother's respect and admiration for what might be called physical coordination. And this, as any trained athlete will affirm, is attained only with discipline. However, Mrs. Davis never disciplined her sons. She just set an example. She most certainly was a very proper person, but hers was a robust propriety. She was a tennis and golf champion and an excellent horsewoman. Her diary reveals an unexpected interest for a proper Philadelphian lady:

"I was always fond of carpentering, and my wedding present from my father-in-law was a completely equipped tool chest, of which I certainly made good use."

With such a mother it is not surprising that all of her sons excelled in at least one athletic sport and embarked on careers related to engineering.

Perhaps the earliest evidence of Francis' talent in what became his life occupation was a working steam engine he designed and constructed with the aid of his oldest brother, William Morris.

*   *   *

Ten years had passed since the Davis family came to Colorado Springs. The boy who had taken walks out on the plains so he could study the mountain was growing up. He was tall—six feet two—and straight as an arrow, sinewy as the venison gut the Arapahoes used to string their bows, and he was ready to take on that mountain.

In the beginning, Francis Davis had intended to climb Pike's Peak on foot. Of course, it had been done that way many times; by horse and mule-back, too. But no one had ever climbed the mountain with a motorcycle. So on an August morning in 1906, Davis and two friends, George W. Sheff and Glen W. Blake, gunned their engines and rode out of Manitou Springs headed for the summit 28 miles and 9,000 feet away.

Their route was the mule path used in the construction of the cog railway in 1892. Since that time the path had been abandoned and only a few sections used by prospectors and trappers below the timber line were in semi-passable condition.

About 9 A.M. when the group stopped for a light lunch they had progressed 22 miles. The last six would take the rest of the day. The engines were beginning to lose power from the altitude and much pedaling was necessary. These cycles didn't have gears or clutches and were started by running alongside and jumping on. This wasn't too difficult on a flat highway, but was another story up a stony 20% grade. From 9 o'clock until nightfall the procedure was to run alongside until the engine caught and then jump on, pedaling for all

IN AUGUST, 1906, DAVIS AND TWO FRIENDS CLIMBED BY
MOTORCYCLE TO THE SUMMIT HOUSE (14,108 FEET) AT
PIKE'S PEAK, COLORADO . . .

"At 9 a.m. we stopped for a rest just below the timberline . . ."

"The last mile . . . nothing but rocks. We are forced to push and carry
our bikes."

"Through patches of snow, we neared the summit before nightfall."

27

they were worth until they collapsed from exhaustion. Toward the end, as the altitude began to affect them, they were falling asleep between climbing sessions. For the last two miles the road became so bad that they had to disconnect the cycle chains and push or carry their machines the rest of the way.

They stayed in the Summit House at 14,018 feet for the night and started back the next morning. After the first few miles, which again saw them carrying their machines, they were able to make it down by noon with the help of the down grade. When Davis stood on the scales he was 16 pounds lighter. He said of this trip something he would say fifty years later about power steering, "If I had known what it would take when I began I would never have started."

In both cases, Davis was speaking out of character, momentarily forgetting his own technique or methodology which is to never see or tackle a mountain or a technical problem as a whole, but to reduce it to a collection of levels, cubes, or arenas of study.

CHAPTER III

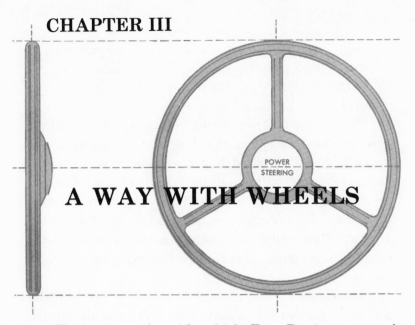

POWER
STEERING

A WAY WITH WHEELS

The motorcycle with which Fran Davis conquered Pike's Peak was called a METZ. His older brother, William Morris, had acquired the Colorado Springs franchise for the vehicle when he went east to attend Harvard University. Morris ran the agency in the summer but when he returned to school in the fall he left fifteen-year-old Fran in charge of the business. This was Francis W. Davis' first contact with motor transportation and there has always been some doubt on the part of his friends whether he has ever recovered from the initial spell cast by the poetic sales rhetoric of C. H. Metz. Here is a sample from a Metz brochure, circa 1903.

"Ever since man first bestrode a fleet-footed horse and felt the keen excitement of swift passage through the air, he has longed for a pair of wings. Man's keenest ingenuity has been employed in devising means for faster and more buoyant travel. But it remained for the despised coal oil brought from the depths of the earth to furnish an essence, the breath of a metal horse that would not only surpass its four-footed prototype, but would emulate the flying of the eagle. Such is the Metz Motorcycle.''

Well, almost. They might be eagles but somewhere between the factory in Waltham, Massachusetts, and Colorado Springs they'd had their wings clipped. Fran Davis' job was selling, riding, racing, and repairing the motorcycles. The competition was even since all the makes of those early years—Indian, Reading Standard and Metz—used the engines manufactured by the Aurora Automatic Machinery Company of Aurora, Illinois.

Because Colorado Springs has an altitude of 6,200 feet and Aurora is about sea level, Davis started tinkering with the carburetion to get back some of the lost feathers. By changing the spring rates and increasing the amount of the valve lift, he was able to improve the breathing sufficiently to get an extra 5 mph out of the Metz. With his modified cycle, Davis began to win races on the small dirt tracks which once knew only sulky racing but now were being taken over by those two new speed demons, the automobile and the motorcycle.

Barney Oldfield and his racing car, the *Ford 999,* filled the nation's imagination. A flamboyant, guileful promoter named Bill Pickens was making money on that imagination. He headed a troupe that featured Oldfield and the renowned ''999'' and included a crack team of motorcyclists from the Indian motorcycle factory. Posters announced they were coming to Colorado Springs.

The program called for the Indian crack team to take on the local motorcycle talent in a series of races and then, as the grand finale, the great Barney Oldfield would give an exhibition of his speed, driving skill, and cigar smoking.

Naturally Fran Davis was going to enter those motorcycle events. He and his Metz had considerable local backing because of the way he had been winning against local competition. And this led to his undoing. Observing that the chief of the Indian factory team was watching him circle the track in a practice run, Fran couldn't resist letting his Metz out. Young Davis didn't know it but he did the half mile a full second faster than the Indian company's fastest stripped-down racing model. Rather than be defeated by a rival machine "hopped-up by a yokel," Indian withdrew its crack team from the race.

Davis won an easy victory over the same local competition he had trounced so often before, and while he was disappointed, he was also elated. A picked team, handling what was considered the finest engineered motorcycle in the country, had withdrawn its vehicles from a fair contest because of modifications made by a fifteen-year-old youth. Maybe he should go on to Harvard and get an engineering degree as both his parents urged.

The day was not over. Davis was to have his first personal contact with a representative of the automotive industry. He describes it in this manner:

"Bill Pickens, Mr. Oldfield's manager, came up to me and patted me on the back and said, 'Frank, you've run a fine race; go down to Strang's Garage and pick up a Solar headlight.' Of course everyone in Colorado Springs knew Mr. Strang and that the Ford 999 was garaged there. So I thanked him even though I didn't like his calling me "Frank" and went down the next morning to the garage. I said, 'Mr. Strang, I've come to pick up that Solar headlamp that I won yesterday.' 'Headlamp? Solar headlamp?' 'Why yes, Mr. Pickens told me to come down here and pick it up.' Strang snorted, 'Those guys left here last night and they didn't leave a damn thing.'"

This was Fran Davis' first encounter with the ethics and behavior patterns of Detroit. At least, the men involved were the first whom he identified with that far-off center of the new automotive industry. In those days Barney Oldfield's name was indelibly linked with Henry Ford, for the elder Ford, in his first bid for fame, had built a racing car dubbed the "999" for the cigar-smoking race driver. Reproductions of photographs of Henry, Barney and the "999" graced as many walls as Budweiser Beer's vivid lithograph of Custer's Last Stand, and today the car occupies a conspicuous place in the Ford Museum at Dearborn, Michigan.

As Davis mulled over his bilking, he came to realize that he had also experienced a confrontation with the engineering "know-how" upon which the much-vaunted superiority of America's rubber-wheeled product rested. For in the motorcycle world, the name that ranked above all others was "Indian."

And another name rankled. One of Davis' marked prejudices is his aversion to ever being called "Frank," an idiosyncrasy he shared with his great golfing contemporary Francis Ouimet. The name is linked in his mind with a particularly dislikable figure of his youth. All through his life, Francis W. Davis has sidestepped people who insist upon calling him "Frank."

He also sidestepped any early association with the Ford Motor Company. Any researcher who wonders why Ford never had the opportunity to introduce power steering might find the answer in a due bill for a head-lamp issued by a scamp with the roguish name of "Pickens"—and in the pictures of Henry Ford, Barney Oldfield, and the "999" that hung on the wall of every barber shop in this country five decades ago.

32

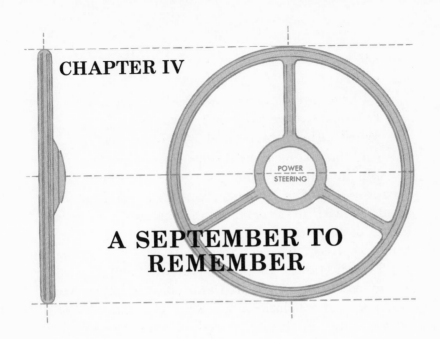

CHAPTER IV

A SEPTEMBER TO REMEMBER

It was the Indian Summer of America's age of innocence, or so a great many writers were to declare years later. But Francis W. Davis and other freshmen who entered Harvard Yard for the first time that mellow September of 1906 were not aware of this. The one thing they were beginning to realize was that now, and for the rest of their lives, they would be known to Harvard men as "the Class of 1910." In retrospect, that class has taken on a charisma of its own; perhaps because for four full years its members moved in a serene atmosphere of sublime self-confidence that they and the western world would never know again.

"As I look back I think we all thought we were paladins of some sort or another," a member of the class was to admit in the decades of doubt that were to follow. And one among them who was marked for early immortality did indeed live by the paladin code. This was America's Sir Philip Sidney, the poet-soldier, Alan Seegar, who enlisted in the French Foreign Legion but felt no hatred for the German enemy, who sensed and wrote:

"I have a rendezvous with Death
On some scarred slope of battered hill,
When spring comes round again this year
And the first meadow flowers appear."[2]

But in 1906, the guns of August were still nearly a decade away. The freshmen registered, got lost, shook hands, vowed to remember and promptly forgot the names of their classmates: Eliot, T. S.; Jones, Robert Edmund; Reed, John S.; Seegar, Alan; Little, Clarence C.; Sumner, James; Lippman, Walter; Broun, Heywood C., to name but a few. It was a class of future Nobel laureates and revolutionaries: Reed in politics, Eliot in poetry, Jones in theatre set design, Broun in journalism and labor relations, Sumner in chemistry, Little in medicine and Davis in transportation, but early indications of this were strangely lacking.

Twenty-two-year-old Francis Davis posed for his Harvard graduation portrait.

A member of the Harvard water polo team, Davis appears in the top row, third from right.

Francis Davis kept up his athletic interests and since there weren't any mountains handy to Cambridge he took to the water. On the water polo team he got to know and like an engaging, restless young man from Portland, Oregon, named Jack Reed, and they became roommates the following year.

When asked what it had been like to room with the only American honored by burial within the Kremlin wall, Davis' answer is first to grin broadly and then count off on his fingers a list of Jack Reed's Harvard activities: Ibis on the Lampoon, president of the Cosmopolitan Club, author of the lyrics for the 1910 Hasty Pudding Show, staff member of The Crimson, letterman in water polo, and one of the greatest pranksters who ever enrolled at Harvard.

Davis has never been able to take Reed's espousal of Communism seriously because he believes it was just another phase of his friend's need for constant excitement and activity. "Today, Jack would have to be an astronaut, and don't think he wouldn't have wangled it."

The only sign of socialistic thinking Davis observed in their two years of living together was a tendency on his roommate's part to consider all wearing apparel

35

community property. Reed was constantly helping himself to Davis' shirts, socks and ties. And this, Davis insists, was based on Jack's reluctance to check out his laundry and a compulsion to be the best dressed man at any party, rather than due to any reading of Karl Marx.

Rooming with Jack Reed certainly was not conducive to study. The two roommates felt bound to attend every "deb" party in Greater Boston and they stretched the city limits to include Cape Cod; Newport, Rhode Island; and Bar Harbor, Maine. It was considered a quiet evening when T. S. Eliot or Heywood Broun were in their room debating the future course of literature and art at the top of their lungs.

Real concentration went into ground-work preparation for practical jokes. One that Davis recalls was quite elaborate. For a week or more Davis' and Reed's friends in the plot reported that Jack seemed to be sinking into moments of deep depression. They planted these gloomy expressions of concern so they would be passed on by faculty members to President Lowell. As Jack Reed always wrapped a sullen shroud around himself when anyone in authority, such as a housemaster, inquired about his health, he unwittingly contributed to the build-up much to the conspirators' secret glee.

Finally pay-off day arrived. Davis knew that Jack was taking off to meet a girl. Davis waited an hour and then reported to the housemaster that Reed, in a state of despair, was heading for the Fall River boat. The housemaster alerted the police who checked the boat and could find no trace of Reed. A frantic, tearful, and apparently pregnant young woman in a shawl (and also a wig) appeared at dockside and started keening mournfully. A young man told a reporter,

36

"She saw him jump!" The police were unable to find the wailing woman and interrogate her, but by now at least twenty people averred they too had seen a young man leap off the boat into the oil-streaked water.

"His face was the most tragic and distraught I ever beheld," one witness declared, and Davis still insists that the man was neither a student plant nor a drunk with hallucinations.

With the Boston police getting ready to drag the harbor, newspaper reporters descended upon President Lowell for a statement. This was to be the salt of the jest to Fran Davis and the conspirators, the pay-off for the whole affair. Trying to look properly sorrowful and bowed by tragedy, they awaited a eulogistic statement from the university head and a diplomatic cover-up for the undergraduate's transgressions.

It came more quickly than they had anticipated, in the form of a curt official communique to the press which read, "President Lowell attaches *no importance* to Mr. Reed's disappearance."

*   *   *

To what extent Francis Davis' creative instincts were dulled and blunted by Harvard's social whirl can never be established, but the reawakening of his interest in things mechanical and technological can be attributed to one member of the faculty. Davis' academic record was indifferent until he encountered Lionel S. Marks, Professor of thermo-dynamics at Harvard's Lawrence Scientific School. Only mystics can tell you what inspiration is or how it occurs; only fortune tellers have the temerity to predict accidents. But accidentally, or predictably, Professor Marks collaborated with student Davis in some inspired experiments with engines that had constant burning cycles—the gas turbine principle. Though Davis did not continue to work in thermo-dynamics, years later (1954) he acknowledged his debt to the encouragement he had received from Professor Marks by endowing a fellowship at Harvard, honoring his teacher.

As graduation day approached, Reed tried to persuade Davis and Waldo Pierce to work their way to Europe on a cattle boat. Pierce succumbed to Reed's siren song but jumped off the bovine ferry before it passed Boston Light and swam ashore. Davis refused to be tempted and headed for Buffalo and a job with the Pierce-Arrow Company.

In 1910 business was so hungry for young engineers that Pierce-Arrow put Davis to work for $12.15 a week inspecting with micrometers. Davis' next job was grinding a valve assembly for the transmission, and then he worked on a carburetor assembly line. All the time the young man was thinking of ways to advance. The last thing he wanted to do was stay on the assembly line.

The first step he took was to help his feet. They hurt, and he couldn't see any real necessity for it, so Davis found himself a packing box and sat down. The line boss said that while sitting down might not have anything to do with grinding valves, the front office would take it as a sign of laziness. He further explained that the idea was not necessarily to grind the best valves but to make the foreman, Mr. Welker, think you were. Davis got rid of the box and in a few years he was in charge of Mr. Welker.

About the time that Davis joined the company and began to move up, Pierce-Arrow went into the trucking business. Davis was offered a position with the truck division and took it because he knew there would be more opportunities with a new operation. He helped assemble the first 5-ton truck that Pierce-Arrow, or any other American manufacturer, had produced and was given the job of test-driving the truck 10 hours a day on the roads around Buffalo. On what was a venturesome cross-country trip to Pittsburgh, Davis was made forcibly aware that added weight and size presented steering problems.

Davis is a tall rangy man with powerful arms but only by fighting the wheel and the truck's accelerating weight until his hands blistered, did he escape what could have been a serious accident on Negley Hill. Pittsburgh's Negley Hill is one of those steeply inclined streets it is a joy to drive up if you like to hear the whine of an engine destroying itself in low gear, and fun to coast down while the muffler pops out the tailpipe as the engine backfires braking down. Davis was trying to keep control going down Negley Hill when the truck hit a pot-hole and bounced Davis against the cab roof. When they reached the bottom, he found to his surprise that he was again in control, but he couldn't remember regaining it. He stopped the truck to count his teeth and see if the truck had lost anything.

While examining the tires and steering linkage, Davis realized that power-assisted steering was going to be necessary if large trucks were to be practical. At that time he did not have a solution, but he placed the need at the back of his mind for his imagination to work on. "You could say I was bounced onto the right track as far as my career was concerned."

Until Davis was hit on the head with *the need* for power-assisted steering, his fecund mind had been working overtime on such fanciful ideas as evening up the two lengths of a bow-tie, adjusting the height of a bed pillow, keeping the light out of a sleeper's eyes. In 1916 he patented a pocket-size cigar cutter. Other ideas of his Pierce-Arrow years appear in his notebooks:

1. *Scheme for getting perfect scavenging of 4-cycle motor.* Rotate crankshaft in eccentric bearings (probably ball bearings), said eccentric bearings to be at 1/2 crankshaft speed and to be driven through internal gearing at either end of the crankshaft. This would give full intake and full exhaust strokes; the other strokes to remain same.

2. *Steam jet multi-stage compressor.* The apparatus is based on the known data that air can be raised in pressure by an amount equal to 1/6 of the steam pressure used, i.e., 60 lb. steam will give 10 lb. air. By means of the multi-stage principle, the air could be raised to any desired pressure.

3. Suggested type of *universal joint* with leather or canvas fillers and a ball and socket joint in the center to hold it in line.

4. *Key Holder* arranged like a penknife: supply the handle and simple tools for forming the butt end of (Yale type) keys to fit handle.

5. The value of salt is well known as a stimulant of thirst and hunger; bars would like to place on the free counter alongside the potato chips and olives, salted peanuts or salted almonds; however, due to the cost of same, it is impracticable. Would it not be desirable to prepare an artificial product about the size of a pea out of bread, potato, etc., and heavily coat it with salt to take the place of the more expensive but desirable salted nuts?

6. *Hydraulic clutch:* a new type of clutch wherein there is arranged a series of spur gears in mesh, each pair acting as an oil pump, then by merely throttling the outlet we tend to stop the rotation of the gears. When the

Fig. 1

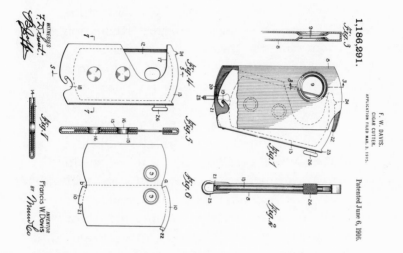

Davis' fifty-year-long inventive career is bracketed by his earliest patent,
a cigar cutter (1916) and his most recent, a cigarette holder (1966),
neither of which have anything to do with power steering.

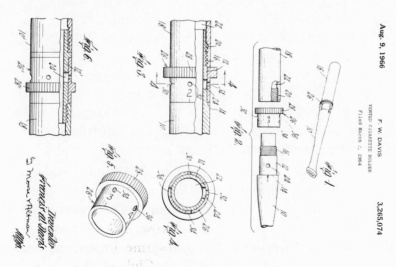

Fig. 2

two shafts have reached the same approximate speeds of rotation the pin could be shot home in its hole.

7. *Self-starter for gas engines.* Type: A turbine wheel driven by compressed air. Reduction gearing an epicyclic train.

Location: A. in front of the engine, B. between fly wheel and transmission, C. on idler shaft of transmission.

8. Assume the given engine can be started as follows: 80 pound torque at 12" radius at 50 rpm: assuming an efficiency at .6, we would require a turbine hp of approximately 1.27 (turning at approximately 10,000 rpm). We will assume it is necessary to use a turbine wheel capable of delivering 1.5 hp at 10,000 rpm.

9. *Amusement park idea:* Large tub full of water, false bottom in the form of a disc arranged to be rotated by a bevel gear and handle extending out one side. Numerous tin fish with rolled-over edges, fish poles, lines, floats, and gang wire hooks. Operator stirs up tin fish in tub, customers pay five cents for pole and line, then at signal, operator turns crank and customer holds lines in water; tin fish catch on hooks; first customer to land three fish gets the prize (candy, etc.).

Interestingly, thirty years later, Davis built such a fish tub for a Children's Fun Fair at Nantucket, and he recalls proudly, "the kids went crazy about it."

While Davis was at Pierce-Arrow, he was moving up in several directions. His golf game improved; he won the championship of the Park Club of Buffalo in 1918. He became a member of the Greenback Club, a poker group made up of friends of "Eddie" Green, whose father, when he wasn't dealing cards, was Edward B. Green, architect of the Albright Art Gallery in Buffalo and other noted buildings.

Possibly more socially significant, but to prove less important for Davis than the experience gained at the poker sessions, was membership in Buffalo's exclusive Saturn Club. Davis received an invitation from his cousin, Tom Cook, whose wife Frances was the daughter of Ansley Wilcox, who had been host to President McKinley during the Buffalo Exhibition at which the President was shot.

Davis considered these associations acknowledgments of his professional progress. In seven years, he had risen to be chief engineer of the Pierce-Arrow Truck Division.

While Davis was moving up the ladder in the Pierce-Arrow organization, war broke out in Europe. Pierce-Arrow found itself supplying thousands of trucks to the English armed forces. The British War Office needed a qualified engineer familiar with the Pierce-Arrow trucks and also the service requirements, who could help them by training personnel, drivers and mechanics to take care of the Pierce-Arrow trucks in service. They sent over a man named Perry, a capable engineer who spent approximately two months in studying the operation and maintenance of these vehicles. He booked his return voyage aboard the *Lusitania* and was among the 1,198 persons who lost their lives when that vessel was sunk by two German torpedoes 12 miles off the Irish coast. When the British War Office cabled the Pierce-Arrow Company for a qualified American engineer to take the place of Mr. Perry, Davis was selected.

If one is to believe the letters and reports Davis wrote back to Buffalo friends, crossing the submarine-infested Atlantic didn't faze him but London femininity did. One night he and a friend were watching a Charlie

Chaplin movie when a German Zeppelin raid interrupted the performance.

"Outside, beams of searchlights were flashing back and forth, people hurrying here and there, street lights going out, buses running by in total darkness at 30 miles an hour, fire engine bells ringing, and numerous reports from anti-aircraft guns punctuated by terrific bomb explosions that seemed just around the corner. I have often read of the scenes during earthquakes and surely this resembled one. We dodged into a subway entrance and went down perhaps 40 feet. Of course this was a place of comparative safety; however, several hysterical women grabbed us and implored us not to go outside for fear of getting killed. This we had no intention of doing until the fervor of their embraces made us decide to choose the lesser danger and go back outside."

Along with assisting the British War Office in the training of drivers and service personnel, the planning of maintenance and spare parts procurement, Davis was able to make recommendations to Buffalo about changes in shipping methods that solved most of the complaints about vehicles and parts arriving damaged. But he felt his job was to find out how the American trucks held up in the theatre of operations, not discover better crating methods. In spite of the books and films about Zeppelin raids, gallant aces, and heroic dog fights that since have depicted the struggle, Davis immediately sensed that the war was not going to be decided in the clouds. He also realized that *the internal combustion engine had made the horse obsolete as a military instrument.*

Realization of this staggering fact had come so suddenly that every nation was faced with the problem of what to do with numbers of cavalry-trained, politically-influential officers who were totally unfit for infantry or artillery command. A few bemused historians have hinted that America solved it by giving them higher commands and point to Pershing as an example. Davis believes that Britain used them to staff the upper echelons of Motor Transport. Anyway, it was a very horsey ex-cavalryman who coldly informed him that the Pierce-Arrow trucks were performing very badly in the war zone. Pressed for details, the British officer charged *all* the American-made vehicles with something he called "mechanical misbehavior."

"Did you say all our vehicles?" asked the astounded Davis.

The officer nodded and fiercely slapped the desk top with his riding crop. It was evident the ex-cavalryman did not wish to be interrogated about these petrol-drinking monsters that had replaced his beloved horses, but Davis learned the ailment, which the officer once called "colic," usually appeared the third or eighth day after the vehicles reached France.

Even fifty years later Davis tells the story with a twinkle in his eye. "I was sure that a veterinarian had written the report he was quoting, but I was equally sure that something was really wrong over there; and that it wasn't a carburetor adjustment or anything like that, because the English motor pool mechanics, even with a cavalry remount officer commanding and a veterinarian writing their reports, were damn good. Some were bound to be Rolls Royce men. I knew I had to get to France."

Davis wrote:

"In my first attempts to get over to the British lines in France, I approached the French Consulate in London for the necessary passports and stated my mission, viz: for inspecting of convoys of Pierce-Arrow vehicles. After much arguing back and forth and considerable correspondence, I was greeted with a stereotyped letter politely but firmly refusing the desired permission. However, with this refusal, I learned enough to know I was approaching the subject from the wrong end. The new quest was launched and just two months later the essential letter arrived."

To this day Davis has never revealed what strings he pulled to get to France, but get to France he did. And the first thing he saw was what was causing the "colic" and "mechanical misbehavior" of his trucks:

"One day I was taken over some carefully selected bad roads and they were very aptly described as a row of holes tied together with string. All of these roads are of the typical "pave" or Belgian block construction, and the bad stretches of road consisted of the "pave" road entirely broken through. Off to the side of the paved center portion you strike the incomparable Flanders mud. When a horse steps off the center part it does not come to rest until its body rests in the mud, and it must be pulled out before it can get back on the center portion.

"When convoys would meet on these narrow sections they had inches to spare; if a driver misjudged those inches, one rear wheel might slip off into the mud. One wheel or two, the truck was just as stuck because the differential transmitted all the power to the wheel in the mud."

After returning from France in 1916, Davis went to work and devised a limited-slip differential, so if only one wheel had traction the truck would move. Although using principles different from those used today, the invention was almost ready for general production when the war ended and the urgent need was over. Considerations such as cost, which in war are no object, took over and Pierce-Arrow dropped the project much to Davis' disappointment and disgust.

One cannot say that the war shaped or changed Davis' character. All of the elements which marked him as an individual were already present and evident to some degree, but against the background of war he took on stature and individuality and emerged a complete and mature personality. The singleness of purpose which could be called his *character signature* was forcibly demonstrated in his lack of concern regarding the dangers of crossing the U-Boat-infested Atlantic. He gave it no consideration whatsoever, even though the man he was replacing had gone down on the *Lusitania*. Again, he seemed to view the Zeppelin bombing in London like a Payne's fireworks display, "The Last Days of Pompei," he had seen as a child at the Colorado State Fair. It was a creative engineer's reaction. As a child he had thought there must be some better way of setting off the fireworks displays than by men whom the audience weren't supposed to see, but did. During the Zeppelin attack he thought that both the searchlights and anti-aircraft fire could be electrically and mechanically coordinated in a "detect-and-destroy" system with the elements then available. With the additon of radar, this, of course, is the basis of today's advance warning systems.

If Davis shared a somewhat isolationist view that this was not America's war when he departed for Britain, he returned an earnest advocate of preparedness for America as this front page interview in the Buffalo Evening News, April 28, 1916 indicates.

"I left here with ideas of the needs of this

country. I have returned with those ideas greatly strengthened. This country is in a sad prédicament as to preparedness it seems to me. For instance, we read of the three aeroplanes available for service in Mexico. In England the aeroplane factories are turning out from 20 to 30 machines a week and sending them to France.

"Another interesting thing that England's experience has shown us is the need for compulsory service during war times. At the opening of the war it was thought that England would never be able to enforce conscription. As the volunteers went to the firing line, while the slackers stayed home, the unfairness of the system was forcefully demonstrated. The people demanded conscription. If this country should go to war, I think some form of compulsory service should be immediately inaugurated."

It is Davis' attitude and performance in the years immediately following the conflict that really point up his character. While many of his friends and classmates were flocking to Paris and calling themselves "The Lost Generation," he was clearly a man who found himself.

His imagination was working and he had acquired discipline; what he had seen in both France and England made him recognize that the motor industry could do nothing but expand. During his years at Pierce-Arrow, he had become a company man. "To grow with Pierce-Arrow, think Pierce-Arrow" was one of the mottoes on every wall. Davis now found the company policy was a limitation to his creative searchings. Most certainly their failure to proceed with his locking differential, patented in 1921, influenced his view that the Pierce-Arrow Company was no longer a progressive leader of the automotive industry.

During his stay at Pierce-Arrow, Davis gained the respect of fellow automotive engineers across the nation. On December 7, 1920, he was asked to present a paper on motor truck transportation at the annual meeting of the American Society of Mechanical Engineers. In his paper Davis stated a problem that was to occupy his imagination for years to come, "The question of possible increase in the size of motor trucks is an economic one. There isn't a mechanical limitation preventing an increase in carrying capacity. But if the size increases beyond the present five- or six-ton capacity, the vehicle becomes unmanageable. . . ."

Large mercantile firms such as Jordan Marsh Company of Boston, Marshall Field of Chicago, and Armour in Philadelphia were beginning to convert from horse transportation to motor trucks. These firms did not know how to use the new transportation form effectively. Davis saw the need and left Pierce-Arrow to start a consulting firm to handle the economic problems of routing, maintenance and repair of trucking fleets.

While he was becoming one of the first consulting engineers in motor transportation and starting a new profession, Davis acquired a small shop in Waltham and embarked on the mission of making motor vehicles more manageable.

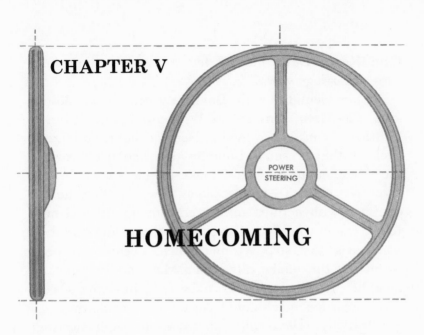

CHAPTER V

HOMECOMING

POWER STEERING

The years between 1922 and 1926 are a splice in the cable of Davis' life. They connect a decade of employment in automotive engineering to his entry in a game of high stakes with the automobile industry. During this period, several new strands are introduced to the story. These are woven in like the colored threads that code electric insulation while the energy-carrying core remains a constant.

In a way, Davis' departure from Pierce-Arrow was more of a homecoming than a leave-taking. When he went to Buffalo, he had left his heart behind in the custody of a young lady named Margaret Cushing Underwood who lived in Belmont, which is just up the road from Harvard and Cambridge. Davis felt that his prospects for success in this new field of consultant engineering were sufficient to warrant his embarking on that most hazardous of careers—independent invention. Miss Underwood did too, and affirmed her faith emphatically with marriage. So, in this small, pleasant suburb of Boston, just a few miles from Harvard and the scene of many of his youthful shenanigans with

John Reed, Davis cut his fetters as a company man with a marriage vow.

Coincidentally with Davis' return to the Boston area, the Metz Company of Waltham became defunct. Waltham is just over the hill from Belmont, and Davis decided that a small building that had been part of the Metz complex would make an ideal shop for his inventive efforts. At this same time, he became acquainted with a quiet master craftsman named George Jessup whom the Metz debacle had also made available.

Davis' first step as a mechanical inventor had been to modify the intake valves on a Metz motorcycle, and now he was beginning a professional inventive career with discarded machinery from the same company.

Initially, Davis did not work on power steering; he had to eat. Contacts made while he was with the Pierce-Arrow truck organization enabled him to quickly build up what was one of the first consulting firms in motor transport engineering. His experience with the British during the war helped him to set up maintenance systems for American companies that had neither experience nor knowledge in short-haul and long-haul operations.

Almost at the start of his consulting business Davis invented a cushioned steering system that received wide and immediate publicity. Early steering gears were rigidly mounted either by bolting them to the frame, to the engine block, or to both. Because steering columns were solid, all vibrations from the car and the road were transmitted to the driver's hands. Without protection, blisters and dangerous fatigue resulted. Davis' first patented steering improvement eliminated this vibration.

Davis' solution was very simple: rubber is a shock absorbing material, so Davis provided a rubber coupling in the steering column.

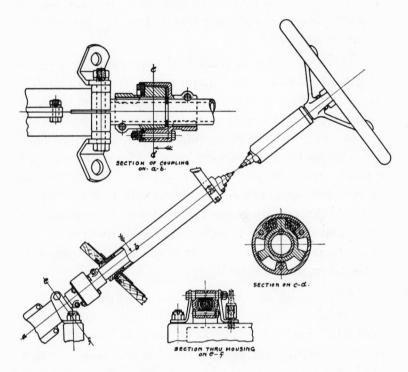

SECTION OF COUPLING
ON A-B.

SECTION ON C-D.

SECTION THRU HOUSING
ON E-F

Fig. 3

Fred S. Duesenberg used the couplings in his cars that won the Indianapolis 500 in 1923 and strongly endorsed the product: "The steering gear coupling certainly worked out 100% right. I believe the coupling is very satisfactory and all our boys are strong for it, as those who drove through the entire race did not experience any sore hands as other drivers did."

But Davis had a problem with this coupling and it was going to plague him for a long time to come—

he could not get it into standard production. The reduction of driving fatigue from noise and vibration should have justified making the coupling standard equipment, but it didn't. Only a little over 100 units were built and installed. However, the coupling lived up to every claim that was made for it and the simple, excellent engineering established Davis' reputation in professional circles.

Davis was not satisfied with the coupling because it did not solve the major steering problem—high steering effort. Newton's laws of inertia state Davis' problem in its classical form, "Objects at rest remain at rest, and objects in motion remain in motion, unless acted upon by some outside force." Davis had to apply enough force to park a car without exhausting the driver. However, combining driver effort with mechanically advantageous gearing would not be enough, because Davis also had to apply that force quickly enough to get a car around a corner without either going off the road or hitting something.

It's one thing to talk about Newtonian forces in neat equations, but quite another to apply them in practical machinery. A short look at the history of power steering will give some idea of Davis' temerity in 1924 when he decided to solve the problem of steering effort by successfully inventing power steering.

The first steering devices that met the design criteria for practical power steering were developed during the nineteenth century for use on ships. The development was international: an American, F. E. Sickels, obtained the first patent; the first British application of steam steering occurred on the "Great Eastern"; and a Frenchman, Joseph Farcot, wrote the first book on the design factors of successful power steering.

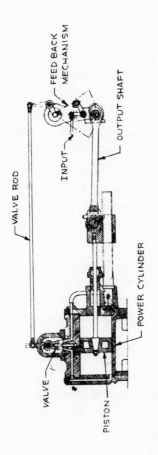

Fig. 4

The input shaft is connected to the steering wheel and the output shaft to the rudder. When the wheel is turned the input shaft works through a series of linkages to displace the valve and power is applied. As the output shaft moves it works through a linkage to replace the valve in a neutral position. When the valve reaches neutral the mechanism becomes stable and the rudder is held in position.

The linkage from the output shaft to the valve is called a feedback because it "feeds back" information about the position of the rudder to the controls. If the information it feeds back says that the rudder is in the position ordered by the steering wheel, then the power is automatically shut off. The system is closed because there are no monitoring or adjusting mechanisms outside it. The steering gear maintains at all times a perfect correspondence between the position of the input (steering wheel) and the output (rudder); any difference in position between these two is immediately sensed and corrected by the valve linkage. The gear might be said to have "intelligence" while following the orders of the helmsman. The control acts as the driver's slave, hence the name "servo." All successful power steering mechanisms have been positional-servo-feedback control devices.

The earliest attempt to apply power steering to automobiles closely followed the design described by Mr. Farcot. Developed by Charles F. Jenkins of Washington, D.C., (U.S. Patent No. 818,967, Automobile Steering Device, April 24, 1906) the device used the pressure of exhaust gasses as the power source. The attempt was never successful. However, Mr. Jenkins' design had one feature that has been incorporated into most power steering units to the present. In his patent he states:

It will be understood that, should the power drop to nothing for any reason whatever, the driver does not lose control of the machine, the steering simply being then performed in the usual way with the consequence, increase in labor. . . .

Another device was patented in 1915 by Henry A. Lardner and George F. Challis of San Francisco. Their mechanism used an electric motor as a source of power. In this gear a movement of the steering wheel would close an electrical contact; as the motor turned the output shaft, the contacts were opened. The device was a positional servo; however, there were problems of stability and it was never generally accepted.

The next application of power to steering was

patented in 1923 by James Sumner of California. His device was a very complex system for applying hydraulic pressure to assist steering. For several reasons, among them complexity and cost, the attempts by Sumner did not result in a practical design. However, Sumner's efforts are important because they represent the first attempts to apply fluid pressure to power steering.

When he started his work Davis was almost totally ignorant of the solutions that had been attempted. He did know that several men had failed with complicated mechanisms and that was about all he knew. Davis did not want his mind cluttered with ideas that would fetter it in any way, so he did not have his lawyers research patent literature until he had a gear designed and built for bench testing in 1925. Davis was only interested in building a servo mechanism that would power assist steering in motor vehicles. He did not worry much about someone else's doing it first. He hoped no one would, but the important thing was to solve this engineering problem.

Davis began his attack by dividing the problem into three sub-problems and solving each. First, he needed a power source; second, he needed a control device; third, he needed a power applicator.

Davis' decision to use hydraulic power is a classic demonstration of the necessary part intuition plays in invention. Davis saved himself much time he might have wasted in experimentation. His guess was so correct that over 95% of all power steering units in use today are hydraulic. Yet looking back, his decision seems quite daring. In the middle 1920's adequate hydraulic pumps, seals, and transmission lines had not been developed. Deciding upon hydraulic pressure, Davis had to invent a complete hydraulic transmission system.

Fig. 5

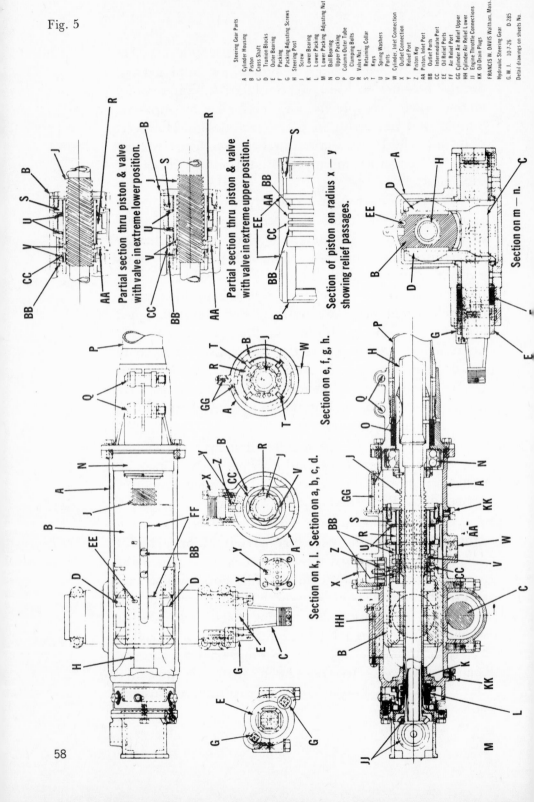

Partial section thru piston & valve with valve in extreme lower position.

Partial section thru piston & valve with valve in extreme upper position.

Section of piston on radius x — y showing relief passages.

Section on m — n.

Section on e, f, g, h.

Section on k, l. Section on a, b, c, d.

Steering Gear Parts

A   Cylinder Housing
B   Piston
C   Cross Shaft
D   Trunion Blocks
E   Outer Bearing
F   Packing
G   Packing Adjusting Screws
H   Steering Post
J   Screw
K   Lower Bearing
L   Lower Packing
M   Lower Packing Adjusting Nut
N   Ball Bearing
O   Upper Packing
P   Column Outer Tube
Q   Clamping Bolts
R   Valve Nut
S   Retaining Collar
T   Keys
U   Spring Washers
V   Ports
W   Cylinder, Inlet Connection
X   Outlet Connection
Y   Relief Port
Z   Piston Key
AA Piston, Inlet Port
BB Outlet Ports
CC Intermediate Port
EE Oil Relief Ports
FF Air Relief Port
GG Cylinder Air Relief Upper
HH Cylinder Air Relief Lower
JJ Engine Throttle Connections
KK Oil Drain Plugs

FRANCIS W. DAVIS Waltham, Mass.

Hydraulic Steering Gear

G. W. I. 10·7·26   D 285

Detail drawings on sheets No.

58

A hydraulic pump may be easily driven by an automobile engine, but in 1924 suitable pumps could not be bought. So Davis designed and Jessup built a three-piston, cam-operated reciprocating pump. The pistons were machined and lapped to very close tolerances by Jessup and the pump proved very satisfactory, operating for hundreds of hours with little attention.

Since rigid transmission lines would have fractured from the vibrations present with an internal combustion engine, Davis created a flexible hydraulic hose by splicing the accordian section from a water thermostat into a solid pipe section. Yet he was never able to adequately seal his system when oil was maintained at a pressure of close to 1,000 psi (pounds per square inch). Existing systems were only 200 or 300 psi. Finally he eliminated the necessity for continuous high pressure sealing by eliminating continuous high pressure oil. While Davis looked for a solution to adequate sealing, he proceeded with the design of the other components.

For reasons of simplification Davis decided to modify the basic screw-and-nut steering gear of his Pierce-Arrow.

When the wheel was turned the nut was displaced and moved the Pitman shaft and arm; the Pitman shaft transmitted the force to the wheels through a linkage. Davis needed two components for his gear: a servo valve (to control the hydraulic fluid) and a power cylinder. These components could have been either separate or together. For example, each wheel could have had its own power piston. Davis decided that the control and power mechanisms should be integral with the steering gear.

Since the nut on the Pierce-Arrow gear moved, he decided to make the movement operate the valves

59

directly; that is, make the valves part of the nut. Second, he decided that hydraulic pressure on the nut was the most economical way to power assist. His first gear was immensely simpler than the steam gears developed for ships.

When the wheel was turned the nut was displaced inside the piston; the displacement opened the valves and hydraulic fluid was applied to the piston. This piston formed an outer sleeve that was part of the valve mechanism, so when the piston moved it closed the valves. If power was lacking, the nut moved until it butted into the piston and steering was manual. Within a year of starting, Davis designed and, with the help of Jessup, had a power steering mechanism working on a bench.

They had all the components of a gear. They had a pump and tanks and oil; but when the pump forced the oil into the tanks, pipes came loose and swung around like a garden hose dropped with the water on. Davis and Jessup were working days and nights to get a workable accumulator and relief valve. They were always aware of the danger of broken lines and packings and were always in a mess of leaked oil.

Davis was certain he could find the seals, until one night he looked up in the dim light and saw a pipe snaking across the room. He did a double-take; there wasn't supposed to be a pipe there. He couldn't figure why Jessup would string plumbing across the middle of the shop. Of course—it wasn't a pipe; it was a jet of oil at 1,000 psi. Davis just stood there and stared at the accumulator tank and the snake of oil connecting it to the opposite wall. He just stood there, discouraged and quietly cursing. That snake meant defeat.

Davis was about ready to admit that hydraulic power presented too many problems to warrant further exploration when "it" happened. "It" was one of

those sublime moments only men of imagination know
—a moment when the mind bottoms out and rebounds
as the energy of an idea carries the spirit to a new
height—a rebound from failure that seems to prove
there are not problems without solutions. Davis' moment came while he was driving home from town down
Concord Avenue. Today the answer seems obvious,
but the answer Davis got that day makes his invention
special. He thought, "Why not have the valve open
just a little bit when the gear is neutral? Such a valve
is called an open center valve." This valve allowed oil
to circulate freely with a minimum of back pressure
as long as the gear was in neutral position.

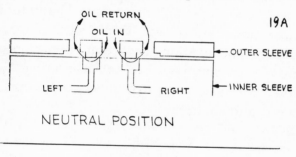

NEUTRAL POSITION

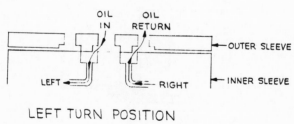

LEFT TURN POSITION

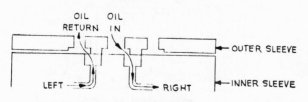

Fig. 6   RIGHT TURN POSITION

When the valve was incorporated into the mechanism, Davis no longer needed elaborate sealing because he had eliminated the need for an accumulator. What he had now was a reservoir of oil at atmospheric pressure.

Once the problem of handling high pressure oil was solved, Davis had a gear running in his Pierce-Arrow immediately. He describes how it worked, ". . . the first time we tested it and tried our steering gear we didn't have any reaction in the thing! You could turn it with a feather, with a touch of a finger, and it had no tendency to come back. You'd turn it and it would stay there, and the car would go round and round and round. That's when I came up with the question of reaction in that mechanism, whereby you had to function against either spring load or hydraulic reaction or a combination of both."

In his first gear Davis experimented with two kinds of spring loadings, either with or without stops.

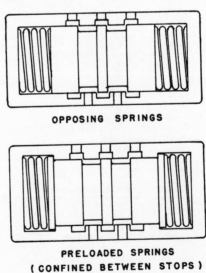

OPPOSING SPRINGS

PRELOADED SPRINGS
(CONFINED BETWEEN STOPS)

Fig. 7

Each type gives a different kind of feel. If the gear has springs with stops, the driver has to overcome a pre-set load before the valve moves and he gets power assist. Without stops the springs only function to center the valve so the driver gets power assist immediately. The second system might seem better but it gives less feel of the road. At high speeds, without stops, the steering wheel feels as if it is not connected. This can be dangerous because a driver feels as if he isn't doing anything and can easily over-correct.

Springs with stops give manual steering below a certain load. Thus, at highway speeds the car does not use power steering unless it is needed; the driver retain the feel of manual steering and is in better control. When he included springs with stops, Davis had completed the design and construction of a steering gear containing the essential features of all steering units produced today.

With his design Davis retained the features of the best manual gears. He did not have noticeable backlash (the lost mechanical motion always present during a reversal of the direction of torque transmitted through a series of gears). He had good directional stability without excessive driver attention, and good feel (a subjective quality referring to the gear's tendency to transmit information to the driver). Finally the gear was self-righting; that is, the front wheels returned to straight ahead after the turn was completed.

In addition to these qualities, Davis added four new ones. First, his steering ratio was selected on the basis of optimum maneuverability instead of a high ratio for parking. Second, he dramatically reduced the force necessary to steer under difficult conditions. Third, Davis effectively damped the steering mechanism, removing annoying noise and vibration. Finally the gear assisted the driver to retain control of the vehicle under severe and surprising conditions.

If the front wheels were deflected by a pothole the steering wheel did not break the operator's thumbs. Instead, the wheel deflected the radius rod, which deflected the Pitman shaft, which deflected the power piston. This opened the valve and pressure was applied to straighten the wheel. Thus the gear operated as a shock absorber.

Davis' gear was selectively reversible. Stable under shock loads, it was reversible under light conditions and therefore self-righting. Now he had his entry: the Davis Hydraulic Control. (He saw additional hydraulic power assists: brakes, windows, hoods, etc.) His gear was safer and better than anything the industry had to offer. He was positive that success must be his for the asking.

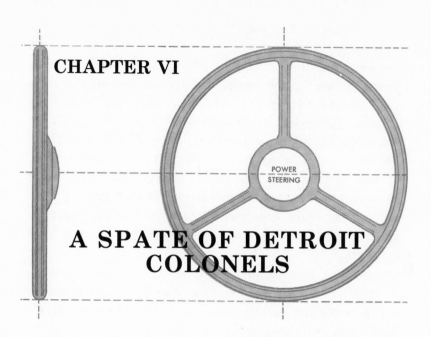

CHAPTER VI

POWER STEERING

A SPATE OF DETROIT COLONELS

Successful inventions have three-step histories: conception, execution, adoption. Inventors don't have trouble with the first; if they were not creative they would not be inventors. The second can cause trouble, but although sometimes they don't have the money, most inventors have the skills to build prototypes of their ideas. Acquainted with machine shop practices himself, Davis had an additional advantage in Mr. Jessup. The third step stops most inventors; adoption can take forever. But Francis Davis felt he had that one licked because he knew he was timely.

In 1926 automobiles were no longer amusements for the rich; the Model T changed that. As early as 1919, Ford, by his wide and effective use of assembly line techniques, had been able to sell flivvers for $360, so practically anybody could afford to buy a car and practically everybody did. The Model T brought the farmer into town, moved the Southerner north, and transported cities to suburbia.

By 1926 automobile transportation was essentially modern. As highway systems improved to handle 20 million cars, they made the Model T obsolescent. With paved highways the nation demanded comfortable cars and bought Chevrolets. On May 31, 1927, the last Model T, serial number 15,000,003, rolled off the assembly line. Henry Ford could justifiably say, "The Model T was a pioneer. It had stamina and power. It was the car that ran before there were good roads to run on. It broke the barriers of distance in rural sections, brought the people of those sections closer together, and placed education within the reach of everyone."

As the automobile came of age in the twenties, it created the nation's largest manufacturing industry which, over the decade, consumed 90% of the country's petroleum products, 80% of its rubber, 20% of its steel, 75% of its plate glass, and 25% of its machine tools. Francis Davis believed that this industry, the largest in the world, would leap to acquire the rights to power steering. And he had solid and ample reasons for this belief.

Balloon tires, introduced in the twenties, provided a softer more comfortable ride, but they had one major drawback everyone was complaining about. Their larger sections placed more rubber on the road with a corresponding increase in traction, i.e., better braking and cornering. But at parking speeds better traction meant more steering effort. This effort increased as cars became heavier and six-, eight-, and twelve-cylinder engines replaced lighter four-cylinder power plants.

To Davis the incident he had witnessed in Waltham epitomized the entire situation and dramatized his golden opportunity. The huge, heavy, twelve-cylindered car with balloon tires, which the stylish young matron couldn't extricate from an ample parking space, represented the direction in which Detroit styling and engineering was moving. That every sidewalk viewer expressed only admiration for the unwieldly monster and a desire to possess a dreadnought of similar gigantic proportions, convinced him that public taste would never permit the automobile manufacturers to retreat to a lighter, safer, far more economical, and more readily handled product.

Davis had received his "entry cue." It was time for him to make his move.

In Detroit the motor moguls had received the same message several years earlier. They were quite successfully filling the public demand for bigger and heavier "Detroit iron." And while it would be four decades before Ralph Nader would call a much superior product "unsafe at any speed," they were re-receiving a sufficient number of complaints to recognize that steering was a *tender* area.

The manufacturers tried two remedies for the steering problem. First, they removed friction from existing steering gears. The Marles gear was the first to have rolling instead of sliding contact; it combined a worm gear with an offset roller mounted in the Pitman arm. The Ross Gear Company added roller bearings to their cam-and-lever steering gear, and Saginaw adopted a ball-bearing roller tooth gear similar to the Marles gear.

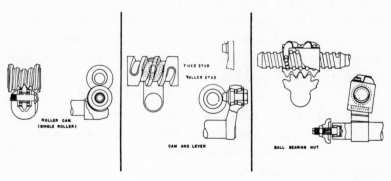

Fig. 8   Fig. 9   Fig. 10

These improvements increased efficiency but they also increased control problems on rough roads. With less friction steering gears were more reversible. Road shocks were transmitted to the driver and potholes became more dangerous. Removing friction from steering gears did nothing about friction between the road and the tire which was the principal resistance to turning.

As a second solution, automakers increased steering ratios, sometimes as high as 24 to 1. While this made it possible for wheels to be turned, with effort, it had a major drawback: high steering ratios reduced responsiveness. Davis saw that maneuverability could only be limited so much before the loss in safety became prohibitive. A 16/1 ratio is 1.5 times faster than a 24-1 ratio. This is significant when you're avoiding pedestrians.

Davis admits that he felt very confident that October day in 1926 when he and Jessup drove out of Waltham. "They were in a squeeze and I had *openers,*" is the way he puts it.

The "openers" was the Pierce-Arrow roadster that he was driving equipped with a smooth efficient power steering unit.

It was a glorious day, the earth basking one more minute before the late fall rains would rinse the blood out of the oaks, but Davis only noted that the weather was fine. His imagination was occupied with plans for his attack on Detroit. He was confident that he was going to win but he was also aware that he wouldn't win unless he played his cards well.

When he arrived in Detroit on October 19, 1926, Davis did not go charging into the corporate maze of General Motors, and as an aftermath of his youthful encounter with Bill Pickens he had no desire to either meet or negotiate with Henry Ford. You can't very well stand off and observe Detroit like you do a mountain, but there are ways of studying it before you try to scale its summits. Davis got on the phone to find out what was happening and to make some scouting appointments for the next day.

On October 20 he had lunch with Percy Barter of McCord Radiator. Davis did not expect McCord to build power steering, but Percy Barter was an old friend and Davis wanted to find out which companies would be the most likely to need the competitive advantage of power steering. Percy advised Davis to see E. F. Roberts, Vice President of Packard.

That afternoon Davis demonstrated the car for the first time when he spoke to Colonel Glover and Colonel Alden of the Timken Axle Company. He knew that Timken would be in closer contact with steering engineers because they supplied suspension parts. Davis felt they would help him to anticipate engineering questions and arguments.

When the colonels advised Davis to see Colonel G. A. Green of Yellow Coach, General Motors, and Pontiac, they told him to expect some resistance because Westinghouse was making a big effort to introduce air brakes, and Colonel Green might object to mounting an oil pump in addition to an air compressor.

This spate of colonels made Detroit sound like a camp-out for the Grand Army of the Republic. Briefly inundated by the military titles, Davis decided to pause a day to get his head above water before he acted on the advice of Colonel Glover. On the twenty-first he demonstrated the car to the Gemmer Steering Company and arranged to contact them again later in the week.

On the twenty-second Davis followed up Percy Barter's lead and called on Roberts at Packard. Roberts was busy in the morning so instead of giving a demonstration, Davis had lunch. After lunch Mr. Roberts was still in meetings and suggested that Davis get in touch on Monday morning.

The afternoon was more profitable. Davis demonstrated the car to Colonel Green and left with a letter from him to Major G. E. Hallet of General Motors Research Laboratories. Green's letter read, "I believe power steerings are going to be necessary in connection with heavy-duty equipment—this particularly in view of the rapid development of balloon tires." The foot was on the accelerator now; with this letter Davis arranged a conference with Hallet for early the next week.

Even though things were beginning to look favorable at General Motors, Davis persisted in talking about the Davis Hydraulic Control to anyone who would listen. Monday morning, the twenty-fifth, E. J. Roberts at Packard put him off again; Davis waited two hours to get an appointment for 2 o'clock the next day. In the afternoon he went to Cadillac. There he met H. M. Denyes of the Saginaw Products Division of General Motors. Denyes immediately began to talk about producing the Davis Hydraulic Control.

On Tuesday, the twenty-sixth, Major Hallet drove the car and was extremely pleased with its handling on all kinds of roads. Hallet did express concern with the performance at low speeds when the car was in high gear. Davis didn't answer the objection because he hoped that Hallet would downshift eventually.

Later the same day Davis finally got in touch with Roberts and Morehouse at Packard. They drove the car and said, "We are very impressed with its smooth operation; however we aren't interested at the present. Please keep us informed of all developments." Later Davis called the Gemmer Steering Company and they said, "We were very impressed with its smooth operation; however . . . etc." Davis finished the afternoon going in the wrong direction; he tried to locate the

Chrysler plant but got the wrong one on Jefferson Avenue and was told the engineers were at the Highland Park plant.

On Wednesday, the twenty-seventh, Davis spent the day at General Motors roughing out a 14-month option at $200 per month. If General Motors took up its option for an exclusive license the royalties would depend upon the price of the automobiles on which the units were installed. General Motors guaranteed Davis a minimum of $5,000 in 1928, $10,000 in 1929, and thereafter. Davis was to provide all possible assistance in General Motors' development work in addition to his patent license. Apart from this basic agreement, Jessup was to go to Saginaw and help General Motors engineers and draftsmen. Denyes of Saginaw was to pay Jessup's salary of $75 a week and expenses.

Davis, the poker player, was playing his hand with assurance now; he had General Motors talking in concrete terms, although he was dissatisfied with the royalty schedules. But it wasn't time to ask for a new deck. In fact Davis did not know how much he should ask in royalties. He did know that what General Motors offered was low. So he showed the car to Sidney D. Waldon, Vice-President of Packard Motor Cars, who agreed to find out what some of the engineers at Packard and elsewhere might think about royalties.

In case the deal with General Motors fell through when he asked for greater royalties, Davis took out an insurance policy with Chrysler. Mr. Maynard of Chrysler engineering was very impressed, especially when he drove the car over a railroad track and the wheel didn't move. With Chrysler's engineering reputation one can speculate what might have happened if Davis had found the right Chrysler plant before the negotiations with General Motors started.

71

Davis spent the twenty-ninth at General Motors negotiating. He agreed to the basic points outlined on the twenty-seventh. He also received the right to deal with any claims of interference on his patents and to come to financial agreement with interferers. General Motors agreed not to license anyone else should a claim of interference be made.

When Davis left Detroit on October 30, 1926, he felt he had achieved his goal. Not only did he have an agreement for the development and eventual production of his invention but, in a single fortnight, he had demonstrated the Davis Hydraulic Control to a wide top segment of the automobile industry and everywhere his innovation had commanded interest, respect and, in most instances, enthusiasm. He traveled home convinced that the industry was hungry for power steering and with the heady feeling—at least for a poker player— that he held a winning hand and his timing was right.

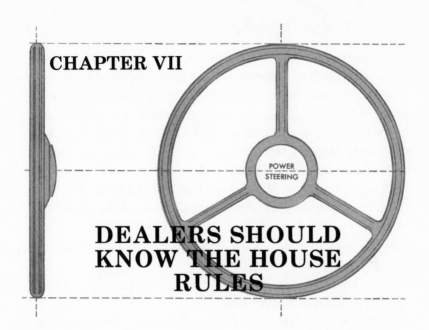

CHAPTER VII

POWER
STEERING

DEALERS SHOULD
KNOW THE HOUSE
RULES

Of the three major power assists on the modern automobile, starting, steering, and shifting, the first, Kettering's self-starter was the only one to have a practically instant introduction.

Self-starting owes its sudden acceptance to an accident. In 1910, while driving across the Belle Isle Bridge in Detroit, a good Samaritan named Byron T. Carter stopped to help a stalled woman motorist; and as he tried to crank her car, the starting handle kicked back and broke his jaw. He died of the injury.

Henry Leland, President of Cadillac, happened to be a close friend of Carter and was very shaken by the tragedy. He was also a friend of Charles F. Kettering, who headed General Motors Research. So when Kettering remarked that he could crank an automobile electrically, Leland placed an order for 4,000 starters sight unseen, and the 1912 Cadillac became the first car with a workable self-starter. Kettering and his Dayton Engineering Laboratories Company, DELCO, already had a reputation that helped, but Leland made the decision because of Carter's death.

Davis had every reason to expect that he would have success as immediate as Kettering's. He knew that his invention was as necessary, though he wasn't prepared to establish that anyone had died for lack of power steering. And he quickly found out that all the truck drivers with broken thumbs were not going to excite General Motors executives to make power steering a matter of honor. But still, Davis did not think that death or cosmic disaster should be required of him or of the universe to effect the acceptance of power steering. Of course, Ralph Nader probably could have told him differently, but certainly not in 1926 when that prober of the automotive industry's attitudes was yet to be born.

When he left Detroit in October, 1926, Davis was convinced that success was only a matter of working out a few small bugs and tooling up for manufacture. He knew pumps were going to be something of a problem but he felt that they would be no more difficult to develop than power steering. General Motors had given him an option at $200 a month and they were assuming Jessup's salary for the development period.

With one more push he'd be all set, then he could go to Hawaii and play tennis or pursue the hard-fighting, land-locked salmon in the wilderness lakes of Maine.

The first interest at General Motors was in the application of power steering to trucks. By the end of 1927 they had a successful linkage-type steering gear in a five-ton truck. The gear presented some problems with oil leakage, but on the whole worked quite well. On the basis of this success General Motors took up their option and signed an exclusive contract with Davis to run for one year beginning January 1, 1928.

Denyes of Saginaw Products Division had the principal responsibility for the development of power steering. He had ample encouragement from Colonel Green of the Truck Division and from Strickland and Prentis of Cadillac. Denyes decided to proceed with the design of production type gears for both Yellow Coach and Cadillac. Because the piston pump was too expensive for production, Davis designed and Saginaw built a rotary gear pump based on a gear tooth suggested to Davis by Professor Earl Buckingham of Massachusetts Institute of Technology.

Denyes proceeded with the Cadillac gear first; it was ready for bench testing by the end of August, 1928. General Motors put the gear on the bench and there it sat. By December of 1928 the gear was still on a bench, even though it had tested satisfactorily. Denyes said that development had stopped because of increased efficiency in manual gears; he refused to proceed without the whole-hearted support of both the Truck and Cadillac Divisions. Davis felt trapped; with an exclusive license, General Motors controlled the progress of power steering within General Motors. Davis realized he had to build a fire under Denyes; but how could he do that without gaining the enmity of Denyes and possibly impeding all further progress?

In poker, as Davis had learned the game in the Colorado gold camps, it was time for a "force play." On December 11, 1928, Davis wrote Lewis M. Spencer, who now headed General Motors Patent Department, as follows:

> "If you desire to continue with the steering gear I am sure that we can arrive at a satisfactory arrangement. If not, then I would appreciate it very much if General Motors would agree to a conclusion of the contract now existing, so as to enable me to proceed in other channels."

From a poker standpoint, at least Western style, it was a brilliant move, for it took Denyes out of the dealer's spot, a position Davis had concluded Denyes did not especially relish.

Then, since no one else wanted to make the decision, the question was turned over to the General Motors Technical Committee. Because interest was tepid at most, the Committee decided they had best hedge their bet; they recommended that the company continue with Davis but on a nonexclusive basis. Under this arrangement General Motors was protected. If power steering began to be accepted by the industry, they could proceed under contract with Davis. But they gave up their speculative, exclusive position of using power steering for a competitive advantage. Under the exclusive agreement they had control and could have sold rights or frozen out competitors at will. Under the new arrangement they still had the inventor captive, or at least on a leash, and they could beat any competitor to the punch, or at the very worst be on equal terms with any other company that decided to offer power steering. The Technical Committee had proved they were pretty good poker players themselves, but they were playing the game as Davis knew it.

However, the Technical Committee made another decision that moved power steering farther away from production: they turned the development responsibility over to the Research Department. Denyes was concerned with production. At Saginaw, Research was concerned with ironing out bugs; that is, Research had the freedom to be leisurely. They also had the freedom to be energetic, but with power steering they chose to take their time. The sample Cadillac gear was turned over to J. O. Almen of the Dynamics Section of the Research Laboratory. Mr. Almen of Dynamics got the Cadillac gear installed in a car and on the road by the end of 1929, one year after bench testing began.

When the Cadillac gear was designed, a significant departure from the Davis design was made. Instead of springs against stops to hold the valve in a neutral position, General Motors used a split ring device.

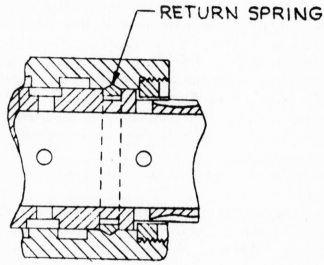

RETURN SPRING

Fig. 11

When a force is applied to the ring the V-shaped groove compresses the ring and it moves, allowing the gear to operate. An important feature of Davis' design was springs against stops. With the split ring General Motors was obviously trying to find a method of gaining the performance of Davis' gear without incorporating his designs. Obviously they were trying to patent around him.

Almen had only one problem with the split ring; it didn't work. The force required to compress the ring was so great and the driver had to expend so much energy to get the power part of the steering into operation, that he could have done the same

77

steering job without power assist. Almen solved the problem by removing the split ring. He claimed that he had good directional stability with the gear after it was modified. This may be, but the gear would have possessed the same problems as those in the early experimental gears that Davis built in Waltham. First, it would have had little feel of the road since the power assist was always on. The purpose of springs against stops had been to provide this feel. Second, although it would have directional stability, the gear was not reversible. The driver of the Cadillac would have had to bring the wheels back to straight ahead after making a turn. Davis incorporated springs in his original gear to make it reversible. The modified Cadillac gear had no such feature. In subsequent gears General Motors provided spring centering against stops, confirming the unsatisfactory nature of the Almen alterations.

The truck gears that were laid out in 1928 remained on paper; but Davis had succeeded in getting a gear he approved of installed in a twelve-cylinder Cadillac. However, as 1929 passed, Davis grew more discouraged. His contract with General Motors was nearing termination and he felt quite certain they intended to let it lapse. But when he returned to Detroit in December, he found more enthusiasm than he had encountered since his initial trip in 1926.

For the first time, Davis met Charles F. Kettering, and found he had an ally in the most respected engineer in the industry. Kettering not only believed in power steering, but said he would gladly pay $100 more for a Cadillac equipped with power steering. Speaking of Denyes' lack of interest in power steering, Kettering remarked, "It only takes 100th of a second to get a message around the earth, but three years to get the same message through ½ inch of bone."

As a result of Kettering's enthusiasm, the power steering equipped Cadillac became the most popular car at the General Motors Proving Grounds. It became the fashion for officials and engineers from all divisions to drive the experimental car around the high speed course, over the Belgian block pavement, the hills, water tanks, sand and other test obstacles. Davis, being human, was there as often as possible, not only to accept congratulations, but to answer any questions. One day he saw Kettering, W. J. Davidson, who was Sloan's executive assistant and Colonel Green, head of the Truck Division, climb into the car and drive off. They were gone about twenty minutes and when they returned Kettering waved to Davis and gave him the "O" sign with his thumb and forefinger. As the trio walked away, a mechanic called the inventor's attention to what, in those days, was called a 'drag-link.' Davis discovered that metal fatigue had caused a break that went half way through the link. He still shudders when he thinks about the incident.

"If that thing had let go during that test drive, power steering would have gotten a black eye it might never have recovered from."

Despite the stock market tumble, everyone Davis talked to had enthusiasm and individually stated that they wanted to move. The problem was to get all these people pointed in such directions that they didn't run into each other and wreck the program. At least this was the way Davis first appraised the situation.

Davis always took notes and here are the comments he collected on one day, Friday, December 6, 1929:

"Lunched with Mr. Spencer. Talked with Blackmore. Pointed out Kull's statement about offer to furnish experimental gear to General Motors truck at their expense, $5,000. Asked who the financial man was back of Denyes. He said Wilson was the man. Asked me to advise Denyes to outline situation in letter to Wilson and arrange for me to see Wilson. Wilson has taken I. F. Johnson's place in the financial scheme of General Motors. Wilson is the man to say *yes* or no on this project.

"Talked with Ball of General Motors Truck. He explained their desire continued for power gears more so than ever. He further explained the negotiations with Denyes and Denyes' proposition to contribute $5,000 for purchase of gear. Ball explained that they could not afford and didn't feel justified to pay out that. *There's the rub.*

"Talked with Green for a couple of minutes. I just happened to run into him. He seemed rabid on subject of power steering and said he proposed to go thoroughly into subject in a few days. Green just arrived from Europe yesterday and is rushed to death.

"Talked with George Hallet, General Motors Research. Hallet is in complete agreement about the desirability of power steering for *all motor vehicles.* Says it must come for buses and trucks and large cars and when cheap enough, will go on small cars as well."

Perhaps today this sort of thing is rapidly recognizable and even has a name—*corporation run-around.* Davis certainly had encountered some of it before at Pierce-Arrow and other companies, but he had never run into a "snow" blast of such proportions.

"It was like those rotary snow plows the railroads were later to use to clear the railroad tracks in the Rockies. I could feel myself getting buried deeper and deeper in their praise for power steering."

As a mountain-reared boy, Davis knew all about the dangers of getting trapped under a snow avalanche. His goal had always been to get his power steering unit into production. So on Tuesday, December 10, he went back to Denyes, who headed production at Saginaw. Denyes greeted the inventor warmly and apparently held no hard feelings for Davis' poker power play. But what Denyes had to say contradicted practically every impression Davis had picked up four days earlier.

Here are Davis' notes:

"Talked with Denyes; he is still a believer in power steering, however from business standpoint he refuses to spend any more money nor will he ask for appropriation of money to try to back the power gears on General Motors Truck, Cadillac, and others in General Motors Corporation. Also says he is not interested in developing possible outside business (Mack, White, etc.).

"He said General Motors Bus was at 'white heat' short time ago but the thing died down when he offered to build in gear for $5,000 and the General Motors Bus said 'no.' He and Green must get along like a couple of strange dogs."

This was one of Davis' lowest moments, for he realized that Denyes' attitude was a roadblock to any approach to Charles E. Wilson, the man who controlled the corporation's spending. One must remember that this was 1929, the year of the market crash, and the man who held the purse strings was the fount of all action.

On December 11, the situation brightened. Davis and Blackmore discussed a new contract that would give General Motors exclusive rights again. Davis was to get $5,000 on signing and a guarantee that would increase $5,000 per year through 1933. Blackmore left, saying he'd let Davis know the final decision.

Davis closed his stay in Detroit talking to Kettering. Kettering felt that Denyes should shoulder the responsibility of building the bus gear and of arranging for production. He claimed the muddle was Denyes' mistake, "Denyes should have gone out and applied power steering gears and made them like it or not. He only did half his job."

Coming from the most famous automotive inventor in the land and a charter member of General Motors inner Round Table, these were heady words indeed. And Davis left Detroit assuming he would know where he stood very quickly. A month later nothing had happened.

Davis returned to Detroit January 17, 1930, and on the next day reached Blackmore, who informed him that the company refused to pay him the $5,000 during 1930 that they had talked about in December. Davis showed Blackmore his notes.

Blackmore recalled that Davis mentioned a saving of $35,000 for General Motors over the old agreement. But word came down to the General Motors bargainers from Vice President Ormond E. Hunt, to stand pat. Davis said that he would return $5,000 during any year subsequent to 1930 (under controversy) but that he wanted to give General Motors a chance to live up to their agreement of December. This discussion took place on Saturday. Everybody agreed to make a decision on Monday.

Monday started slowly. Blackmore, J. H. Hunt, and Spencer said that O. E. Hunt would not retreat on the $5,000. Finally Davis said he'd take the loss if General Motors would change the cancellation clause in the contract from 90 days to 1 year. Davis noted the reaction to his demand that General Motors commit itself:

"They tried to impress me very strongly with the fact that Kettering, Green, Denyes, and Almen had voted strongly to go ahead on power steering and the hydraulic gears in particular; furthermore, that it was intended for Almen and Denyes to proceed independently on different gears of two different types, and that already they had submitted designs that 'appeared to fall under your patents.' Also, that Almen and Denyes had money and authority to proceed as rapidly as possible in the building and installing of experimental gears. One for buses by Denyes, and one for Cadillac by Almen.

"As a result of all this, I finally broke down in order to wind the thing up and said to go ahead on the six-month cancellation clause."

Davis did not take offense at the statement that the new designs *appeared to fall under his patents.* The name of the game that any independent inventor must be prepared to play when he deals with a large engineering organization is "They'll Invent Around You if They Can." In 1927-1928, General Motors had approximately 9,000 engineers in its employ and Francis W. Davis was well aware that he was matching his wits and his skill, and practically issuing a personal challenge to this army brigade-sized group when he drove to Detroit and asked General Motors to appraise and test his power steering unit.

He was pretty certain that various General Motors groups had spent and would spend thousands of man hours trying to invent around him. And the fact that after three years General Motors was still haggling with him meant that despite their vast resources and 9,000-to-1 advantage they had not been able to find a better answer to power steering.

This was the game whose rules he knew and that he had expected to play when he sat down with the General Motors negotiators. And to all outward appearances this was the game they had been playing—but Francis Davis recalls his own disturbed feelings:

"It wasn't that they were constantly calling for a new deck, which is something the house seldom does. (This said with a Western-like frown.) Of course it's the house's option to set the rules—but when you get the feeling that the *house players* themselves don't know the house rules, well it gets a little eerie and nerve-wracking."

Davis was instinctively right. Half the time the house players, or General Motors negotiators, didn't understand the house rules. In the first few months of The Depression, Alfred P. Sloan, Jr. had effected radical organizational policies that saved the sprawling General Motors business empire from self-destruction. Sloan's daring concepts, which are the basis for large corporation systems operation and management control as we know them today, were little understood by layer upon layer of the company's management personnel at that time.

"Suddenly they were men living in boxes," is the way Francis W. Davis puts it. In explanation he points to the many-tiered boxes of the table of organization charts that illustrate Mr. Sloan's best-selling book "My Years with General Motors," which Davis keeps on his desk. "Mr. Sloan had each one of them cooped up in his own special box. They didn't like it and I didn't know it. I guess you can see why I thought everyone was acting a little eerie."

But the men who had yet to get used to the idea of working in boxes continued their negotiations and on Tuesday, January 21, 1930, Davis signed the contract and received a check for $5,000.

As Davis was handed his copy of the agreement, Blackmore undertook to explain some company procedures *in order to set his mind at rest.* He stated that General Motors might file applications themselves on hydraulic gears but that Davis was not to be alarmed that any interferences might be declared as they often filed applications to smoke out the situation.

Davis got the message. Blackmore was letting him know that General Motors was still trying to invent around him in every way possible, and at the same time send up smoke signals that would draw a response from anyone else working in the field. It was a clear invitation announcing that others could buy into the game.

"I really felt considerably more at ease," Davis explains, "for the game was now back in the right ball park. I had learned something too; that once they knew the house rules, Mr. Sloan's 'box men' could act with vigor and authority."

Davis put this new information aside for future guidance. He had other more important things on his mind. He recognized that his opponents were setting up a "squeeze play." The signed contract he was carrying back to Waltham really meant that General Motors would now commit more of their research facilities and resources to the power steering problem. The pace had quickened and Davis realized that he and Jessup would have to scramble to retain their lead in the race.

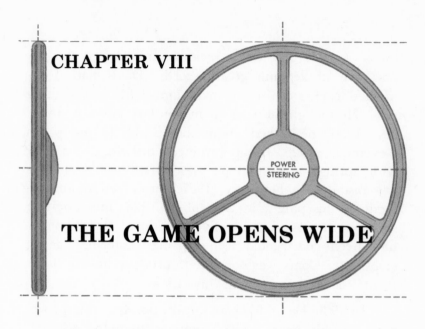

CHAPTER VIII

POWER
STEERING

THE GAME OPENS WIDE

While Alfred P. Sloan, Jr. was installing management techniques at General Motors that would change the whole nature and directional flow of American business, and Davis played poker in a non-stop game where each relieving "house dealer" seemed to have a different concept of the house rules, other American engineers were not unaware of the rewards that inventing a workable power steering device promised.

Early in 1931 the United States Patent Office advised Davis that a notice of interference had been filed on his first steering patent. The other contestant was Roy G. Coats of Pasadena, California. Mr. Coats had applied for a steering patent in October, 1927, and his gear used spring centering against stops. This was an essential feature of Davis' first gear. Since Davis' patent application dated from February, 1927, he was declared the senior party in the dispute.

When a patent claim is disputed the decision is based upon seven types of evidence: 1) conception; 2) drawings; 3) models; 4) written description; 5) disclosure to someone else; 6) operation; 7) application for a patent. The Coats incident emphasized the importance of keeping good records. Davis had documented each step in the invention of his first steering gear. He thought of using springs in late 1925; in January, 1926, he talked about the springs to Jessup. In November, 1926, Jessup produced drawings of a gear with springs against stops. The first gear with stops was installed in February, 1927. Davis filed an amendment to his patent in December, 1926, incorporating spring centering. Finally, five additional steering gears had been constructed using spring centering against stops. Mr. Coats was not able to produce similar documentation in support of his invention.

In 1930 Davis filed an application for an improvement on his gear. More compact than the original, this gear incorporated the usual open center valve and spring centering against stops, but in this valve the outer member was stationary and the inner member was fixed to the steering shaft. The inner member and the steering shaft were allowed a limited amount of axial movement; thrust bearings were used to limit the movement.

On November 28, 1927, B. S. Aikman of Milwaukee, Wisconsin, filed an application for a steering gear incorporating four closed center valves that were actuated by axial movement of the steering shaft. Aikman's application clearly preceded Davis' conception and Aikman was awarded priority. Mr. Aikman had attempted to interest the automotive industry in his invention but had failed. Davis purchased Aikman's rights for a considerable sum and was thus able to maintain his control of the patent position. Davis was anticipated in this development, but that should not detract from his independent conception or from his continuous imaginative improvement of power steering.

Davis was also facing competition from industrial research organizations. The first device developed by industry was the Bethlehem steering gear. This gear never got anywhere but it did serve notice to Davis that other solutions were being sought. The Bethlehem gear had two drums rotating in opposite directions; inside the drums were two clutches. A steering input would engage the appropriate drum, and power from the engine was transmitted through the clutch to assist steering.

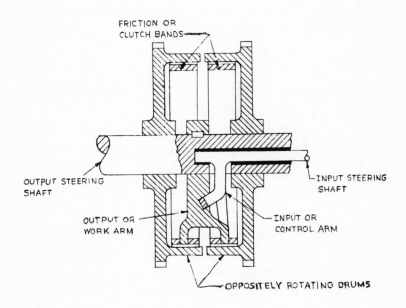

Fig. 12

The Bethlehem gear had too many problems. The clutch and the drum hardly ever rotated at the same speed, so the gear had the failing of all friction devices —it would wear out. Also, the gearing necessary to transmit torque from the steering wheel to the clutches occupied too much space.

The first system to come into commercial use was the Bendix-Westinghouse. This gear was very similar in appearance and operation to the steam gears developed in the nineteenth century for boats.

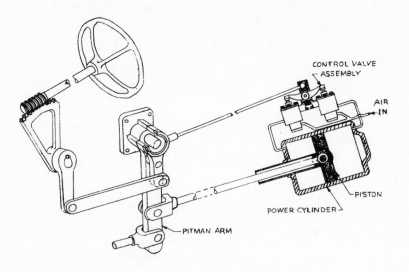

Fig. 13

Bendix air brakes were standard on heavy equipment, so a supply of high pressure air was readily available. Even though air systems are used today, the large piston sizes necessary with air pressures of 100 psi limit use to large, expensive installations. Also, air is a compressible fluid, this makes an air steering system relatively insensitive, compared to a hydraulic system.

In 1931 the first hydraulic power steering gears were commercially manufactured by Vickers Inc., a small independent company founded by an able engineer and inventor, Harry Vickers. Vickers' interest in power steering dated back to 1925. In 1927 he reached the demonstration stage. Although they attacked the steering problem along similar lines, Vickers and Davis were only in indirect competition. Vickers concentrated on heavy vehicles, while Davis was mainly interested in the larger passenger car market.

The Vickers gear was a linkage type, so it would be adaptable to many different installations. Since he was a supplier to several truck manufacturers this flexibility was mandatory. On the other hand, Davis could design more compact integral gears since they were going to be used in vehicles produced by one company.

On the Vickers gear the valve and power cylinder were located in one housing between the Pitman arm and the frame. Vickers also used spring centering against stops and adopted the open center valve prin-

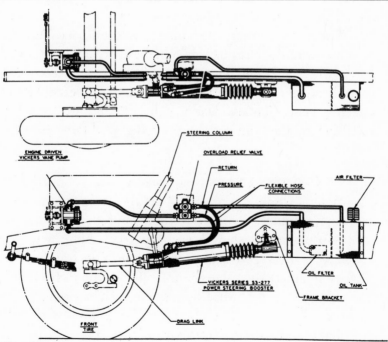

Fig. 14

ciple after Davis' patents were published in 1931. Even though his gears were different from Davis' designs in many details, the spring centering principle was clearly Davis' and a licensing agreement was worked out. The rewards from Vickers were insignificant compared to those Davis would have received had General Motors made power steering optional equipment on even one line of its passenger cars.

But the Vickers gear did mean that Davis must run all the harder to remain even, let alone stay ahead. If Vickers could produce a commercial power steering unit for heavy vehicles, then somebody else could come up with one for passenger cars. It would only be a matter of time before engineering staffs at Ford, Chrysler, or General Motors designed a power steering gear that didn't fall under Davis' patents. Davis not only had to think up his own designs, he had to anticipate those of everyone else.

Then, as though the high command at General Motors weren't causing him enough grief, during the early thirties Davis encountered his first mechanical roadblock since the initial success of the Pierce-Arrow steering gear. Today Davis can joke about what he calls one of the toughest engineering problems he ever faced:

> "General Motors had one of the experimental trucks on the floor at the plant in the early thirties. I was out there and they said, 'We want to show you this truck here; we have a power steering setup on it. You watch, we'll start the engine and jiggle the wheel and you'll see what'll happen.' They jiggled the wheel and that great big truck started to shake and shimmy in the front end. They said, 'You know what we call it—Little Egypt.' "

The oscillation began when the valve was displaced from the neutral position, and the oscillation grew worse every time; the gear could destroy itself. Davis attributed the oscillation to inertia in the heavy components of the truck gear; they just couldn't move fast enough to keep up with the valve. The solution was either speed up the heavy parts or slow down the valve. The first was not possible because the massive parts were necessary for large vehicles. So Davis tried two methods to friction dampen the valve. One didn't work and the second was so stiff that the gear might as well have been manual.

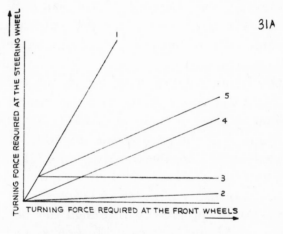

31A

I. MANUAL STEERING
2. HYDRAULIC POWER STEERING WITHOUT RETURN
   SPRINGS OR HYDRAULIC REACTION.
3. HYDRAULIC POWER STEERING WITH RETURN SPRINGS
   BUT WITHOUT HYDRAULIC REACTION.
4. HYDRAULIC POWER STEERING WITH HYDRAULIC
   REACTION BUT WITHOUT RETURN SPRINGS.
5. HYDRAULIC POWER STEERING WITH RETURN SPRINGS
   AND HYDRAULIC REACTION.

Fig. 15

Davis and the Saginaw engineers dismantled the valve and changed the portings. When they put it back together, it still oscillated about as badly as it had before. Finally, the problems were solved with a new design that introduced hydraulic reaction: the valve was constructed in such a way that the hydraulic fluid would dampen valve movement in amount proportional to the steering force. Hydraulic reaction slowed down valve movement enough to eliminate chatter.

While General Motors was constructing truck gears that didn't work, Jessup applied for a patent on a new design. The patent was granted in 1934 and assigned to Davis. This gear was a major change from earlier Davis designs. All previous gears had used a power piston of some type; this gear had a rotary power pack. The outer valve member was connected to the Pitman arm, the inner member to the cross shaft from a manual gear. The valve was of the open center type and was maintained in neutral by springs against stops. The three movable vanes on the valve and the three stationary vanes on the casing formed six power units. When the valve was displaced from neutral, hydraulic fluid entered three of these units and rotated the outer valve member in the appropriate direction. This valve was installed in the Pierce-Arrow in 1931, and in a 1932 Buick. This gear performed very well and offset the poor performance of the truck gears.

But Davis' progress with design did not seem to get General Motors any closer to power steering production. Each new improved gear he took to Detroit brought additional enthusiastic comments to fill his notebooks. Every executive he encountered agreed that power steering would be a necessity on cars, but each inferred that progress was being held up by departments other than his own. Later, in describing the situation, Davis compared it to the hedgerows bordering every plot of land in Normandy which did more to hold up the Allied advance after their successful landings in World War II than enemy mine fields or tank traps.

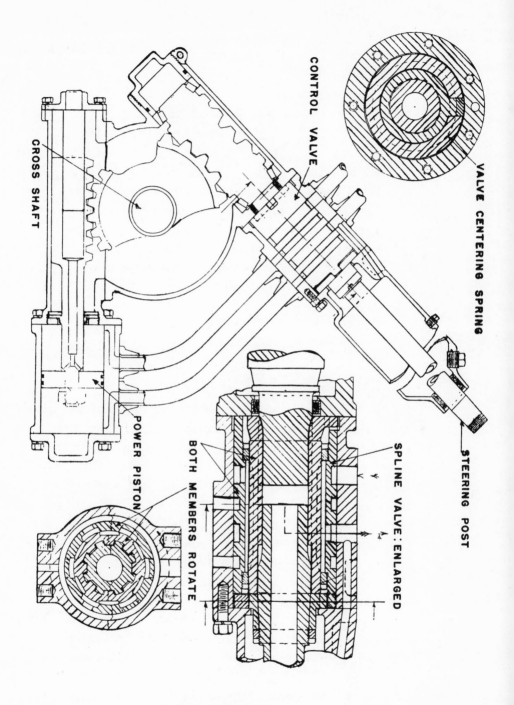

CONTROL VALVE

VALVE CENTERING SPRING

CROSS SHAFT

STEERING POST

POWER PISTON

SPLINE VALVE : ENLARGED

BOTH MEMBERS ROTATE

Fig. 16

Finally, on January 22, 1934, General Motors acted:

Dear Mr. Davis:

Re: Power Steering Gears
License agreement dated
January 1, 1931

In accordance with the provisions of Section 10 of the above-identified agreement, as modified by the understanding expressed by your letter of December 28, 1933, please accept this as notice that General Motors Corporation will exercise its right to cancel the above-identified agreement at the close of the second calendar quarter of this year.

Very truly yours,

O. E. Hunt
Vice President

LMS:GS

From far up above someone had dropped the big one. Davis might have reacted violently to such a disruption of his aims and dreams; some men would have got drunk and stayed that way a while. Not Davis; he wrote Hunt a letter, not an angry letter, but a reasonable one in which he stated:

"You are now using a 24-1 ratio steering gear in your Cadillac car and it takes from 45 to 60 pounds of pull on the wheel rim to park the car. The large Buick with a 23.5 to 1 ratio is but little better off. Recent tests at the Cadillac Company indicate a required torque of 10,000 lb.-in. necessary to swing the front wheels of the 1934 Cadillac on dry pavement.

"It is generally agreed that you have about reached the limit of efficiency in the hand-operated gear. It is fantastic to believe that no further progress will ever be made in steering passenger cars. The gradual lowering of tire pressures is not helping this situation. Furthermore, the reversibility in the high efficiency steering introduces a dangerous factor with tire blowouts and other heavy reactions on the front wheels. Further development must logically come from power-assisted steering. The combination of hydraulic steering and hydraulic booster brake offers an economical and compact installation.

"In the bus and truck fields, legislation is forcing the transfer of more and more weight onto the front axle. The latest models of 'Camel-Back' (seat over the engine) trucks will give a weight distribution of about 33% on the front axle amounting to 9,000 to 10,000 pounds front axle weight. This change is bringing power steering forcibly into the picture as these vehicles cannot be properly handled without power steering. There is talk of legislation requiring this equipment in the interest of public safety."

Certainly Mr. Hunt's reply, which Davis received on March 2, 1934, was one of the most amazing revelations of disregard for the safety of the public and its own customers ever typed under the letterhead of a corporation of any consequence, and signed by a responsible executive. Unfortunately for O. E. Hunt's future literary fame, it was neither short nor pungent and will never achieve the wide circulation of Commodore Vanderbilt's "The public be damned!" It reads:

Dear Mr. Davis:

This will acknowledge your letter of February 6th with regard to power steering gears.

All the points you raise were given consideration at the time we made our decision to discontinue our agreement with you.

We came to the conclusion that the cost of the protection to us under the then existing arrangement was greater than its value to us either now or for the future.

If you have in mind some plan whereby the cost could be reduced we would be glad to have your suggestions.

Yours very truly,

O. E. Hunt

Vice President

What makes this chronicle even more fantastic was Francis Davis' reaction. He was not shocked then, or is he shocked today, by Ormond E. Hunt's statement.

"My first conclusion was that Mr. Hunt felt that power steering would add an extra hazard to driving. After all, as an engineer he knew the 24-to-1 steering gear ratio in the Cadillac was pushing the safety margin close to the limit."

But Hunt's letter brought a recent incident back to mind. Davis relates it in the following manner:

"While in Detroit with my Pierce-Arrow Runabout after General Motors had shown interest in the power steering unit, they requested that I loan them the car for a couple of days so that they could run some tests. I consented to this, and at the end of the two days, I went out to the General Motors building to pick up my car. I noticed that the little padlock that held the spare tire in place was missing.

"I asked one of the men what had happened to my padlock. He smiled and then proceeded to tell me about the test that they had put the car through known as the 'shotgun test.'

"In this test, a shotgun shell is used to blow out a front tire unexpectedly, so the handling and control of the car under stress could be checked. They didn't want to blast one of my tires, so they cut the padlock and removed the spare tire from the rim, and put on another tire of their own which they changed to the front wheel, and then proceeded with the test.

"The General Motors drivers, who were both engineers, reported that the power steering equipped Pierce-Arrow had passed the tests with flying colors."

As an automobile man, Davis knew that test drivers don't go around breaking padlocks and giving non-company cars secret proving-ground tests without orders from pretty high up. He was then convinced that Mr. Hunt and the "we" in the letter were well aware that their own proving criteria had demonstrated that power steering would greatly aid safety in driving.

The more he considered it, the more Davis became convinced that the cost factor, which was mentioned in the last paragraph of the letter, had no real significance.

No, something else was preventing General Motors from adopting power steering. Davis remembered how, during the long game sessions, he had had the feeling that the house men weren't sure about the house rules. He had yet to make his crack about their being "box men," but he did know that the man who had signed that letter was a member of the small upper echelon that wrote the house rules. Up there on the summit, hidden in the clouds, was the real reason that General Motors was not going ahead with power steering.

Davis decided that it was time to stand back and study the mountain. He realized that the short man, given to wearing formal black attire "every damn day you saw him," who had signed this letter, blocked his path more effectively than any Colorado chasm or cliff.

Just as he had once studied Pike's Peak, Davis observed Ormond E. Hunt from every available angle. He kept fitting the insights together as he acquired them, and gradually the person who had been chief engineer at Chevrolet when "Chevy" ran Ford off the road began to emerge in a form Francis Davis was not quite able to identify—the modern corporation man.

The reason, of course, was that Alfred P. Sloan, Jr. had barely finished creating him.

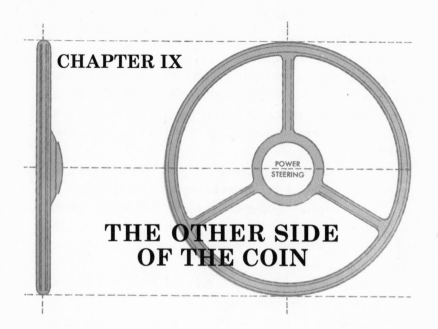

CHAPTER IX

THE OTHER SIDE
OF THE COIN

In 1905 the Rough Rider occupant of the White House and advocate of vigorous living, Theodore Roosevelt, bowing to public disapproval, somewhat ruefully admitted that on two occasions he had ridden in an automobile but pledged he would not do so again. In 1907, Woodrow Wilson, president of Princeton University, about to be elected governor of New Jersey, and well on his way to the presidency, felt it politic to denounce motoring as a moral menace. Castigated from pulpits, ridiculed by the press, harassed by village ordinances and rural constables who ardently enforced 10 mile an hour speed limits, the pioneers of the American automotive industry early developed both thick skins and a rugged sense of self dependence. Outside of the cities anything that could qualify as a suitable road for their vehicles did not exist, but instead of seeking Federal aid such as canals, steamboats and the railroads had received in such great abundance in their infancy, they went ahead and built cars. And the American people in what now seems like a gigantic grassroots anti-Establishment protest movement bought them and with a mud-spattered, dust-sprinkled jaunty attitude of defiance drove them, with the result that there were 300 different makes of American cars when William C. Durant formed General Motors Company in 1908.

It was this background of rugged independence that gave the automobile business and Detroit, which became its capital because Ford and General Motors happened to center there, the brassy self-assurance and insular attitude many have found annoying and which found its fullest expression in Charles E. Wilson's unembarrassed statement, "What's good for General Motors is good for America."

Whatever retractions Mr. Wilson made under the goading of his horrified public relations staff, he undoubtedly deeply believed what he had said and for what, to him, were sufficient and obvious reasons.

He was still a relatively young and active man. In his short life time he had seen the early-maligned and still-ridiculed automobile industry practically pull a nation mired in recession and depression back on the road to prosperity on three occasions. Also, as president of General Motors, he was acutely aware that he had been part of a management team that, without government aid, had rescued that corporate giant when it too had momentarily faltered. He probably shared a belief that, had this giant of industry toppled, it would have pulled the entire nation down to economic ruin with it.

Like every automobile man, Francis W. Davis was equally proud of the self-reliance of the industry to which he belonged. His Colorado Springs boyhood had made him acutely aware of the huge land grants the railroads had obtained from the government before they would consider extending their roadbeds westward. And Davis had a personal acquaintance with exactly how

102

roadless the United States was as late as 1921. From April 7 to May 24 of that year, Davis headed a transcontinental trip for Pierce-Arrow which Sidney A. Walton, Vice-President of the Packard Motor Company, prophesied would be a failure due to bad roads, mud, and snow. Davis was accompanied by John Talcot, an experimental engineer, and Charles Hodge, Pierce-Arrow's publicity director. The presence of the company's publicity director reveals the importance the company attached to the venture and Davis' description is almost unbelievable reading today.

"We completed the first leg from New York to Los Angeles in 12 days, 9 hours" (which, apparently, was some sort of a record or Davis would not have recorded it).

"The progress to St. Louis was quite easy; west of St. Louis there were no paved roads excepting in towns. We plowed through Missouri muck, Kansas gumbo and Colorado adobe. At that time of the year the roads were thawing out from winter storms and with plenty of rainfall. We used chains on all four wheels and broke the chains many times. On Raton Pass, between Colorado and New Mexico, we by-passed a snow-blocked roadway by using horse wagon tracks on the side of the mountain. Aside from tire replacements and broken front and rear springs and other minor mechanical troubles, we had no serious problems with the car.

"During our stop-over in Los Angeles and San Francisco, I gave several talks before auto groups on the experiences on the trip.

"On the return we traveled more leisurely and made several detours to the Grand Canyon and Colorado Springs (where Davis' family

In 1921 the Pierce-Arrow Motor Car Company sent Davis on a transcontinental automobile trip. The drive from New York to Los Angeles took twelve days.

"We disembark from the Missouri River ferry."

"West of Kansas City. Our first experience with Kansas 'Gumbo'; four days of continuous rain had put the roads in a frightful condition and the natives pronounced them impassable. However, we moved along just the same with chains on all four wheels and occasional stops to chop the mud out from between the wheels and fenders."

"Through the Main Street in one of the little Kansas towns."

On the Raton Pass (Colorado) "with car up against snow bank which extended for three or four hundred yards at a depth of two to four feet."

"The little town of High Hill, Missouri, is to be congratulated on its excellent quality of mud."

lived). On reaching Buffalo the Pierce-Arrow workers lined up the roadway parallel to the factory and greeted us like returning heroes. The trip gave the company lots of valuable information on the working of the car under extreme road conditions at that time of the year."

Apparently, urgently needed state and federal co-action is not a recent development, for this trip was taken five years after Congress had, in 1916, belatedly recognized that an adequate highway system might be just as important to the national defense and general welfare of the country as dredging the rivers and sub-sidizing the railroads with mail contracts. In that year Congress passed a measure matching state appropria-tions for what we now call Interstate highways.

If Teddy Roosevelt and Woodrow Wilson did not realize what was taking place in the country, Francis W. Davis did. As an engineer he was aware that both the internal combustion engine and electricity had already changed the age-old patterns of living. He recognized that they represented a new wealth that could not be saved but had to be used. This, of course, was a very revolutionary theory and Francis Davis, by the wildest stretch of the imagination, could never be called a revolutionist.

The explanation is that Davis has always felt and thought like an automobile man. And even when his negotiations with General Motors were their most baffling, Davis was aware and proud of the fact that during the days of darkest financial panic, the financial genius of Alfred P. Sloan, Jr. had enabled General Motors to avoid disaster and without the aid of the President of the United States. It was fairly common knowledge, during the bank moratorium of 1933, that the President instructed his treasurer to keep the doors of what is now the largest bank in the world open at all costs, dispatching three specie trains to California if necessary.

All this must be considered as background to the position Davis now found himself in. For if Francis W. Davis was not the first inventor of a major invention to tangle with the management philosophies of what its acknowledged parent calls *the modern corporation*, he certainly made and kept more copious notes on his entanglement than any other inventor. And if these notes reveal a certain myopic quality in regard to what are commonly accepted and expected management attitudes and operational procedures today, it is well to remember that the modern corporation, as created by Alfred P. Sloan, Jr. "needed techniques never used before." At least, so boldly states Mr. Sloan in his book "My Years With General Motors." [3]

Today everyone has a pretty good image of the corporation man. He has been fictionalized in numerous novels, dramatized on motion picture and television screens, lauded or jibed at in men's style magazines, and the younger third of the nation's male population seems engaged in a major effort to either look like him or unlike him. But, Davis was completely unaware that such a type existed. Davis had seen local banking figures attempt to emulate J. P. Morgan by wearing frock coats and smoking huge cigars. As a boy in the West he had even seen men try to look like Buffalo Bill, and the early silent movie stars like Wallace Reid and Doug Fairbanks had their imitators in every town. Possibly, if this new breed of corporation men at General Motors had tried to dress like Mr. Sloan, Davis would have caught the idea immediately but, while none of them tried to dress like Sloan, all were thinking in channels and acting within limits that Sloan had prescribed.

However, both Davis' notebooks and his accurate memory reveal that while their thoughts and actions were channeled and prescribed at that time, these men had not mastered what today is called "corporation double talk" or possibly Davis' unattuned ears did not recognize it. For his notebooks are crammed with direct quotations from General Motors men praising his invention, and constant personal assertions and predictions of when power steering would go into production and use. For instance, every time Davis encountered Charles E. Kettering, whom he greatly respected, the inventor of the self-starter went out of his way to praise power steering.

As Davis explains it today, "There were tables of organization charts everywhere, but I was unable to take the concept seriously. I couldn't believe that men like Kettering would allow themselves to be fenced off in those little printed boxes. I still find it hard to believe that they did." At this point Davis is apt to refer a listener to a small volume in which he has marked a paragraph that reads:

"Probably the most effective mental container ever devised is the t.o. (table of organization) box—it lets little fresh thoughts in, and none out. If that is its main purpose, it is certainly successful. But if the encouragement of creative thinking and action is an objective of a firm or organization, then it is the greatest barrier Man has ever erected against himself. Every week more ideas are smashed, squashed and ignored within its four ruled sides than were suppressed by the Spanish Inquisition in the four centuries of that institution's existence." [4]

As Davis took time out to study the mountain—in this case the behavior patterns within Sloan's new organizational structure at General Motors—he neglected to notice that Kettering had clashed with O. E. Hunt, then chief engineer of Chevrolet, over the use of copper-cooling in the 1924 engine. In explaining this omission, which he termed "the copper cooling bit," Davis said: "While I knew the company had been forced to recall those copper-cooled cars, they continued to publicize Kettering as General Motors' engineering genius and, at that time, I couldn't believe that Kettering was no longer a major figure in engineering decisions. In other words, he had been boxed out. I'm sure now that's why he turned to the development of the GM two-cycle railroad diesel which took over that field."

What Davis is saying here is that O. E. Hunt, the man who opposed power steering, was not only the chief engineer of the car that overtook Henry Ford and forced him into the ditch, but earlier had taken the measurement of and had dimmed autodom's brightest creative shining light, at least in the higher inner councils where the company's big decisions were made. Sloan's book, published many years later, indirectly confirms Davis' diagnosis. Sloan describes his decision to back Hunt in the controversy as one of the most difficult he ever had to make, and undoubtedly this was because of his warm personal relationship with Kettering. That this friendship survived is a tribute to Sloan's diplomatic gifts and his ability to inspire complete loyalty even when hobbling the former free-wheeling individualists of the auto industry This was an accomplishment comparable to Louis XIV stripping all power from the barons of France by luring them to Versailles and making them idle courtiers, except that Sloan, by means of his then novel corporation organizational techniques, made men work more efficiently than they ever had before. Confirmed by decades of General Motors earning statements, Sloan's concepts have only recently begun to be challenged.

Sloan's own summation of the "copper cooling" episode is significant as an example of top corporate management thinking. To Sloan it proved that management must subscribe to the firm policies which "we had been working on." Which in *corporatese* meant that from then on at General Motors the divisional and corporate functions in engineering, advanced product engineering and long range research would be determined by upper management committee policy decisions.

The first three decades of automotive history belonged to high-soaring individualists, but their sun was setting when Davis headed for Detroit. Accustomed to an environment where a new name lit up the sky every year and men like Henry Ford, R. E. Olds, Charles Nash, Barney Oldfield, Louis Chevrolet, William C. Durant who seemed to orbit like blazing comets, and who—even when they went down—crashed noisily and spectacularly, is it any wonder that Davis often found himself groping for reasons and answers in the muffled atmosphere and subdued indirect lighting of the new General Motors complex?

It was a world where all policy decisions were made by committees, not one, but pyramids of them. Davis was under the impression that he was meeting and dealing with individuals vested with authority and responsibility but who necessarily in a matter as complex as power steering would have to consult with other department heads. He did not immediately grasp that while these men appeared to have unlimited power, it was confined to an area defined by the tables of organization. Nor did Davis realize that the actions these dukes of the realm could or could not take was described and prescribed in a series of loose-leaf manuals guarded as closely as a military code book in time of war called departmental, divisional or organizational procedures.

It was Sloan's way of bringing order out of chaos and is possibly the only way to manage a giant corporation. At any rate, Sloan, in his writings, makes clear that he considers this delegation of authority, within clearly defined boundaries, which he terms *decentralization,* a necessary and basic principle for successful large scale industrial enterprise, and certainly it has since been adopted by many large and successful corporations. The study and application of Sloan's principles and concepts has supplied the major part of a curriculum to numerous schools and colleges of business administration and given birth to a highly paid and respected ilk, if not a profession, called "reorganization experts."

While Davis willingly admits that Sloan's *decentralization* principle helped bring order out of the chaos that Durant's forced abdication as head of the company had left in its wake, he was probably one of the first persons to observe and note what has become one of the most obvious disadvantages of the system. "All of these men had drive and ambition. By confining them to these little boxes or cages, Sloan turned their ambitions inward. They became what are now called *empire builders,* each intent upon making his own little empire bigger than the next guy's."

Davis "who was there," as the saying goes, credits the success of Sloan's brainchild, *the modern corporation,* to a man rather than to Sloan's concepts and now almost sancrosanct guiding principles.

"You might say that Sloan's great idea is a literate expression and extension of O. E. Hunt," is Davis' amazing tribute—left-handed though it be—to his principal adversary. According to Davis, Hunt was not only the prototype of the corporation man in a techno-

111

logically-oriented society, but he was reacting and functioning like one before Sloan created the species.

Detroit is a winner-take-all town. It's a Ty Cobb "slide with your spikes high and sharp" kind of place. And Sloan acted in the Detroit tradition when he used the Chevrolet team that had knocked Ford off the top to take over the controlling reins at General Motors. It was this Chevrolet triumph that enabled Sloan to install his system which his publisher calls "an idea so big it changed the whole nature of American business." Davis does not deny Sloan his accomplishment but he credits O. E. Hunt with making it possible.

"The heart of Sloan's concept was inflexibility. It put ideas as well as men into what Robert Rines calls mental containers," states Davis. "The whole thing is a system which, if you study it as I had to, is geared to make it practically impossible for an individual to make a major mistake and, of course, the surest way not to make a mistake is not to adopt or push a new idea."

"Stick to the tried and tested" according to Davis, was O. E. Hunt's philosophy. When Hunt, backing the old Chevrolet water-cooled engine against Kettering's new copper-cooled concept, stood his ground and was vindicated when the air-cooled cars had to be called back to the factory, Sloan annexed both Hunt and his philosophy. And it is a matter of record that in 1929 O. E. Hunt succeeded Sloan as Chairman of the General Technical Committee which directed and coordinated advanced engineering for the whole corporation.

Davis would be the first to admit that he never made anything that could be called a study of Sloan's *modern corporation*. "I formed some personal opinions and jotted some of them down when I was trying to figure out how this new set-up would affect me."

("Me" in this case meaning power steering.) While sparse, these jottings indicate that Davis clearly grasped the basic principles of Sloan's concept and, even at that early date, sensed that a built-in resistance to change was fundamental to the structure.

The following are some of the Davis' 1934 notes on the subject:

"A giant bookkeeper's dream—predetermine and control costs by standardizing effort and accomplishment (product)."

"They are trying to reduce the *play* between human parts."

"If the objective is to create an environment, resistant to change of any kind and hostile to invention and innovation, they can't miss."

"Anything not conceived *in*-house will have tough sledding."

In 1967, in a book entitled "Technology and Change: The New Heraclitus," Donald A. Schon, president of the Organization for Social and Technical Innovation, appears to have furnished ample confirmation that in the intervening years since Davis made the above notations, not only large business corporations but entire industries and government agencies have "succeeded in creating an environment hostile to invention."

Among the points Mr. Schon makes are that while business and industry, and also government agencies, cannot live without new inventions and innovations, they cannot readily respond to them because they are constituted to maintain what he terms a "steady state." As "closed-loop feedback systems"—self maintaining and self-reinforcing systems of communications and control— "They tend to welcome new inventions in theory but often ignore them or resist them in practice."

113

This, according to Mr. Schon, is a matter of their very nature. "They are superbly organized to deal with the known; the partly unpredictable, a fundamental new discovery or innovation, makes them unsure and fearful."[5] He contends that the more radical the innovation, the more thoroughly it will be resisted, which is just about the same conclusion Davis reached three decades earlier.

Perhaps one of the few bits of amusement Davis had during his prolonged and discouraging negotiations with General Motors was the treatment one of Alfred P. Sloan's own pet ideas received at the hands of the monster he created.

It seems that Lawrence P. Fisher, one of the famous body building brothers, visited Hollywood in the late 1920's. And, amidst restaurants shaped like derby hats, apartments fashioned like Egyptian tombs or Chinese joss houses, and movie starlets wearing high-heeled satin slippers with slacks, he spied a car pointed at both ends like a ship's dory, and its hood and trunk planked with caulked teak. It didn't matter that the young man driving this nautical-styled automobile later escaped from his male nurse and leaped to death from Hollywood's only limit height building; Fisher decided that Detroit needed the designer of this custom body job.

The designer's name was Harley J. Earl, and Davis has always held the opinion that Earl was a man of quiet good taste, whose carefully concealed antic sense of humor decided that what Hollywood, of that fantastic period, needed was a teak-decked automobile. Whether this same sense of humor or an acute understanding of national taste levels caused him to bestow tail-fins on Cadillacs a few years later has never been revealed. But this young man came to Detroit and to the attention of Sloan when he worked with the Cadillac Division body engineers on the design of the new La Salle. The La Salle was neither a great success nor a failure, but it was the first *stylized* car to be mass produced, and Sloan then and there decided to add this new element, *styling,* to the General Motors production formula.

As Davis tells it "His own dog bit his own boy." The General Motors organization was so attuned to rejecting any and all new ideas that Sloan found that the support and prestige that Fisher and the Cadillac Division gave the newcomer and his styling innovation was insufficient. Sloan had to personally support the new section to get the styling concept considered by the other divisions.

An ironic footnote is that a Davis power-steering unit was installed in one of the experimental La Salles but, not having Alfred Sloan's personal sponsorship, "silently drowned in one of the lower pools."

Davis generally considered his tilt with General Motors a poker game in which he held high cards but the house controlled the play. In later years he likened the obstacles he encountered in getting his power steering invention into production and public use to an ascent of the longest fish ladder in the world—referring to the series of steep flumes and small resting pools which their builders claim enable salmon to surmount the highest dams and return to their up-river spawning waters. An avid salmon fisherman himself, Davis undoubtedly felt a kinship with those lion-hearted silver-scaled fighters that found their way back to their birth streams blocked by massive towering concrete barriers and, instinct driven, desperately had to turn to these escalating concrete torture chambers man had designed. Someone has written that inventors and most creative persons are "instinct driven," and certainly something stronger than a stout heart, infinite patience

115

and perseverance must have sustained Francis W. Davis during his long ordeal. For unlike many creative men he did not patiently wait for recognition, he fought for it. It was an upstream battle every inch of the way. And like the Columbia River and other dispossessed salmon, it was not up familiar natural water courses but up new strange injurious forms designed by men who publicly declared their strongest desire is to encourage invention or help wildlife survive.

However, when Davis read the preceding paragraph he objected to it as being too harsh an indictment of both corporate management and big dam builders. When it was pointed out that his agreement with The Academy of Applied Science placed interpretation of both the biographical material he supplied and their own research in the hands of the authors, he did not withdraw his objection but chuckled. "If you've got to compare me to a salmon on one of those fish ladders, at least credit me with some good leaps—I did make a couple, you know." He also admitted that several times he mistook some of the resting pools for the summit. He had thought he had won his battle before he had.

Though he sometimes considered both distractions that enabled management to avoid adopting power steering for years, Davis feels that with "styling" and the "annual model" Sloan made great contributions to the automotive industry. "They certainly enabled General Motors to attain the leadership it has maintained ever since."

Davis also credits both "styling" and the "annual model" with providing financial stability. These enabled the industry to avoid disastrous gambling risks by creating a demand for a slightly restyled and mechanically-proven product every year. This, the inventor admits, they would not have been able to do if they had relied on technological innovations like power steering, automatic transmission, etc., to stimulate new sales every year. He points to the hundreds of thousands of cars that were called back in 1965 and 1966 when the companies, influenced by Congressional criticism, perhaps too hurriedly introduced mechanical improvements.

It is evident from these later judgments that Davis has always remained an automobile man. It probably enabled him to play the game without shooting up the house like Ralph Nader, an outsider, did forty years later. In fact, the tone of his reaction to Nader's criticism of automobile safety was very much that of an automobile man of Davis' most active period. "We were engaged in designing and selling transportation—in other words, movement. I was concerned about the high steering gear ratio, and I am sure that Mr. Hunt was too, even if he did not admit it to me. But I'm sure not one of us thought a car should be a padded cell equipped with straitjackets."

But while Francis W. Davis remains a creature of his environment, and will always consider himself an automobile man, it is possible that his early recognition that invention and the philosophy of corporate system management represent principles that are incompatible, may be a far greater contribution to technology than his power steering invention.

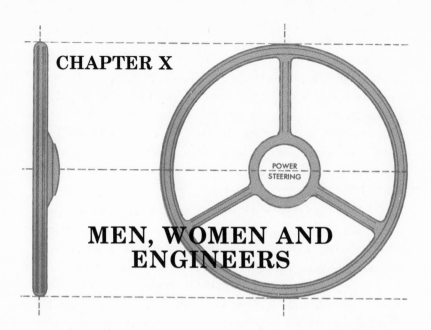

CHAPTER X

MEN, WOMEN AND ENGINEERS

One of Davis' close friends has said "Francis Davis is not an ambiguous person, he just takes considerable knowing."

Strangers have tried to explain some of his actions by resorting to the trite "men, women and *engineers*" catchall, inferring that Davis' Harvard University engineering training locked him in the particularly unimaginative mental container these persons reserve for the engineering fraternity. They overlook that Davis is one of the most financially successful inventors and original innovators of this century, was far ahead of the statesmen and leaders of his country in recognizing the nation's unpreparedness for World War I, and has been proven a seer in predicting that the bureaucratic structure of giant corporations would stifle inventive activity.

Yet it is these indications of his remarkable vision and profitable practicality that make Davis' conduct so baffling to many who were a part of the Detroit production picture in the Thirties and Forties when O. E. Hunt cancelled the General Motors contract.

There is general agreement that O. E. Hunt's letter releasing Davis from his obligation to General Motors could have been quickly turned into a golden passport to almost immediate success if "Fran hadn't pulled back into his turtle shell." The turtle shell referred to being the machine shop in Waltham, to which Davis retreated and huddled with Jessup for the greater part of the next two years.

What everyone expected was that Davis would waste no time in approaching the one man in Detroit who had the taste, foresight, technological background, financial independence, courage and, more important, the right vehicle to introduce power steering—Edsel Ford. His *Lincoln Zephyr* was considered the most advanced American production car and during the period of Davis' Waltham hibernation, Edsel Ford was formulating the concept which many authorities on both sides of the ocean still consider the finest expression of American automotive design, the *Lincoln Continental*. Edsel Ford, seeking to create an engineering masterpiece as well as establish a style superiority, which the years have increased rather than diminished, would most certainly have launched proven power steering in the initial *Continental* which made its bow in 1939. Probably he would have pre-tested it earlier in the Lincoln Zephyr.

At least that is a concensus gathered from men who knew his aims. But he was never even given the opportunity to test the Davis Hydraulic Power Steering unit.

Why?

Francis Davis has never really admitted that his youthful fleecing by Bill Pickens, Barney Oldfield's manager, might have subconsciously dampened any desire to ever do any business with anyone associated with Henry Ford. He expresses most enthusiastic and

120

vigorous admiration for Edsel Ford, calling him "the least appreciated, and one of the most gifted men Detroit ever produced." All of which makes his failure to contact the younger Ford more mystifying.

Those who try to pin the "men, women and engineers" label on Davis would have it that Davis was unable to see that if either the Lincoln *Zephyr* or *Continental* had come out with power steering other class cars would have quickly had to follow suit. This is belied by Davis' comment in 1951 at which time Chrysler used several of his expired patents to produce a power steering unit. "Looks like you've lost the store, Francis," a friend commiserated. "No," Davis grinned, "Chrysler just put me into big business."

If one is seeking the reason why Davis did not approach Edsel Ford, it is probably found in the fact that he didn't go calling on Chrysler in Highland Park either. Most certainly he would not have taken the wrong turn this time if he had. What becomes evident is that Francis Davis had no desire or intention of having any organization other than General Motors produce the Davis Hydraulic Power Steering unit.

Again, the question is . . . Why?

Here it is necessary to look behind what its owner thinks is a canny New England grin that accompanies the remark "General Motors were the biggest and best. I always aimed for them." The grin is a smoke screen and the remark is an evasion.

In 1926 when he set out for Detroit, his own notebooks state that Davis spent the first few days after his arrival reconnoitering the field, and these same notes show that he considered Chrysler, with its reputation for engineering leadership, a better target than General Motors. This was pointed out to Davis recently at his summer home that faces Nantucket's busy boat Harbour. He ruminated for a moment and then said

121

"Let's get out to the Cut, I think the blues will run this afternoon."

The *blues* did, and one gave Davis a terrific battle before it broke the leader and got away. A little boy ran up crying "Hey, Mr. Davis, wasn't that the same fish you hooked last week?"

"Yes, I think you're right, son," Davis agreed.

"You said, last week, you had your initials on him and you'd get him," the boy chirped on, giving an answer to other matters besides surf-fishing.

It was James C. Kyle, Manager of Bendix Power Steering Sales, who said "Francis is not ambiguous, he just takes knowing." And anyone who knew the athletic background of the Davis family, the competitive spirit that saw his brother Harry win the Panama Pacific Exposition Golf Championship, remembered the fierce struggles of the 1910 water polo teams at Harvard, that dogged motorcycle ascent of Pike's Peak in 1908 which still remains in the record books, would have recognized that the negotiations with General Motors somewhere along the line had changed from a high stake poker-game with revolving sets of house dealers to a personal combat in which the opponents were O. E. Hunt and Francis W. Davis. Davis' stubborn, competitive nature could no more ignore the challenge Hunt had tossed at him in stating "if you have in mind some plan whereby the cost could be reduced," than he could resist going after the big cagey bluefish that broke his line.

Like giant elk, two very stubborn men had locked antlers, and it was not in Davis' nature to ever retire from a fray, particularly one in which he was certain he would be the victor.

One mark of Davis' fecundity is that whenever he set out to solve one problem he generally came up with an entirely fresh approach or answer to another.

And, while working out methods to reduce the production cost of his power steering unit, he perfected his third major contribution to hydraulic engineering— *the fluid booster.*

When Davis started his original work on power steering, hydraulic accessories (fittings, seals, pumps, etc.) were non-existent. Davis managed to find easy solutions to all of these accessory problems with one exception, pumps. A good power steering pump meets contradictory demands. It must provide a supply of high pressure oil; it must be small, and it must be silent.

Oil pressures of 1,000 psi mean that the steering gear power cylinder can be more compact. To provide oil at this pressure when it is needed most, at parking speeds, the pump is running at from one to two times engine speed. Rpm must go up as the pump becomes smaller if the pump is going to supply sufficient oil. All of these demands increase the possibilities for irritating chatters, whines, squeaks and even low howls. Pump noise is all right on large commercial vehicles because they make enough other noises to drown it. But a chatter or squeak won't do for that mythical little old lady from Pasadena. She will instantly head for the dealer, waving her warranty.

Davis worked on the problem of supplying continuous high pressure oil for twenty years getting several major patents. For a while, in the last half of the Thirties, Davis thought that his first financial returns, as an inventor, would be from his pumps. They could be used in everything from oil burners to variable pitch propellors.

Years later, J. H. Hunt (O. E. Hunt's brother) was to declare that pumps were the bottleneck that held back steering. "Well, Davis," he said in 1953, "I think that if it weren't for the pump problems that you have been faced with, power steering would have been used in the industry in the early Thirties."

A short look at Davis' developmental work on pumps will show that this was not the case.

The three piston cam operated pump used on the first Davis power steering gear admittedly was too expensive. However, this pump had one breakthrough in its design; metal to metal seals. These seals were permanent; they did not require periodic maintenance. There was no need to worry about losing oil because one forgot to tighten down the leather packing that had been used to seal rotating pumps prior to Davis' innovation.

As soon as Davis had an option agreement with General Motors, he began to seek a better pump design. First he investigated existing hydraulic pumps. The machine tool industry was the only significant user of high pressure oil in the Twenties. But the pumps they used were too large and too noisy for automotive purposes. But Davis felt that maybe he could modify existing designs to suit his needs. With this in mind, he purchased a pump from Pratt & Whitney. This rotary spur-gear pump was used to supply oil for long drilling operations such as producing gun barrels. The pump supplied oil at 1,000 psi and up to 1,500 psi for a short time at 550 rpm. Slowed to 225 rpm it still produced 750 psi.

The Pratt & Whitney people told Davis that it wouldn't run faster than 1,200 rpm. Davis and Jessup knew that they would need higher rpm's than that. So the first thing they did was push the Pratt & Whitney pump to 1,800 rpm, just to see what would happen. Hydraulic fluid is not compressible, and at 1,800 rpm the pump trapped fluid between the gears. Davis and Jessup discovered that they might as well have tried to pump ball bearings.

124

After the two men had cleaned out the bits and pieces of the Pratt & Whitney pump, Davis knew that he had to go elsewhere for a solution, but he didn't quite know where. Like any intelligent person who is temporarily lost, he started asking directions. Finally, he got them. While Davis was demonstrating the Pierce-Arrow at the Rolls Royce Assembly Plant in Springfield, Massachusetts, he got talking to Maurice Olley the chief engineer for Rolls. Olley gave Davis a letter of introduction to a former MIT professor who was an expert in gear design, Earl Buckingham.

Buckingham suggested a gear tooth design that had two important features: 1) the faces of the gear teeth met in a line that moved in such a way that trapping could not occur; 2) the teeth were helical, assuring uniform flow.

Fig. 17

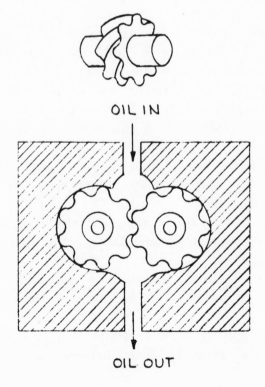

OIL IN

OIL OUT

A pump using the Buckingham tooth design was installed on the Pierce-Arrow in 1928 and moved to a Buick in 1932. The pump worked very satisfactorily.

However, Davis found that he was picking up noise at certain pump speeds from resonance. That is, the hydraulic lines had a diameter that was related to the distance between the wave fronts of certain sound frequencies. Davis contacted Dr. Ernest J. Abbott, of the Physicists Research Co., Ann Arbor, Michigan, who told Davis that if he would use hoses of varying diameters the sound patterns would be broken and he wouldn't have to worry about resonance.

Next, Davis redesigned the tooth on the Buckingham gear so it would produce a little more volume per revolution with the same diameter gear. Then Davis reduced the gear size and connected it to the back of the generator on a 1934 LaSalle. Hydraulic pumps had never been run at more than about 1,800 rpm before. Since a generator runs about twice engine speed Davis was going to push his pump to about 8,000 rpm, four times the previous high. At these high speeds, Davis knew he was going to encounter cavitation which is indicated by a high scream created as the oil column breaks up, and then claps back together. The output curve of the pump goes up until cavitation occurs and then it levels off; the energy that would normally be increased oil flow is dissipated as sound.

When driving the LaSalle, the pump worked fine at 50 mph, but at 52 mph Davis got a high scream that disappeared when the car dropped back to 50 mph again. To prove the scream was caused by cavitation, Davis hooked a bicycle pump to the oil reservoir; Jessup sat beside Davis, and when they hit 52 mph and got the scream, Davis had Jessup pump air into the reservoir. The increased pressure was enough to hold the oil together, demonstrating they had cavitation.

Davis solved the problem of cavitation with an invention that has been valuable wherever compact high pressure hydraulic systems are necessary. Called the Davis Fluid Booster, this invention has brilliant simplicity; it uses the Venturi principle to increase oil pressure at the pump intake.

The Venturi principle states that in a moving fluid the product of the velocity and the pressure is a constant: V x P = C; further, the volume of fluid passing a given point is also a constant. This means that if the tube is restricted, velocity must go up to get a constant volume past the restriction. Since V x P = C, if V gets larger, P gets smaller.

The oil supply tank is open to the atmosphere and normally the air pressure is high enough to fill the gear spaces with oil, however, at high speeds or high altitudes the atmospheric pressure is not enough to accomplish this and the result is cavitation and noise.

By means of the Davis invention, it is possible to increase the oil pressure entering the pump at high speeds without cavitation and noise. This method is also used in the lubrication system of airplane engines at high altitudes. With airplane engines having the usual oiling system, the oil from the main oil pump (under pressure) is supplied to the various elements of the engine, such as cylinders, crankshaft, camshafts, etc. The oil that collects in the crankcase is then forced out through a filter and cooling chamber by means of a separate pump. Any surplus oil supply needed is furnished from a tank open to the atmosphere, and connected to the oil flow from the cooling chamber. The flow of oil then passes through a Davis Fluid Booster enroute to the main oil pump. Consequently,

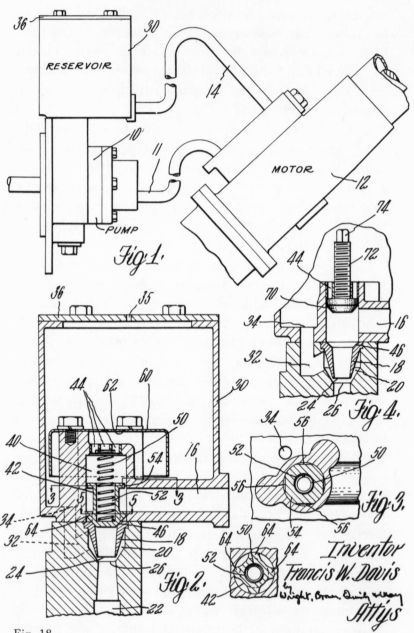

Fig. 1.

Fig. 2.

Fig. 3.

Fig. 4.

RESERVOIR

MOTOR

PUMP

Inventor
Francis W. Davis
by
Wright, Brown, Quinby & May
Attys

Fig. 18

the airplane can ascend to any desired altitude without cavitation, noise, or interruption of the oil flow.

Since 1955 the automotive industry has manufactured and sold many millions of lubricating systems each year incorporating the Davis invention which permits of high pump speeds thus reducing the size and cost of the units.

Unfortunately, although the patent on the Davis Fluid Booster was issued in 1941, the principle was not put into common use until the patent life was in its last stages. Davis endeavored to work out license agreements, but with the promise of delays and legal frustration which he had experienced previously, he considered that it was not worth the effort. Today there are millions of pumps in the automotive field as well as in airplanes which use this principle.

With the completion of the design work on the Davis Fluid Booster, Davis felt that he had the job done. His part of the bargain was to design a good power steering system. General Motors' part was to produce it. But Davis found that every time he fulfilled one demand, General Motors came up with another.

Davis presented a new design for the power steering unit that represented substantial savings in cost and weight over his previous designs. O. E. Hunt liked the Davis power steering and pump development enough to start negotiating a new contract. Then the Engineering Department and some vaguely named cost production committee explained that the Buckingham gears were too expensive to produce, so Davis designed a lapping machine to produce the gears.

Davis realized he was still being given the same old merry-go-round ride, but O. E. Hunt had ordered the new contract negotiations. Davis was still not aware or would not accept that even a man with Hunt's power was shackled by committees in Sloan's corporate edifice.

Fortunately for Davis during these contract talks, he encountered an unusually candid man in the General Motors corporate structure. His name was Lewis M. Spencer, and at that time, he was a member of the Patent Office staff which he later headed. According to Davis, the meeting that made him aware that the poker game he thought he was playing was as unreal as Antonioni's tennis game in the motion picture "Blow Up" went like this:

"In April of 1934 I was in Detroit for conference. General Motors had thrown up their hands all at once and said, 'We can't continue this $10,000 minimum; we want to get out of that because the country is in a Depression and we don't know how long it will last and we want to re-write this contract. We'll go along as long as we don't have to pay this guaranteed minimum, and we believe that this thing will come into use.'

"Well, Spencer and I went into a huddle, and he drew up another contract, and it had a lot of wording—'we undertake and we plan and we propose,' and what they were going to do about power steering. Finally, sitting across from Spencer at his desk, I said, 'Mr. Spencer, what does this new contract obligate General Motors to do?' 'Not a goddam thing,' he replied."

That conference marks the effective, if not the apparent, end of Davis' formal relationship with General Motors. As late as December of 1934, Davis would jot in his notebook "Looks as if G.M. is coming to life on the Hy. Steering," but negotiations never really got started again.

During 1934, the Great Depression gradually lessened but Davis' depression became steadily worse. He had spent a decade of development on power steering since he first sketched out his ideas with Jessup in Waltham, and Davis had moved hardly at all toward his goal. During that time, he had received $45,000 from General Motors, and he had spent much more than this in expenses connected with development.

In the late fall of 1934 even the personal contest of skills and wills with O. E. Hunt seemed to have palled. Davis suddenly decided that he wanted to get at least his cash investment out of power steering. During the year Davis had met F. E. Deem. Deem was a broker in "blue sky." He had a few formal connections and hoped to make a fee if he could bring Davis together with a developer. In December, Davis told Deem that he was interested in selling a half interest in power steering for $50,000.

This marks the bottom point of Davis' spirits and fortune. Before Deem could find a buyer with the cash, Davis picked up what his Arapaho Indian friends of his Colorado days would have called some "good signs" and he decided not to sell. The signs were the personalities and attitudes of three men: D. O. Scott, president and general manager of Hydraulic Brake Company "Lockheed" Division of Bendix; his chief engineer Wallace F. Oliver, and Karl Wise of Bendix Aviation Division.

It wasn't their enthusiasm for power steering that really swayed Davis for, as he said "practically everybody I ever talked to was for it," but an intangible quality, on which Davis could not immediately put his finger that imparted a great sense of reliance.

For one thing, they did not communicate in stilted guarded corporatese or play their cards close to their chest. Instead they came out with whatever was on their minds, even if it might later detract from their own company's bargaining position. As an example, Davis still possesses an early letter from Scott which reads in part:

"Perhaps I don't need to tell you that I have a fantastic idea of what can be done with that hydraulic steering job. Enthusiasm carries you a long way, I have found. I hope that you will be able to get the fellows down at South Bend really hopped up on this thing and get going soon.

"One thing that I think should be done— and without delay—is to demonstrate this thing right and left to truck operators. The Union movement in connection with operators is strong all over the country, and one of the things that the unions are striving for is better working conditions; and if operators won't recognize in the Davis gear better working conditions—and holler for it—then I miss my guess by a long way. I only wish that I had a finger in the pie."

This letter from Scott demonstrates the kinds of concern for both truck and passenger car drivers Davis always expected, but never found at General Motors. And nothing could be more unlike the atmosphere that prevailed at General Motors headquarters than the environment in which Davis got to know Don Scott and Karl Wise.

"I'd run into this Don Scott and I went over to his office one day because he said he wanted to show me something. He took me out to a back room. There was something that looked like old dirty laundry on a shelf and there were motors and all kinds of things

—pipes, hoses around it. He pulled some of that dirty stuff from the shelf, threw in some water and moved a switch. The thing went through some motions and jumped around, and the motor ran out and the thing stopped. He said, 'This is an automatic washing machine.' 'Well,' I said, 'it certainly is a neat little job if you can smooth it up and make it work properly so that the ordinary person can operate it.'

"This was the beginning of the Bendix washing machine but it had flaws and, when Scott took it down to South Bend and turned it over to the South Bend division, it didn't function quite properly; it bounced about and all hell broke loose.

"Fortunately there was a guy there named Karl Wise; I got to know him very well indeed for he had a great deal to do in promoting power steering at Bendix. They put Karl in charge of this collapsing, defunct, paralyzing situation called a washing machine. He was a very able engineer and executive to boot. And Karl took hold of this washing machine and corrected the defects and put it on the lines that developed into a tremendous industry."

Davis sensed that the creative energies at Bendix were spent on developing products rather than developing new corporation procedures. Maybe the back room filled with odd mechanical bits recalled the shop in Waltham, or that first shop in Colorado Springs. Whatever it may have recalled, meeting an executive who didn't mind a little grease and who could handle tools, certainly made Davis feel at home.

Davis had also acquired other important supporters in the Bendix organization, Wallace F. Oliver, Scott's chief engineer. Davis talked with Oliver in August, 1935, and records that "He was much impressed with the safety feature of power steering as he recently blew a tire and his car turned upside down when it went out of control. He will report to Mr. Scott. No arguments or questions raised by Oliver. He is sold on the whole thing."

With enthusiastic support from Scott, Wise and Oliver, negotiations at Bendix proceeded smoothly and on March 10, 1936, Davis signed a contract with Bendix. With some modifications this agreement was to run for more than 20 years.

In tying his fortune to Bendix, Davis was not forgetting his mountain. Having failed to scale the steep frontal massive, he was trying a flank approach with easier gradients and establishing a base-camp for the summit strike, as mountaineers say.

Bendix, at one time, had been a part of the General Motors organization and was still a big supplier of parts to the automotive giant. Davis figured that there must be men in the Bendix sales operation who knew their way through the corporate labyrinth that Alfred Sloan had created. You might say that after so many years of playing a lone hand against professional house dealers in this high stake game, he felt it was time for "pros" to take his seat at the table.

It was both a gambit and a gamble—highly successful in the first instance but a gamble that nearly cost the cool Coloradian his store.

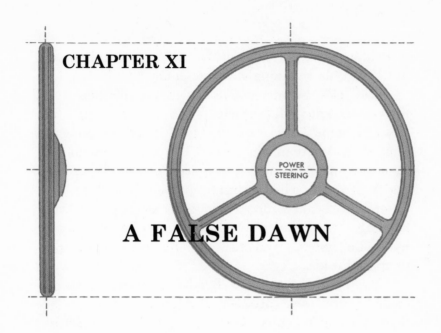

CHAPTER XI

A FALSE DAWN

A new optimism was sweeping the country and there was a marked business recovery during 1934 and 1935, which augured well for Davis and power steering. But, by the time the Bendix engineering staff had worked out production techniques for Davis' designs, the economy had slipped into what is called the Recession of 1937. Bendix suggested a renegotiation, objecting to paying Davis minimums when power steering had yet to bring any returns. This time Davis went along because in return he was able to obtain an increase in the royalty schedules.

Considering the complexity of starting a new manufacturing operation and a fluctuating national economy, things progressed rapidly at Bendix. They were involved in developing three major pieces of equipment: a pump; a closed-center valve steering gear, and an open-center-valve steering gear.

The open-center-valve gear with spring centering and hydraulic reaction was the final development in power steering made during this period and Davis was able to hold off on the patent for this design until 1940, thus gaining valuable patent life.

The closed-center valve design was developed for use in commercial vehicles, and this was the first closed system Davis had designed since his early attempts in Waltham in 1924. The closed system had some advantages since it required a tank to hold oil under pressure. This hydraulic pressure could be used to operate brakes, doors and other accessories. Davis had always dreamed of developing a multi-purpose hydraulic system, and this was his first opportunity to apply his ideas.

By the end of 1938 Bendix had proceeded far enough with their product development to begin actively seeking markets. The first significant application of Davis' power steering was a pilot project in New York City. Twelve of the Fifth Avenue buses were equipped with Davis-Bendix Multipurpose Hydraulic Systems, including power steering. The purpose of the project was to obtain extensive data on the performance of power steering under actual operating conditions. Regular drivers can abuse equipment in many ways that would never be anticipated by the ablest engineer.

During one of the test runs, Davis heard the driver grumbling and asked him what was wrong. "I'll tell ya what's wrong with this bus, buddy. Only one thing, and that's that I don't drive it all the time. After I turn this baby in, driving the regular junk, the company bus, is hell. I can't never get used to it again."

Another front that Davis and Bendix actively explored was the market for pumps. The most significant company they talked to was the producer of the Hamilton Variable Pitch Propellor. Davis and Bendix showed Hamilton how the Davis pump could be used in the hydraulic system that operated the airplane propellor. Other areas that were explored to exploit the pump varied from oil burner applications to the machine tool industry.

During this period Davis also demonstrated that his pump could be used as a motor by feeding high pressure oil into it. This led to further possible applications in aviation and industry. For example, in a discussion on January 27, 1939, with Commander Austin S. Kibbee, procurement officer for all PT boat squadrons during World War II and a battleship officer during World War I, Davis demonstrated both steering gear and pumps and Commander Kibbee stated that the Navy might be interested in applications for gun pointing on battleships.

All of this activity led Kettering to remark to Davis that he might find, like many other inventors, his greatest rewards would come from a secondary invention, or other applications that he had not anticipated when he set out.

But as far as Davis was concerned the most exciting development during the years from 1938 to 1940 was the awakened interest at General Motors Buick Division. Not only did the Bendix sales staff know their way about in the Sloan labyrinth, but they knew how to make a pleasing presentation.

Once the direct development was being handled by an outside firm, so that research expenses did not show up on division balance sheets, divisions at General Motors became interested. Davis realized that in this way division profits were not adversely affected by development, so executive bonuses were not jeopardized by progress. Davis calls it "Lesson One, Paragraph One" in dealing with any modern corporation man.

By 1938 Davis and Bendix had worked the bugs out of the designs that Davis had originally presented to O. E. Hunt in 1934. They took these new designs to Buick in 1938 and received an immediate favorable response. By the end of 1938, they had one gear running in a Buick and by 1940 Buick felt ready to commit themselves further than any division of General Motors had ever gone. That year Buick, Davis and Bendix installed power steering units in three new Buicks. This does not seem like many but, for the first time, General Motors did not haggle over who was going to write off the cost of the cars.

The first privately-owned automobile equipped with power steering was custom-built for the owners of the King Ranch in Texas.

For once Davis found that he had all the cooperation he could want and more. By the time they had completed the three installations they had learned enough to work out all of the details that had inevitably bothered the one-of-a-kind power installation in the past.

Progress did not stop with the installation of the units on the three Buicks. Since the units worked so well, Buick decided to proceed with production. They made arrangements with the Saginaw Steering Gear Division to produce power steering, and Saginaw started designing the machine tools to turn out the units.

The commitment was made at last; the 1942 Buick was going to have power steering. It would have, too, were it not for Pearl Harbor. What Franklin D. Roosevelt called "a day of infamy" put an end to Davis' dream along with a hundred million others.

Another effect of Pearl Harbor was the termination of the New York City pilot project on buses. This would also have to wait until after the war.

But Davis did not wait. In 1916, he had claimed that the United States could not afford to remain unprepared in the midst of a world at war. Recalling the lessons of that conflict which again were being ignored, he was determined that the development work he had completed at Bendix should not go to waste. He insisted that the machine tools that Saginaw had designed to turn out Buick steering gears could be modified a little to turn out power steering gears for armored cars and tank recovery units. The experience with the New York buses helped here because they had required heavier equipment.

Davis also profited from the constant urging he had put up with from O. E. Hunt to make the steering gear lighter and smaller. His work to shrink pumps also paid off handsomely, for an armored car may be heavy but its interior is not large. Its economy of space was impressed upon Davis during the testing of one of the armored cars. He tried to climb into one to get the feel of the controls, to discover that he would never have to worry about serving in a tank command. Davis got half-way into the car before he found that the space available would not let him by any further; he then tried to get back out and found that his contortions getting in had wound him around to the point that he could not get out either, at least not without a fresh approach to the problem of egress.

During the war, Davis was in almost constant consultation with the Chevrolet Division of General Motors. This was the division that produced military vehicles for the U. S. Armed Services as well as the allies, particularly the British. The British army had, from hard experience, learned to appreciate the steering problem with heavy armored vehicles, particularly on the desert terrain of North Africa. During 1942, they ordered a large quantity of armored cars from the Chevrolet Company, all equipped with the Davis Bendix power steering units.

The Saginaw Division of General Motors built the basic steering gear, Bendix Corporation supplied the valves and cylinders. As Prof. John R. Markham of M. I. T. has pointed out, the United States Army's large tank recovery units would not have been practical without power steering. The Ross Company supplied power steering gears for these vehicles equipped with the Davis valve under license to Bendix. In addition, the Bendix Corporation manufactured the valves and cylinders for these units. All in all, Davis' power steering units were installed in over 15,000 armored cars and tank recovery units. And it was their record of success

that gave Davis the self-confidence to continue with power steering after more than fourteen years of struggle had considerably eroded his faith.

If ever machines have to be "goof-proof" and rugged, they have to be under battle field conditions. Chasing Rommel across North Africa, or moving into Normandy from a narrow beachhead, under heavy fire, is no time for army units to pause and make adjustments in their complex military equipment. Records show that with Davis' power steering they did not have to.

Davis also made an indirect contribution to the war effort that cannot be measured as easily as his contribution to armored car warfare. This contribution was in aviation. In over twenty years of experience in hydraulics, Davis acquired a "know-how" that was not patentable but proved to be valuable. This kind of knowledge cannot be labeled, one could not turn to the blueprints of the hydraulic system of a B29 and systematically list the contributions of any one man. Nevertheless, the individual contributions are there.

The B29 had a 10,000 pound bomb load; on the ground this weight plus that of the plane itself was distributed over a three point landing gear. The nose wheels of a B29 demanded power steering. Also, the control surfaces of a modern aircraft could not be managed any longer by the muscle power of the pilot. Some of these power assists were electrical, some were hydraulic, most were a combination. Multiple systems were necessary because of the nature of warfare; if one system was knocked out, another had to be available so the damage to the aircraft would not prove total.

Bendix Aviation was a major contributor of components to the airplane industry during the war and Davis was always available to Bendix for consultation.

To this day, no one has been able to estimate the extent of Davis' contribution. In 1942-'45, the United States was engaged in a war for national survival; to wage that war, it needed strategic aircraft capable of operating at high altitudes of 30,000 plus feet. Davis was well aware that these aircraft needed hydraulic systems and pumps that would not cavitate, and at 30,000 feet pumps cavitate at much lower speeds than they do at sea level. And, if some hard-pressed aviation engineer or designer used some Davis ideas to keep those planes up there and didn't mention it, Francis Davis hasn't seen fit to either.

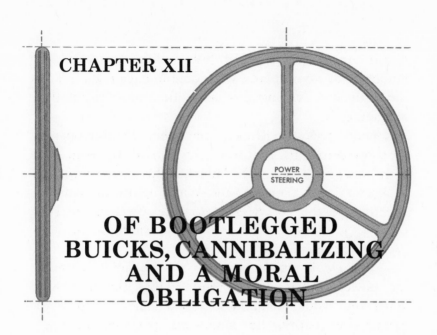

CHAPTER XII

OF BOOTLEGGED BUICKS, CANNIBALIZING AND A MORAL OBLIGATION

The year 1945 dawned with the scent of victory in the air. The German assault on the Bulge collapsed in January, in March the Allies crossed the Rhine and by April only half the world was at war. Even though the Japanese were hanging on, signs of the coming return to civilian production began to appear in Detroit. Henry Ford II was pulled out of the service and sent home to hold his grandfather's company together as the government prepared to release the Ford facilities that had been commandeered for military production. Even as the Marines landed at Iwo Jima, Detroit was making blueprints for retooling.

The slick magazines began to blossom with articles about the post war world that lay just ahead. Among the wondrous things promised were pre-cooked frozen meals and small family airplanes for every other garage. Francis W. Davis wasn't particularly excited about frozen dinners as he had tasted a few on Air Force trips and he didn't believe America was ready for family planes. In this, he was proven correct, for

143

North American Aviation lost millions in trying to launch such an airplane with double page color ads in the Saturday Evening Post and other mass circulation magazines.

Davis was determined that when Detroit opened its showrooms, its post-war cars would be equipped with power steering. He launched his own campaign by presenting a paper at the War Engineering Annual Meeting of the *Society of Automotive Engineers* held in Detroit, January 9, 1945, which appeared in the *SAE Journal* April issue.

The Davis article began by reestablishing the need for power steering but, sensing that the post war generation would demand some excitement even in an engineering paper, he made his presentation both direct and vivid.

For instance, he attacked the "road shock" problem on large trucks and commercial vehicles head on by stating:

> "At high front-axle weights the reversibility of the modern steering gear and its tendency to transmit road shocks to the driver's hands becomes a serious problem. A firm grip is inviting serious injury and many accidents involving broken hands occur.
>
> "Some drivers, in fact, cultivate a 'thumbs up' attitude, for the sudden striking of an obstruction may cause the front wheels to swing violently against their stops, also rapidly whirling the steering wheel the spokes of which can easily dislocate or break thumbs. Steering wheels have been known to burst from the sudden accelerations they thus receive, and it is a common matter to have the axle stops hammered over by repeated whips of the

front wheels. In one case, this phenomenon resulted in the unusual complaint by drivers that their steering wheels had become square. These were four-spoke wheels, and because of repeated high decelerations as the spinning wheel was brought to rest by the front wheels striking their stops, the spokes had become bent resulting in a square wheel." [6]

Judging from the reaction throughout the industry, the frank style of the paper and the timing were perfect. Davis received a call from James C. Kyle, sales manager of hydraulic apparatus for Bendix, summoning him to Detroit. Jim Kyle's greeting was, "Everyone wants a demonstration of power steering. How quickly can we put one on?" Davis was sure they could do it almost immediately. All they had to do was borrow one of the three power steering equipped Buick passenger cars General Motors had assembled in 1941 and tune it up.

But the Buicks had disappeared. And no amount of record searching revealed what had happened to them. When paper trails gave out, Jim Kyle and Davis combed Detroit and Saginaw looking for the cars. They ran up long distance tolls calling Buick dealer service managers and asking if, in the past four years, they remembered servicing any cars equipped with power steering. None had, but they all wanted to know more about "this power steering thing."

Davis admits it was probably the only time in his career he ever turned down an invitation to talk about power steering. "We didn't have time. We had to find those cars." But they never did. As to how three very costly experimental cars, that should have been stored away safely for the duration, could disappear along with all inventory records of their existence, is a complete mystery. The best conclusion is that in a well-planned operation they had been lifted and bootlegged, for car bootlegging became an ingenious and lucrative art during the war years when the manufacture of civilian pleasure vehicles was completely curtailed.

Though stunned by this disappointment, fortunately, neither Jim Kyle nor Davis completely lost their sense of humor. They were still able to laugh when the head of a nation-wide detective service rose to heights of oratorical grandeur telling them how he would go about solving their problem. "It stands to reason that one, two and possibly all three of these cars still exist. But let's assume only one of them does. Do you know what that means, gentlemen? It means that somewhere in this wide and beautiful land a man is driving a car that steers easier and better than any car in existence. Now that man is going to talk about his extraordinary car—I say, if he's an American, he can't help himself . . . he's got to talk about it."

Instead of engaging the detective agency to start a nationwide hunt for "this talkative American," Davis made a hasty retreat to Waltham where he and Jessup set to work installing his latest prototype power steering unit in a 1946 Cadillac. This action, which was undertaken reluctantly and seemed such a disappointing happenstance to both Kyle and Davis at the time because it meant that Kyle had to cancel all the demonstration dates he had set up, was to prove most fortunate. The improvements Davis had made during the war years made this Cadillac unit far superior to the ones that had been installed in the vanished 1941 model Buicks.

Jim Kyle and the people at Bendix couldn't restrain their enthusiasm when Davis delivered the power steering equipped Cadillac to South Bend. And with every demonstration that Kyle set up, enthusiasm mounted. Davis had not received such exhilarating receptions since he and his two companions had driven up to the Pierce-Arrow plant after their record-making cross-continental tour 25 years earlier. Naturally, because of Buick's plan to offer power steering in its 1942 models and Chevrolet's employment of heavy duty power steering gear in military vehicles during the war, General Motors had the inside position, but Jim Kyle was too great a sales genius to let other car manufacturers get the impression they were ruled off the track. Chrysler, whose engineering reputation had always commanded Davis' respect, called Kyle and Davis back for repeated conferences and further demonstrations.

Davis recalls "There was no doubt in our minds that power steering was going to be offered by at least three companies in the 1948 line. Bendix was worrying about what they would do if the whole industry jumped aboard. Then I began to notice that Jim Kyle was steering me away from meetings and conferences I thought we had coming up. It was hard for Jim Kyle to break it to me for he was a naturally exuberant person and a fond friend. Finally Jim muttered 'Fran, you might as well face it, we're going to have to wait for a buyers' market.' "

Bendix later prepared what might be called a position paper, which cogently outlined why the automobile industry was not going to adopt power steering at this time or in the immediate future. The paper stressed that the lifting of war time restrictions had set up a buying demand in which the industry was selling as many cars as it could make and deliver; that installing power steering gears would slow up production schedules; that the public was not demanding such an innovation and might even reject it; and that, despite the excellent record of the military installations, power steering in passenger cars might reveal hidden service and maintenance problems.

While Jim Kyle tried to buoy up their joint hopes by stating that every sellers' market is followed by a buyers' market, Davis admits that he found being stopped by "over" prosperity harder to take than the blow dealt by the Pearl Harbor bombing which set power steering back five years. He agreed with Kyle that a buyers' market would come along some day, but he wondered how many more of his patents would expire before that day came along. This worry or instinct, spurred his next action.

Davis had noted a too casual but mounting interest in the issuance dates of many of his patents. Some extended back to 1926 and had, of course, long since expired. He was quite certain that all through his Detroit negotiations "house" (company) engineers had been trying to invent around him. "So far they hadn't been successful but I was sure they could count—at least on their fingers."

As a good poker player, perhaps the most skillful move Davis ever made was to toss in his cards and announce that he was taking off for Hawaii. As the Colorado-trained poker player explains it "If somebody was keeping track of my discards—expiring patents—I wanted to give whoever it was plenty of time to study them. I figured it might be less embarrassing if I wasn't around."

Hawaii hadn't just popped into his mind. For three generations the Davis family has maintained close ties with the islands. The inventor's grandfather, William M. Davis, made them a landfall on a whaling cruise in 1834 and the log of this journey is displayed in the

Whaling Museum in Nantucket. In keeping with the love of sport which seems to run in the Davis family, this whaling ancestor made what is probably the first appraisal of the sports opportunities offered by the then Sandwich Islands. His selection of the best fishing grounds was confirmed a century later when it was decided to hold the Annual International Billfish Tournament in the waters he named. The inventor's niece, who is an artist, has made her home on the island of Kauai for a number of years while Francis W. Davis has managed to make eighteen trips to Hawaii since this first visit.

All through the winter months of 1949 while "Davey" Davis, as the beach boys called him, took up surfboarding, attended luau feasts, tried out-rigger canoeing and trolled the broadbill grounds his grandparent had spotted off Kona, there must have been a great deal of searching in the United States Patent Office in Washington, debate about infringement in the offices of several leading firms of patent attorneys and considerable activity behind locked doors in machine shops in the Detroit area.

In 1950, word spread through the Detroit grapevine that Chrysler was going to introduce power steering in its 1951 top line. The Chrysler power steering gear was developed by the Gemmer Steering Gear Company and it was soon revealed that the design was based on Davis' patents that had expired.

During visits to both Chrysler and Gemmer, between 1946 and 1948, Davis had discussed and even illustrated how later Davis designs could be adapted to the Gemmer manual gears. But the temptation of getting something for nothing apparently was too great and Gemmer decided they could build a unit employing expired Davis patents and thus save all royalty payments. Davis now warned them that they could expect trouble with certain features of his older designs and that his present steering gear was the result of a considerable evolution beyond his early and expired patents. Both Chrysler and Gemmer arrogantly treated his warning as the bleat of a sheep they had already slaughtered.

As the 1951 season approached and Chrysler heralded its great technological advance with full and double page ads, Davis was accepting the condolences for the years he had expended on power steering. The whole industry was aware that the Gemmer gear was using Davis' ideas.

During the war great numbers of Detroit's management and engineering force had gone into the Air Force and in the far flung global war had seen an old word take on a new meaning. The word was *cannibalize,* and it had come to mean to strip a crashed or disabled airplane of parts to enable other planes to fly. These Air Force veterans pinned this word on Gemmer's action and it was a pretty accurate accusation, for Gemmer had certainly stripped Davis' power steering designs of every *legally* removable part. Deluged with sympathy and tenders of loans and jobs, Davis had one fixed reply, "Don't worry about me. This is what I've been waiting for."

Davis was aware that this remark caused several close friends to feel that he had lost his mind as well as his early patents. But, to Davis, what he calls "the Chrysler bid" was the break he had been waiting for in the deadlocked high-stake game. He still describes the situation in terms of card values.

"Chrysler and Gemmer were sure they held 'jacks' or better. General Motors and Bendix had what you could call 'kings' in their heavy-duty military and bus-truck units, and Saginaw had a shelved 'queen' in the tooling blue prints for the 1941 Buick passenger car unit. I had 'aces' under the hood of that Cadillac. The danger was that if no one took up the Chrysler challenge their 'jacks' could turn out to be 'deuces'—which is what they were—and I would reap the blame because everyone knew they were using my designs.

"Jim Kyle and I sweated blood. We couldn't tell the industry Chrysler held only 'deuces' because that would remove the threat that if others didn't come up with power steering Chrysler would sweep past them. I, of course, felt we should go all out for my 'aces.' I argued with Jim that the driving public was entitled to the most advanced and efficient power steering unit available and one that was designed to meet the demands of the modern passenger car."

At this point, Davis added with a wry grin "I was pretty hot under the collar and since I knew I was going to get the blame for whatever gear was used I wanted it to be the best."

Today, Francis Davis concedes that Jim Kyle understood motordom's mentality better than he did and credits the Bendix sales expert with being quite a poker player in his own right. "Jim let them build up their fears over Chrysler's getting the jump on everybody and didn't dampen them with worries about the cost of the tooling job my new advanced passenger unit would call for."

The decision was to play their "kings" as "queens."

Translated from Davis' *pokerese,* this means that General Motors decided to meet the Chrysler challenge by transforming the existing Ross-Bendix and Saginaw Bendix heavy-duty power steering gears that had been used on military vehicles, buses and trucks into passenger car units. The necessary tooling changes would be slight, and General Motors would be offering a power steering unit that had demonstrated proven ability on the desert sands of Africa, the beaches of Normandy, in the snow and ice of the Argonne, and even on New York City's bus routes . . . but never as a component of a civilian pleasure or business passenger car.

Davis admits he should have expected the decision, should have remembered that ever since O. E. Hunt blew Kettering off the road in the air-cooled vs. water-cooled fracas, the Sloan molded automobile man has followed one rule, "stick with the mechanically tried and proven." Davis acknowledges, "In this case, it wasn't dangerous. It only kept the public from getting *true* passenger car power steering for a few more years." (In Davis' opinion this did not occur until General Motors installed what he calls his 1946 design in the late 50's Cadillac line.)

Davis took no part in this final tilt with his large corporate adversary but it illustrates what Davis contends is all too often the corporate attitude toward creative people and their contributions.

Tooling and setting up production lines for the Ross-Bendix and Saginaw-Bendix heavy duty power steering units was comparatively simple because of the experience gained in war time use of both units in armored vehicles and trucks. But the cross-licensing agreements had to be hammered out anew and the General Motors negotiating team, while perfectly agreeable to paying Bendix a licensing fee, objected to paying direct royalties to Francis W. Davis.

"Buy him off" was the first suggestion, and the sum of $50,000.00 proposed.

Someone in the Bendix faction didn't think the inventor would be interested. "Then let him sue," a General Motors man retorted.

Things had reached an impasse when one of the General Motors team proposed that they bring Lewis M. Spencer, the former head of the motor giant's patent department, in for his advice. Spencer, who had retired from his position, listened gravely as they explained their problem, then he asked:

"Is the manufacturing arrangement satisfactory?"

"Well, yes it is."

"Is the Bendix unit price okay?"

"Yes, there isn't any problem there."

"And the royalty schedule to Davis, is that a fair royalty for a thing like this?"

"The schedule would be all right ordinarily but we think under the circumstances . . ."

Lewis M. Spencer chopped off the man's words in mid-air.

"I consider that General Motors has a moral obligation to respect the Davis patents."

With that, Spencer put on his hat, turned on his heel and left the conference room.

Davis is inclined to agree that it must have been a jolting experience for these younger corporation men. Spencer was one of the company-revered demigods and they had summoned him down from Valhalla. Whatever they thought, they signed the agreement without further quibbling.

When it was pointed out to Davis that, on the very doorsill of success he might have lost the major fruits of thirty years of endeavor or had to go through a prolonged and expensive legal contest, but for the words and action of this one man, he agreed. Then he cocked his left eyebrow at a rakish angle and added "You know what he did to me, don't you? Made it impossible for me to quit and just enjoy my pile. Ever since that day, I've been on a crusade trying to convince both business and government that they are short-changing themselves and cheating the nation if they don't have men with Lewis Spencer's understanding, honesty and fairness handling their patent affairs."

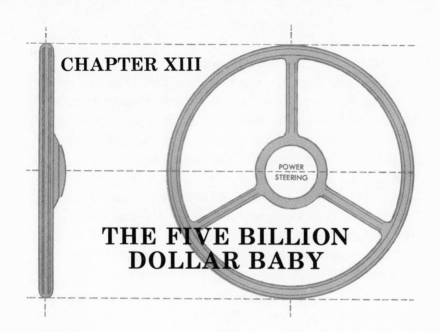

CHAPTER XIII

THE FIVE BILLION DOLLAR BABY

Francis W. Davis never doubted that power steering would find ready acceptance by the driving public. But it is doubtful that, when he and George Jessup set up shop in that small shed in Waltham, either had any idea they were spawning a five billion dollar baby.

In 1950 power steering units were installed in 10,000 new vehicles. (These were mostly the Chrysler-DeSoto Gemmer systems using lapsed Davis patents.) The production figures jumped to 40,000 in 1951 when General Motors entered the picture and topped 300,000 in 1952 with Packard using a Bendix-designed control. By 1964, the number of power steering equipped cars sold reached 3½ million and, including foreign installations, the annual rate by 1966 had climbed to 8 million cars. General Motors observed the sale and installation of 25 million Saginaw automotive power systems between 1959 and 1966. It is estimated that total installations of all manufacturers passed the 50 million the following year.

Daniel V. De Simone, director of the Office of Invention and Innovation, United States Department of Commerce, appearing before a U.S. Senate Judiciary Committee May 18, 1965, stated "What has the power steering gear meant in terms of gross national product? I am unable to compute the figure, but it is certainly substantial. In 1964, for example, 3½ million gears were sold. This amounted to a total sales volume, including the necessary accessories, of roughly 350 million dollars. Crank that figure into the economy and the resultant GNP, employment, etc., are substantial by any measure."

Using this Department of Commerce yardstick it is possible to state that a gifted and stubborn man, aided by a talented assistant, working quietly in a small shop with second hand machine tools, created and developed a unique and original servo-mechanism that added five billion dollars to the national income, a sum equal to the annual sales of the world's largest retail organization, Sears, Roebuck & Company, who must stock 100 thousand different items to attain this figure.

This, of course, is only a monetary appraisal of the value of Francis W. Davis' contribution to his country and modern living. There is no way of estimating the number of highway fatalities that have been prevented, the lessening of injuries and property damage that can be credited to the added control power steering gives the driver. Nor has anyone attempted to determine how much the use of the Davis gear on farming equipment has increased crop yields.

Prof. John A. Markham of the Massachusetts Institute of Technology, and a member of the Science Advisory Board U.S. Air Force, has pointed out that the acceptance of power steering has been so complete that scarcely anyone appreciates "what an ingenious and entirely new mechanism'' Davis conceived. Markham called Davis' use of hydraulic systems continuously in operation "new and splendid" and his invention "a boon to humanity which everyone immediately took for granted."

Another who feels that Davis is one of the great overlooked originators is Bradford Washburn, director of the prestigious Museum of Science in Boston who declared "The public at large has benefited more from the brilliance and patience of this remarkable man than from the output of scores of more-publicized inventions and inventors."

That public recognition did not accompany Davis' great financial success is generally credited to his retiring personality, but any latter day study of the advent of power steering reveals the true culprit was the attitude of the automotive industry. It was to be expected that Chrysler and Gemmer would not publicize the name of the man whose brain they had picked, but Saginaw, Ross and even Bendix, who were to pay the inventor large royalties, went to great and sometimes amusing lengths to avoid acknowledging that the invention was not the result of their own engineering creativity.

"Francis W. Davis was not the first and certainly will not be the last victim of N.I.H. (Not Invented

At the power steering exhibit in the Boston Museum of Science, Davis and Jessup reminisce over models of their early steering gears.

Here)" observed Professor Markham. The M.I.T. authority on the inventive processes could have added that this disease, which is endemic around any enterprise with its own engineering or development group, was particularly virulent in Davis' case.

After repressing power steering for a quarter of a century, the manner in which the industry lauded the part it played in bringing this "boon to humanity" to the public was, at times more hilarious than any comedy writing since the early days of Sid Caesar. For example, here is W. K. Creson, vice-president of engineering of the Ross Gear and Tool Company, in a paper he presented to the Society of Automotive Engineers, January, 1952:

> "Why has power steering grown so slowly over the years and suddenly burst into bloom? Your guess is as good as mine. It is in the nature of things that fundamental ideas seldom come quickly to fruition. The avalanche is not really caused by the falling pebble, but by a myriad of snowflakes, for a long time dropping softly and unnoticed. The joy with which car buyers have greeted automatic transmissions may have contributed to the recently aroused interest in power steering.
>
> "The everyday driver now wants, is eager, to buy the package, and in America still, thank God, he can have what he really wants. Those who provided him with the first production cars having power steering are to be congratulated on their foresight and enterprise." [7]

And whom was the American consumer to congratulate for the fact that they finally were blessed in 1952 with something they could have had in 1926?—

Why, Ross Gear and Tool Company, of course. This is according to the gospel as revealed by Creson of Ross; Saginaw, Bendix and Packard-Bendix told it without "falling snowflakes" and designated their own founts as the source of the great blessing.

While automobile executives were patting each other on the back for the wisdom and foresight displayed in introducing power steering, at least one act of injustice was being rectified. The Gemmer Steering Gear Company was failing. They ran into the troubles that Davis had warned them would occur with the obsolete designs they were using. Chrysler, with its engineering reputation at stake, quickly changed its steering gear to accommodate units of Davis' design which it bought from Bendix and General Motors. So Chrysler ended up paying Davis the royalties they had tried to avoid, and Gemmer ended up being absorbed by Ross.

Davis has never quit developing power steering although he has slowed down some. His last patent in the field was issued in 1958 which means that it will be in force until 1975. Davis received his first steering patent in 1926 for his steering gear coupling that was introduced most successfully by Duesenberg at Indianapolis that same year. Today almost every automobile produced in the United States uses this steering coupling. Besides doing the job Davis designed it to do, the coupling has changed production procedures. With this coupling, manual and power steering gears can be readily interchanged on the assembly line by simply unfastening the joint. Undoubtedly car manufacturers have benefited greatly from this Davis brainchild but it has not enriched his own bank balance. The reason, a sad one far too many inventors experience, is that the life of the patent had expired before it went into general and, in this particular case, universal use.

Whatever the industry's public attitude toward the role Davis played in the development of power steering, inside the industry recognition of his dominance and mastery of the field is such that in 1959, when General Motors introduced a different design to improve valve sensitivity, they turned to the rotary valve first introduced by Davis in the 30's. And though Saginaw commemorates the 25 million power steering units it has produced by displaying this unit like a crown jewel in the Tower of London at the S.A.E. exhibit at Cobo Hall, Detroit in 1966 (but with no mention of the inventor on the plaque), it is Francis W. Davis' original hydraulic power steering gear that occupies a place of honor in the Smithsonian Institution in Washington, D.C.

This is probably why Davis admits that he got an extra fillip of personal satisfaction and enjoyment the year that he was able to say that his take-home royalties from power steering topped the General Motors executive's salary and bonuses. Davis side-stepped stating the sum of these royalties, but the General Motors annual report for that particular year lists that Mr. Hunt received $420,000.

Davis has been honored by his alma mater, Harvard University, with Honorary Membership in the Harvard Engineering Society (1960), a citation "Distinction in Automobile Engineering" (1960), and has been a member of the Overseers Committee since 1947. At the 131st annual meeting of the Boston Society of Natural History (1961) he was named vice-president of the Boston Museum of Science. In 1967, the Board of Governors of The Academy of Applied Science elected him a Fellow of that body, a distinction awarded only once before.

All in all, no one agrees more than Francis Wright Davis that power steering has carried him a long way.

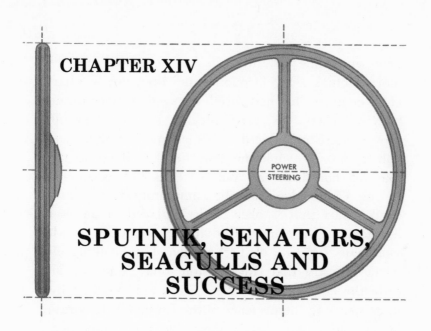

CHAPTER XIV

SPUTNIK, SENATORS, SEAGULLS AND SUCCESS

For 25 years, from 1926 until 1951 when he scored a grand slam in what his close cronies still call "the longest poker session in history," Francis W. Davis admits that he was totally occupied with one thing—getting power steering into production.

He had not realized his involvement had been so total until, in October of '52, he noted the elms change to a lemon yellow, followed by the ash which took on browns and purples as gold came to the sugar maples. Then, like great galleons towering over a multihued armada, the sturdy oaks flung out sails of scarlet, burgundy and brown. He tried to remember when he had last been aware of this great natural spectacle, and he found that he could dimly recall noticing that the crimson was being washed from the oaks as he and George Jessup headed past the Berkshires on that first trip to Detroit in 1926.

His friends' calling his negotiations with General Motors and the automotive industry "a poker game" had become a rather tired joke over the years. But now with time to think, he had to admit they were more factual than facetious and that, for a quarter of a century, he had been engaged in a continuous activity where his card playing acumen had often proved more valuable than his technical originality and ability. For a while he had been inclined to think that his had been an isolated case, but as an *insider* in the Cambridge scientific community he was aware of the part that "poker tactics" played in the establishment of the famed Radiation Laboratory at Massachusetts Institute of Technology. The far-flung electronic industry that rings Boston today, and is practically the cornerstone of New England prosperity, owes its existence to the presence of the Radiation Laboratory in that area, and Davis knew that the United States would not have had successful radar in World War II but for a few brilliant and highly gifted members of its staff.

Even in 1952 the new electronics industry was creating new jobs and fast taking the place of the faltering textile industry in New England's economic structure. The blank staring windows of abandoned textile mills and the shining new electronic facilities suddenly took on significance to Davis. They brought into focus, and vividly illustrated thoughts which, up to then, had been drifting pleasantly on the seas of his new found leisure. Wherever Francis Davis is, there is always a notebook handy, and he jotted down this observation:

> *"In an industrialized society, such as we have become between two world wars, the entire economy is largely dependent upon invention and innovation."*

Then, apparently remembering the highly individual way in which the Radiation Laboratory had functioned during the war and some of the still-classified achievements of its scientific personnel, he added on another day, or with a different ball-point pen (none of them worked too consistently that year) the following:

"Unfettered scientific and technological creativity is the key to national survival."

A few months later Davis remembered these two observations and thought they would be excellent points to make in a lecture he was scheduled to give to a class of graduate students at Massachusetts Institute of Technology. But the professor who had issued the lecture invitation begged Davis to give these graduate students "the real low down" on how he marketed power steering. Davis protested that the truth would be an affront to their intelligence. The instructor, who was a considerable inventor in his own right, did not think so and felt the reaction at least would be interesting, particularly since every one of those students was planning a career in industry.

So Davis advised this group of brilliant graduate students, "the cream of the crop," so to speak, of the top-rated technological school in the world, "A successful inventor should first learn to play good poker." He revealed that a card player's psychology might serve them better than their master's degrees in industry. No one appeared indignant, nor was a single young and brilliant intelligence affronted as far as Davis could tell.

The shifting of a small pebble can start an avalanche. The "cool" of these graduate students, their calm acceptance of the Davis statement that "only by playing the right card at the right time" had he been able to retain possession of his patents and finally market his invention, set off a series of chain reactions that has yet to stop.

Early in his negotiations with General Motors, Davis recognized that Alfred P. Sloan's management philosophy and organizational system had produced an environment that automatically resisted change and was, therefore, instinctively hostile to invention and innovation. Then, largely because of his enthusiastic reception at Bendix, the warm, open and whole-hearted recognition and cooperation he received from the men with whom he worked at that company, Davis came to believe that "men-in-boxes" and "conformity" were things Sloan had grafted on the General Motors structure and were restricted to that company.

After the war, with Karl Wise dead and his friends Scott and Oliver out of the picture, Davis became aware that Bendix, too, had taken on a similar organizational tone. Jim Kyle's ebullient personality and his exciting campaigns to sell power steering gave Davis little time to dwell on the change.

But the attitude of these graduate students alarmed Davis. It indicated that the Sloan type of organizational thinking, with its accompanying attitudes toward innovation, not only permeated American industry but had spilled over into the academic world. The changing hues of autumn and the surf fishing poles stacked in his Nantucket garage were forgotten as the inventor jumped to what he admits was largely an instinctive, and certainly a hasty, conclusion, namely, that during the quarter of a century he had been immersed in his problems:

The climate of the entire country had become hostile to invention and innovation.

At this time, Davis was not aware that he had become a man with a mission, and that any man who tries to rally support for a crusade to change a climate is certain to get mixed reactions. Looking back, after nearly twenty years, Davis readily admits that a good many of his inventor friends had a right to think he sounded peculiar when, in the midst of a genial general conversation, he might remark "We've been taken over by Ottoman Turks."

How were they to know that everything had become grist for this one mill. And that probably the night before he had been dipping into history and his reading had made him identify his country's path with that of the luckless Ottomans.

Davis attributes the demise of the Ottoman empire to its rigid organizational structure and hostility to all progress. "They believed any innovation was an error and should be punishable by hell fire. No wonder the industrial age put them four centuries behind the rest of Europe."

Davis was on the way to being considered a well-tailored Don Quixote tilting at climatic windmills when his fellow inventors became aware that a cold front toward their kind was certainly building up in Washington. At the time of the nation's founding the delegates to the Constitutional Convention, recognizing that creations of the mind enriched the nation, established a policy "to encourage by *premiums* and provisions the advance of discoveries (inventions)." This had been the national policy ever since. Now the Treasury Department was trying to reverse this policy of encouraging invention by pressing Congress to enact legislation that would penalize inventors by disallowing them the same tax status enjoyed by owners of real estate, livestock and securities. The threat was embodied in a section of the new Internal Revenue code of 1954 that would allow favorable capital-gain tax rates only for royalties or payments received within five years from the date of the sale of a patent.

As the number of inventions that reach the market within the first five years of their patent life is practically nil, Davis had no trouble in convincing most inventors that Treasury Department thinking was hostile.

A group of inventors was assembled to go to Washington for the hearings before the Senate Finance Committee. In his presentation at the Senate hearing, Davis was able to make some telling points; one being that the proposed Internal Revenue action "deals with the sale of a patent whereas the inventor sells an invention and an invention is usually protected by several patents."

He was able to get into the record that very few inventions get into commercial production within five years after an inventor transfers his patents. In his own case, it was 25 years after he demonstrated a successful power steering gear and signed a royalty (sales) agreement, that the manufacturer offered power steering to the general public.

Davis argued, "this unreal 5-year limitation offers no compulsion to produce the invention in this period, but to the contrary, would encourage the purchaser to delay development of the invention for this period." He contended that it placed another obstacle in the way of invention and would seriously limit every inventor's earning power.

Davis and the group of independent inventors insisted that they were not asking for special consideration but only requesting that tax-wise they be treated in the same manner as the person who sells a piece of real estate, share of stock, horse, cow, or an oil well. The Senate Finance Committee, chaired by Sen. Eugene D. Millikin of Colorado, agreed. The section that would have severely penalized the majority of inventors financially, and seriously affected the national economy and technical progress in the long run by causing inventors to become wary of revealing their creative products, was eliminated from the tax bill.

During World War II the nation had mobilized completely for the war effort, and production for civilian use was curtailed for many products. The effect was a shortening of the productive life of many existing patents. A great many inventors, with inventions scheduled to go into production in 1941, had seen all hopes of reward for years of effort die, as the war continued and their patents expired. In Davis' own case, Buick was tooling up for power steering when the bombs fell at Pearl Harbor. For others, royalties were not resumed after the hostilities were over because their patents had expired during the war, and the manufacturer was free to produce the very same product without any obligation to its inventor.

Because Francis W. Davis' voluntary contribution to the war effort had been so large, especially in the field of hydraulic controls that later made high-altitude bombing feasible, fellow inventors insisted that he spearhead the group that appeared before both the House and Senate Judiciary Committees in 1956. The inventors scaled their demands down so that they requested only a three year extension to patents which their owners could prove had been directly affected by the war. The bill was approved by both the House and Senate Committees, but powerful forces operating behind the scenes were able to prevent it from reaching a vote on the floor. This political maneuver not only cost thousands of inventors monetary rewards but the nation suffered a greater and unheralded loss.

Davis remarked, "I personally knew of a dozen gifted men who gave up ever trying to invent again after this disappointment. What their decision cost the nation cannot be estimated but in my own opinion it would total billions of dollars and thousands of lives."

Davis can cite some rather chilling examples to back up this statement. The recent autobiography of the great aerodynamicist Theodore von Karman[8] gives the first full account of how similar calloused government action and inaction (which Davis contends "can only flourish in a climate hostile to creativity") practically presented Red China with the nuclear capability that is harassing our mental security today and will necessitate costly changes in the national defense posture. These changes will delay and cripple urgently-needed health, poverty, urban renewal and transportation programs for the next fifty years.

As Davis had studied the mountain he was going to climb in his youth and the structure of the corporation he battled for so many years in mid-life, the Colorado-reared inventor took corings of the soil which nourished this hostility to creative men. He recalled that in his youth inventors like Tom Edison, Westinghouse, the Wright Brothers had been folk heroes. There had even been a comic strip called *"Willie Westinghouse, Boy Inventor."* What had happened to change this image? Why this concerted effort to make a former folk hero a *non-person,* and, in the inner councils of industry, *the enemy?*

Davis knew that mass-production made change of any kind risky and costly. He could see how the maker of a widely-used product, with huge investments in plant facilities, trained servicemen and spare part depots all over the country, would regard an inventor, appearing with an innovation that genuinely improved his product, as an anarchist brandishing a bomb.

Davis began to grasp the insidious magnitude of the Sloan concept, *the organizational system,* that directs man's thinking as well as his actions, dictates his choice of friends and even the selection of a life mate. The inventor recalled having laughed at the many articles in business magazines about how a wife's religion, use of lipstick, or taste in beverages could help or hinder her husband's corporate career. He saw that these and thousands of other articles and news stories, books and periodicals could be called mental soil preparation.

Davis was well aware of the eager acceptance of the economic attitudes of the hierarchy by young employees spurred by ambition and seeking advancement up corporate ladders. He was able to sense the natural reaction of anyone who has acquired position and a seemingly secure future to anything that jeopardizes it.

Davis was able to understand that, to the organization man, innovation was a natural enemy. What he did not immediately grasp was the extent to which everyone had become organized in their thinking. Neither Davis nor sociology have been able to determine whether this change in thinking had come as a bitter harvest from the Depression years or from the threat of coming automation.

But Davis was aware that where the nation of his youth had eagerly greeted every technological change and worshipped progress, the current public attitude was to regard any innovation through suspicious eyes as something that might upset one's own economic applecart.

Davis' choice to continue his improbable crusade under these conditions was perhaps best explained by George Bernard Shaw who wrote:

> "The reasonable man adapts himself to the
> world; the unreasonable man persists in trying
> to adapt the world to himself. Therefore, all
> progress depends upon the *unreasonable man.*"

The most striking, and to many, the most irritating example of Davis' unreasonableness was his refusal to accept what he has always termed the major fallacy of Sloan's modern corporation concept; namely, that creativity can be consistently contained and controlled. During the deluge of literary effort in which scientists, economists, statesmen, businessmen and educators—including two of Harvard's brightest luminaries—sub-

169

scribed to Sloan's doctrine and gilded it with formulations of their own, Davis stood firm and immutable as a granite headland under ceaseless assault by waves, wind and sand.

When James B. Conant, then president of Harvard, declared "Today the lone inventor is as extinct as the American buffalo. In his place . . . (are) the industrial research laboratory and departments of development engineering," Davis made no comment but the same year he set about establishing the Lionel S. Marks Fellowship in Harvard's Division of Engineering and Applied Science in 1954. Davis insists that his action was not the rejoinder of an "extinct" American bison to either Conant or John Kenneth Galbraith, who had written:

> "A benign Providence . . . has made the modern industry of a few large firms an almost perfect instrument for inducing technical change . . . There is no more pleasant fiction than that technical change is the product of the matchless ingenuity of the small man forced by competition to employ his wits to better his neighbor. Unhappily, it is a fiction. Technical development has long since become the preserve of the scientist and the engineer. Most of the cheap and simple inventions have, to put it bluntly, been made."[9]

This statement actually eliminates the creators of most of the material things that epitomized Mr. Galbraith's *The Affluent Society*.

Other noted oracles of the first seven years of the 1950's made the following remarks:

> "We have now reached a stage in many fields where inventions are almost made to order, and where there can be a definite cor-

relation between the numbers of applied scientists employed (and the funds at their disposal), and the inventive results." (W. R. MacLaurin)

"The days when one individual's inventiveness and enterprise could transform an industry are in the past. In this context the big firm again shows to advantage. These are all well-known facts of economic life." (A. Hunter)

"Most discoveries patented today can be anticipated." (Walton Hamilton & Irene Till)

"It is not difficult to predict the effect of industrial group research on invention. As organized invention and discovery gain momentum, the revolutionist will have no chance in explored fields. He will have to compete with more and more men who have at their disposal splendidly-equipped laboratories, time and money. Possibly Edison may be the last of the great heroes of invention." (W. B. Karmpffert)

As this death chant swelled in volume, so did Davis' royalties from power steering, which caused the inventor to remark, "For a Dodo bird, I was collecting a lot of money."

However, the crusade for creativity had slowed to a creeping pace. Editors on a dull day no longer dispatched reporters to interview inventors; instead they ran drawings of newly proposed corporate research and development facilities. These were the new status symbols and every company had to have one.

Davis, in his infrequent speaking engagements of those years, would point out that despite the automobile industry's large investment in research centers, less than 2% of recent motoring improvements were the result of company research. He would list four-wheel brakes, power steering, power brakes, automatic transmission and even the windshield wiper as the creations of independent invention. However, as he has since admitted, he said these things "without disturbing anyone's set opinions in the slightest."

When this faltering crusade for creativity received what Davis was to call a "power assist," it came from an unexpected quarter. On October 4, 1957, the supposedly technologically-backward Russians launched the first artificial satellite and Sputnik's mocking beeps needled the American public as nothing has before or since.

The needling process was unbearably stepped-up 30 days later when the Soviet dog *Laika* began circling the earth in Sputnik II. No cur barking in the night or desecrating a sidewalk ever upset so many American householders as the radioed heartbeats of this animal, which the usually secretive Russians shared with the world. With its pride rubbed raw, the great American public demanded to know what had happened to America's vaunted inventive genius and technological superiority.

"It was crazy, off beat, but in a way, poetic justice," Davis admitted, "For the one thing that does call for an organized systems approach and vast industrial and scientific support is a space shot. But big industry was in a spot and the one thing it didn't want and couldn't afford was to call attention to its scientific leadership and technological capability—not with that Soviet dog up there circling the earth, and monkeys, and possibly Russian ducks, waiting for rides. Yet everyone from the man in *The White House* down agreed that the damage to America's image, as the great inventive nation, had to be immediately repaired."

Davis said, "Suddenly editors, who had been throwing our stuff in the waste-basket, were clamoring for our opinions and information about what we had cooking on the back-burner. Edison, Goodyear and the Wright Brothers were resurrected and dusted off; De-Forest and Armstrong got credit the radio industry had long denied them; and you couldn't pick up a news-paper or magazine without learning not only what a boon to mankind the ballpoint pen was but the name of the man (F. Seech) who had come up with the formula for the ink that went into it."

While Sputnik touched off a windfall of recognition for independent inventors, there was a great deal of embittered talk and feeling in the scientific fraternity that a cut-off in government funding was responsible for the Russians being first in space. These sentiments led Francis W. Davis to make a remark that has plagued him for years. "Charles Wilson[10] thought he could play the space game the G.M. way—hold back and let the other fellow risk the first failure—like they did with power steering."

Davis regrets but does not deny making "this crack." Ten years later, in 1967, he still believed there was good reason for the savage bitterness displayed toward the late Defense Secretary by many who had been engaged in America's early satellite program.

His attitude is supported by an incident that took place when the flag was lowered to half-mast at a large missiles and space facility in respect for the death of Wilson's chief assistant. A member of that earlier space team glanced at the flag, and, unable to contain his bitterness, muttered, "They should lower it the whole way for what he did to this country."

Whether or not a misguided Charles Wilson actually prevented the United States from beating the Russians into orbit by 14 months will never be officially confirmed.

Another irony in the crusade of the independent inventors to achieve recognition is the debt which these men owe to a fairy tale that not one American in ten thousand has ever read.

Called "The Three Princes of Serendipity," it tells the story of three Ceylonese princes who would set out in search of one thing, and always stumble upon something else of far greater value.

Some unknown copywriter, either seeking an unusual and arresting word, or anticipating an outcry from taxpayers about the huge sums being expended for research, spun an even more fabulous fairy tale about the new products which would be discovered in this left-handed manner, products which would enrich the nation a hundred-fold more than the billions being spent in research. He dubbed this alchemic process SERENDIPITY and corporate management like the term so much that, for a couple of years in the early 1960's, one couldn't read an advertisement or hear a speech by an official of a company fattening on research funding that did not employ it.

As Francis Davis has said, it was too striking a word. Everyone noticed it, wondered what it meant and then, because it had fairy tale magic, remembered it long after it had been dropped by its original users. It was this remembering that caused the trouble. When 50 billion or more dollars had been funneled out by the government for research, people began to look for these "serendipity products" and they weren't too impressed by what few they found. (*Teflon*-coated kitchen ware has since had wide popular acceptance but had

174

yet to make its appearance at that time.)

Several government agencies, including the United States Department of Commerce and the National Science Foundation, began questioning whether gigantic research programs nurtured commercial off-shoots. Apparently, after conducting some research that proved they didn't, these agencies started seeking more fertile sources of consumer-oriented invention and innovation, which ultimately led them to the only active and experienced authorities they could find in the matter, Francis Davis and his group of crusading inventors. Davis and his friends were ready not only with statistics and examples but the names and persons of inventors who were inventing, had invented, and would, undoubtedly, continue to invent. Oddly, not one of them was employed by or had the support of any large research organization. Instead, their creative fecundity seemed to indicate that "the huge industrial laboratory does not appear to be a particularly favorable environment for inducing invention." This observation refuted W. R. MacLaurin's contention that there exists "a definite correlation between the number of applied scientists employed (and the funds at their disposal) and the inventive results."

To a young man who had been called to the Commerce Department from the Bell Telephone Laboratories, the basilica of *institutionalized* invention, this must have seemed rank heresy. But Daniel V. De Simone, new Director of the Office of Invention and Innovation in the National Bureau of Standards, and later to become executive director of the National Inventors Council and secretary of the Commerce Department's Panel on Invention and Innovation, was intrigued. And in Davis' opinion, De Simone's study, "The Role of the Independent Inventor," *Some Case Histories of Selected Commercial Inventions,* which was the result of his interest and investigations, indicated that the climate for invention had taken an official and favorable turn in a most important area of government.

De Simone confined his study to case histories of the five outstanding independent contemporary inventions: the shrink proofing of knit goods by Richard Walton; the clock regulator, which was invented by Jacob Rabinow; the mercury dry cell, invented by Samuel Ruben; xerography, a creation of Chester F. Carlson; and hydraulic power steering, conceived by Francis Wright Davis.

But De Simone made many penetrating observations. For instance, he clarified two much bandied-about terms in the following manner:

> "The mental act of conception is invention; the conception itself is *an* invention, either as an idea or an embodiment of the idea. The process by which that idea is ultimately applied to satisfy a need is innovation; and the denouement, the change that is thereby wrought, is *an* innovation, the end for which the inventor and innovator strived.
>
> "The process of *innovation* is not simply *an* act. It is not just design, or market analysis, or investment, or entrepreneurship or the other intricacies that intervene between the concept and the market place. It is all of these, a complex sequence of steps. And it is all the more complex because there is nothing automatic about it: the engines of innovation are human beings.
>
> "Invention without innovation may be intellectually satisfying, but it does nothing to promote the general welfare. If Chester Carlson's conception of xerography had not been

patented, developed, redeveloped, refined, entrepreneured, put into production, and marketed, xerography would not be in our offices today."

It was also difficult to imagine a scion of Bell Telephone Laboratories stating that ignorance can be invaluable. But De Simone did and illustrated it when he wrote "The inventor has to be a bumblebee who doesn't know he can't fly." He also provided what Davis considered the finest assessment of the inventive process he has ever read.

"Outstanding inventors have an extraordinary capacity for associating permutations and combinations of facts and experiences. It is estimated that the human brain consists of something like 10 billion cells, which can be associated with each other in any combination. The number of possible permutations and combinations of 10 billion elements is staggering to contemplate. In any case, by a process we know little about, ideas often spring from the subconscious alignment of these cells. Irving Langmuir once said that the final solutions to virtually all of the scientific problems he explored came to him by a process which was not consciously one of reasoning. I have always believed that truly great invention is not a continuously logical process. The look back may sometimes show a logical sequence, but hindsight is not invention. And the inexplicable part played by unconscious cerebration, which makes the whole process discontinuous, has nothing whatever to do with logical reasoning."[11]

During a slushy March evening in 1963, Francis W. Davis found himself studying what he considered some very slushy wording in a small brochure he had received from his close friend and fellow independent inventor Richard Walton.

"Four hundred years have passed, but every man, woman and child in Spain knows and remembers with pride that men of the town of Palos built and manned the caravels in which Columbus sailed. Only yesterday, an American-built space vehicle soared 30 million uncharted miles to keep a rendezvous with Venus. Yet, how many Americans—even those who live in Calabasas (California), Tulsa (Oklahoma), Iowa City (Iowa), Framingham (Massachusetts)—are aware of the part citizens and firms of these five communities played in creating this historic craft?"[12]

Davis assumed that this must refer to the American space probe by Mariner II. Then the brochure went on to state, "The almost complete anonymity of the men, and teams of men, of firms and organizations, in practically every community who are making significant contributions to human progress and national security— the lack of identity with great achievement and momentous events that in the past was shared by all Americans —was a consideration that led to the formation of *The Academy of Applied Science.*"

Davis' reaction was one of near anger and disbelief. If ever anything seemed organized to serve the interests of *institutionalized technology* and represented just about everything that the inventor of power steering abhorred, this Academy did. Yet, Dick Walton was suggesting every independent inventor ally himself with this body to fight the most serious tax attack yet launched by Washington against inventors. Once again the Treasury Department was out to tax invention at ordinary income rates; but this time, the inventor proposal was included

178

in the President's tax message. And the President was young, vigorous and popular—John F. Kennedy.

Reluctantly, Davis accompanied his friend Walton to the Academy meeting. He recognized many heads of industrial firms and noted the large attendance from the scientific and academic communities who, to his mind, represented *institutionalized* research. Davis had read the published attitude of M.I.T.'s Jerome B. Wiesner, the President's special assistant for science and technology, and was certain that no representative of heavily government subsidized university research would deviate from it. As a result, Davis was ill-prepared when Jack Larsen, a member of the Division of Sponsored Research at M.I.T. took the floor and announced, "The only rational purpose of this bill is to drive the individual inventor into Bell and other corporate laboratories."

Davis admitted he received a liberal education that day, not only in how to block tax legislation sponsored by an immensely popular President, but in human aspirations. He discovered that creative men serving in *institutionalized* research resented their captive anonymity and lack of understanding, encouragement and recognition as much or more than the independent inventor. There was such a thing as creativity in management and industrialists who practiced it were equally aware of the dependence of the economy on invention and innovation. This organization, whose purpose had seemed so suspect, really was engaging in the same crusade as himself, but proceeding on a wider front and employing more effective methods to achieve similar goals.

Davis found himself serving on the Academy tax committee where his previous experience in testifying before Congressional Committee hearings proved most valuable. He was asked to head a special committee to investigate and bring to the attention of the Board of Governors, singular creative achievements of benefit to the nation which had not received deserved recognition. Gordon M. Fair, former Abbott, and James Lawrence, professor of engineering at Harvard University, commented that the committee's first order of business should be to list their own chairman's development of the high speed hydraulic pump used in millions of systems today for which Davis had never received either recognition or royalties because by the time it came into general use the patent covering the invention had expired.

Davis, of course, would not have countenanced such a motion, but the first action of the special committee led to a *contretemps* that made its chairman wonder if a society dedicated to the recognition of scientific creativity wasn't just as wary about recognizing individual accomplishment as any of the corporations he had known. The name submitted in the aviation category was Clarence L. "Kelly" Johnson. It was scratched off the list with no comments or explanation. A somewhat cynical member of the Davis panel observed that the Academy was planning to produce a motion picture dealing with the history of business aviation[13] and might be seeking Lockheed support. This aroused Davis' ire and he would have resigned from the Academy if he had not been shown that the Academy had "full control of content" in the case of the film and full support of the entire airplane industry. This, however, did not explain why C. L. "Kelly" Johnson's highly original contributions to aviation engineering design weren't considered sufficient for Academy recognition.

What had happened was that Martin M. Decker, chairman of The Academy Board of Governors, was at that time also president of the National Aeronautic Association, and being aware of the nature of the highly secretive surveillance missions being carried out by the

U-2 plane, feared that any recognition of its designer might inadvertently draw attention to the plane. After the Cuban missile crisis and the part the U-2 played in definitely establishing the existence of Russian missile sites on Cuban soil was revealed, Davis was permitted to make the following acknowledgment of the Academy's and the nation's indebtedness to Clarence L. "Kelly" Johnson, "Only once before in our history has this nation owed such a great debt to the singular talents of an inventive engineer, and that was when the timely appearance of John Ericsson's *Monitor* prevented the destruction of the completely unprepared Union Navy."

One of the committee's investigations and recommendations was particularly satisfying to Davis because it brought recognition to a creative man who had been completely ignored in what was hailed as a national triumph but could have been a humiliating and tragic disaster.

The big news story of the spring of 1963 was the 22-orbit flight of the Mercury program space vehicle Faith 7. The nation's heart stopped when it was announced that the automatic landing system had failed and Astronaut Gordon Cooper would be forced to depend upon manual controls for the fiery re-entry descent and landing. It started beating again when Astronaut Cooper made a safe and accurate landing in the Pacific.

Davis, reading the three solid pages *The New York Times* devoted to the dramatic story, noted names and praise for the prime and various sub-contractors who had built and designed the orbit vehicle, the rocket that boosted it into space, and explanations and diagrams of many system components.

There were photographs of the launching gantry, the control center, interviews and statements from the public affairs officer, the flight director who bore a name that had caught the public fancy—Chris Kraft—

but not a single clue in 30 thousand words of New York Times reportage as to who was responsible for the manual back-up over-ride which the New York Times, in flamboyant front page headlines, had dubbed "Fly-By-Wire."

A phone call to McDonnell Douglas Aircraft Company, the prime contractor, drew a blank. Their director of information couldn't even name the sub-contractor of the mechanism which had, for the second time, saved his company from the stigma of disaster.

"It was par for the course," Davis remarked, recalling when a magazine writer had tried to learn his own name and address from the Ross Steering Gear people.

Texas Instrument Company, the sub-contractor for the Mercury capsule control system was contacted next. The Dallas headquarters only knew that the manual system was assembled at their Attleboro, Massachusetts, division. At this moment in the search, Davis made one of his intuitive predictions. "I think we will find that this so called 'fly-by-wire' is a complex switch sequence and the heart of it is a unique switch invented by one man."

And so it proved. A fail-safe switch invented by Lyndon W. Burch, who had been a tank commander during the Korean conflict, was the critical mechanism in the complex 36-switch sequence of the manual control. As a result of the Davis committee's investigation and recommendation, the Board of Governors of The Academy of Applied Science honored independent inventor Lyndon W. Burch by electing him a Fellow of that body. In part the citation read, "for the second time a humiliating and possible tragic failure in our nation's space effort was averted by the inventive genius of Lyndon Burch."

182

The Burch story was released to the national wire services and, as a consequence of this, reached the *Boston Herald Traveler* as an Associated Press dispatch not more than an hour later. This caused the newspaper's city editor to angrily accuse The Academy of Applied Science of "delaying important news." Certainly the climate for creativity had undergone a change when a hard-boiled city editor considered the recognition of an inventor by a scientific society important news.

Davis was to receive many other indications that a climatic change had taken place, but probably the most pleasing to the former lone crusader were the requests he received from industrial corporations for advice and counsel on how they should stimulate creativity, invention and innovation in their organizations.

In the half-decade that has seen the rise of a reform movement which, at times, has taken on tidal wave proportions, it might be well to stop and consider what kind of a reformer Francis W. Davis has been and is. Certainly none of his actions have stemmed from what might be called a deep and sensitive social consciousness. When he first assaulted Detroit he never considered that the automobile industry had a social obligation to provide the motoring public with the best transportation. He just felt they were blindly stupid if they didn't, particularly when cars were constantly getting heavier and women had greater difficulty driving them.

Though Davis was possibly the first person in the country to recognize that the modern corporation (as conceived by Alfred Sloan) by its nature automatically suppressed invention and innovation, he never got on a soapbox and accused it of being a private government exercising feudal rights over its employees and he has yet to concede that even a group of corporate giants can long decide "just what will be produced, at what prices and for whom," which is John Kenneth Galbraith's latest contention.[14]

In the early days of the New Deal, Davis declared, "Sloan may be able to put everybody above the supervisory level in his little mental boxes, but doing it will make shop unionization inevitable." That point has certainly been verified.

Twenty years before Ralph Nader, Davis was aware of the automobile industry's preoccupation with styling, but he has never accepted that styling covered a lack of concern with safety. Instead he credits his own great adversary O. E. Hunt's aversion to technological change to a fixation with safety. "Hunt knew better than anyone the problems that even the smallest mechanical change presented to a nation-wide service and maintenance operation. He was always haunted by the recall of those few thousand Kettering-designed air-cooled Chevrolets in 1924. If he had been around he would have never accepted the Corvair design, and General Motors wouldn't have had to recall a million Chevrolets in 1967."

Where Nader's principle concern has been with the way that corporations deal with the public, Davis' interest has been in their method of treating their own employees and suppliers like himself. A social reformer like Ralph Nader is outraged because an engineer or scientist who goes to work for a corporation has "to relinquish his constitutional right of free speech." To Davis, the important issue has been that their ingenuity and creativity is stifled and that this is something that a nation whose economy is dependent upon invention and innovation cannot afford.

To Davis, Sloan's corporation concept was always self-defeating. As early as 1932 he said, "Sooner or later General Motors is going to find out it needs new ideas and that good men will balk at functioning in boxes.''

Perhaps a striking way to illustrate the difference between Ralph Nader, the sociopolitical reformer, and Francis W. Davis, the crusader for creativity, is to compare their attitudes regarding the rear-engine Corvair.

In ''Unsafe At Any Speed,'' the sensational book that brought him national attention and notoriety, Ralph Nader used this General Motors car to sensationally symbolize the abnormal attitude of an industry which he charged ''for great profit, sells cars with built-in defects that they know will kill people.''[15] While to Davis the Corvair was an indication that General Motors had at last, like a mole, come out of its tunnel and was finally willing to try new ways of doing things— namely, by building a car with a rear-engine.

For Davis, the Nader book mainly revealed and confirmed the constriction of the flow of vital and essential information caused by the Sloan tables-of-organization concepts. Davis considered the Corvair the most revolutionary automotive package General Motors had attempted to produce in two decades, and the fact that upper management was totally unaware of what kind of rear-end suspension the Corvair used did not surprise him in the least.

> ''What General Motors terms *coordinated control* supposedly refers to a two-way flow of information at each level of management—the downward flow from authority and the upward flow from initiative—but if just never existed at General Motors. The tragedy is that, living in this dark tunnel of their own making, these people believed it did.''

After thirty years of observation and reflection, Davis is extremely doubtful that such communication can exist in any truly large organization, at least any

185

organized on the Sloan or similar patterns.

To bolster his contention, Davis is apt to bring in a rather unique authority, namely Fred V. Zendar, a former Olympic diving champion who has been a consultant in oceanic research for both government and private industry.

"Zendar noted that in the oceans there is a submerged layer of water that effectively blocks all communications from above and below. When I asked him what this stratum was composed of, Zendar, who was a fishing companion of Ernest Hemingway's, replied 'Suspended silt, plankton and dead minute marine life.' Then he asked me if I hadn't found the same blocking stratum existing in business. When I admitted that I had, he grinned and said 'Now that they're getting around to it the ocean's going to teach big businessmen a lot, if it doesn't drown them all.' "

Davis doesn't think that the heads of the big companies that will engage in oceanic projects in the next few decades will have much personal contact with ocean depths and consequently neither will learn much from them, nor be drowned. But he does believe that the first problem that faces the head of any large business organization is to immediately establish direct unobstructed communications with initiating departments and creative personnel.

"Since tables of organization have become sacrosanct, it would be foolhardy to try to change them; therefore, I think the only way for such a communication channel to be established and to function would be outside the regular organizational structure."

Davis credits Secretary of the Interior Stewart L. Udall with furnishing a workable pattern for this communication channel when Udall engaged a noted scholar and scientist who commanded the respect and confidence of the many scientific breeds gathered under the Interior Department tent to act as a personal advisor or "private line to the Secretary."

"Big business and other government departments should immediately follow Udall's example. And they should not select administrative men but inventive, creative men if they want to command the respect and gain the confidence of their own creative people."

Until recently, Davis has always ignored all requests for a recipe or prescription for creativity. However, after hearing George A. Whittington, former editor of "Research/Development" Magazine speak one evening at the M.I.T. Faculty Club, Davis got together with Whittington and together they drafted a set of "seven reasonable desires" which Davis feels embody things that would make an inventive and creative man more satisfied in a job situation.

According to Davis, the joint effort represents simple common sense in human relations rather than a formula that will create a favorable environment for creativity, though each stated desire is definitely related to helping a man who has this rare ability to be more consistently and frequently creative.

1. The creative man wants to be respected for his ability. He wants to be accepted as a productive member of the team—socially as well as theoretically.

2. He wants to have his work understood—by someone in authority, someone who can further it. He wants it to be used, and to be acknowledged.

3. Like any other human being, the creative person needs emotional support. That is, he wants another individual or group of individuals to show some enthusiasm over a

new idea, to provide encouragement—at least by continued interest.

4. While all good technical men are said to seek challenging assignments, this one is particularly responsive to such work. Usually his interest demands his being involved in selecting the area of investigation and establishing the objectives.

5. Particularly because he is dedicated to trying new approaches to problems this man wants the right to fail, sometimes, without being reproached. He dares to defy conventional methods in the search for new problem solutions, and his courage benefits from knowing that he is free to try without incurring criticism for the effort.

6. The creative man needs a confidant he can trust not to steal his ideas. Some thefts are deliberate—others accidental. There are simple (and common) cases of forgetting where one first heard an idea, or who suggested a line of investigation or a possible explanation of a result. Yet, the latter happenings reflect lack of respect, or carelessness. An individual who depends on creativeness for his livelihood and his future cannot be wasteful of his accomplishments, still, he deserves an opportunity to talk about his work, freely, with someone who will honor his confidences.

7. The creative man also wants to know about all company policies and activities that affect his work, or will affect it in the future. How else can he plan his future, or even his present efforts on the job?

Both Davis and Whittington claim that every employee makes the same seven demands—in some form or other—but the same demands are harder to satisfy when the creative man raises them, than when they are brought forward by others, mainly because he is often much more positive about what he wants. Being positive is essential to the intellectual practices to which he has committed himself. He is more intense because he has schooled himself to a high degree of constant awareness. According to Davis, this is a part of his personal discipline.

The manager's task in meeting the demands of this particular employee are, on the whole, complicated by the other's characteristic personality. Davis agrees with Whittington that it is safe to generalize that creative technical persons are seldom "social successes among members of the staff." They do not, usually, receive personal acceptance as a "member of the group" from their associates. Nor do they generate person-to-person enthusiasm and receive encouragement by that route.

It follows that management must recognize that creative men are, to paraphrase George Orwell, likely to be more individual than other men. And Davis claims he has yet to find such recognition on a department management or supervisory level, and insists that this is the principal reason why creativity does not flourish even in organizations headed by very creative men.

"One thing that should be rejected is that creative persons need to be motivated. The truth is that creativity is compulsive and a person who is so gifted will be creative in technical work *whenever he is allowed to be.*" Then Davis grinned and added, "He will also undoubtedly shock the wits out of any engineering supervisor who goes by the book and any department manager whose main talent is writing lucid memos to upper management.''

The head of a very large corporation recently asked Davis how he should go about attracting creative men to his organization. The man flourished some full page newspaper advertisements that proclaimed arrestingly the challenges his company offered in any number of fields and disciplines. ''You should see the inquiries we are getting from top men all over the country,'' the corporation head bragged.

''Do you want top men or creative men?'' Davis demanded.

''Aren't they the same?''

''Not usually,'' Davis replied. He advised the executive to instruct his personnel procurement manager to give preference to men who had changed jobs ''too'' frequently.

''But that's a sign of a drifter, a man who lacks stability. . . .''

Davis cut in before the man could proceed further, ''It can also mean wife beating, alcoholism, adultery, irritability, bad debts, but it is generally the mark of a man who refuses to stay with a boring job. And it can mask a creative and inventive mind.''

''But it's against everything in our operational procedures. . . . everything our employment people have learned,'' the mighty man protested.

''Probably,'' Davis agreed.

During 1966-67 Davis followed with great interest a dialogue conducted on the pages of campus newspapers between college students and Robert W. Galvin, chairman of Motorola, Inc. The series was introduced with the question, ''Can Business Face the Issues?'' and was accompanied by a letter from Mr. Galvin, which read in part:

''There is an urgent need, I believe, for a

190

serious discussion between campus and corporation.

"I am genuinely concerned about recent studies which indicate that an alarming percentage of college students have no interest in pursuing careers in business. Many of these students show little respect for business and have a condescending attitude towards those who do choose it as a career.

"Some say business leaves them cold. Lacks action. That it's boring, unimaginative, stuffy and self-seeking. Others say they don't want to be lost in the corporate crowd and that there is little chance of early recognition for a young man in business. Some question whether business offers the opportunity for the personal satisfaction.

"However, don't sell business short. If you shrug off a business career because you think it offers no excitement, no challenge, no chance for recognition or to make a meaningful contribution to society . . . I think you're wrong.

"A tremendous opportunity for human and social betterment may well slip away if brighter students turn their backs on business for reasons not necessarily valid. The coming years promise fantastic new developments in the sciences, electronics, transportation or just about any field you can name. However, realization of these great potentials requires fresh thinking, young, vigorous minds able to channel ideas creatively and productively . . . able to make decisions . . . able to generate action, the very thing you crave.

"This is why I'm concerned. If I read some of you right, we're in trouble. Something has broken down, somewhere. Maybe we in business had best undertake a basic reappraisal of our way of doing things. If changes are in order, I'd like to find out."

Francis W. Davis, who followed the discussion in the daily *Harvard Crimson* (it ran in a total 29 college newspapers), wondered if business recognized what Mr. Galvin was trying to do or had any realization of the depth of the trouble it was in. But even Davis was astounded when the undergraduates started hurling back such verbal javelins as "What does business actively do to encourage individual creative action?", "The young man isn't mad at you; he just doesn't like you."

Davis, who once had been practically alone in recognizing that many of the premises of Alfred Sloan's *modern corporation* were self defeating in the long run, was amazed at the virulence of the student attack.

Before making any comment, Davis decided to wait for the results of a program the Harvard Graduate School of Business Administration was conducting. This project was designed to expose fifty highly-qualified management students to the challenging and rewarding aspects of business by having them serve a ten-week internship within a number of leading organizations. When the returns were in, Davis felt it would be immodest to make any comment, but very few men have ever had evaluations they made thirty years before validated so vigorously and emphatically. Here are some of the post internship evaluations:

"The only real split-second decision making we saw was in deciding to pass the buck."

"I was astounded at the tremendous range of mediocrity."

"Only top management is receptive to new ideas."

Many of the student interns noted the same inert

middle strata that Davis had observed and called "a communications barrier," but they diagnosed it as a symptom of the timidity and cautiousness of middle management.

"People have to keep their mouths shut for twenty years before they can speak up or do anything significant."

Lately, with the tide reversed and running full and strong in the direction he has always favored, Davis has found himself defending and succoring the former common enemy and ignoring the reaction of his own sect. For instance, he did not agree with Jim Hill, a Harvard undergraduate, who took part in the dialogue with Robert W. Galvin, the Motorola chairman, that a young man should necessarily regard a corporation "as a device which strangles his talent with organizational inertia and hobbles his ambitions with bureaucratic lethargy."

When William A. Emerson, Jr., the editor of *The Saturday Evening Post,* declared in a first page editorial, "I think that almost everything worthwhile is done by some single irascible human being,"[16] the phrase was not picked up and quoted by Davis as it would have been a few years earlier.

It is not that Francis W. Davis has mellowed or that he considers the industrial laboratory or the corporate engineering research center a particularly favorable environment for stimulating invention. But he does concede that large-scale innovation is logically the province of the corporate world. He feels, that once corporate management recognizes that *invention precedes technological innovation* and accepts this as an ordinary and logical process in which both the individual inventor and institutionalized innovator have recognized roles and responsibilities invention and innovation will accelerate at a rate not imaginable in the past.

Davis further sees this process as the most effective antidote to the threat of corporate concentration which has alarmed so many persons. It has been predicted that by 1975, 200 companies will own 60 per cent of all the assets in the United States which is an alarming increase from the 40 per cent level of 1950. Davis, who has proven a seer in sensing other corporate behavior patterns, contends that despite the record merger rate of the past few years, corporate concentration is already declining. The reason is that new technologies are allowing more companies to enter industry with a minimum amount of capital. He feels that the *State Technical Services Act,* which was passed by Congress in 1965, will play an ever increasing role in furthering this concentration decline.

This Act makes the latest findings of science and technology available to local business and industry. The initial impetus that led to the passage of this legislation was given during a working conference on "Stimulating Technical Education, Invention and Innovation" which was held at The Academy of Applied Science in Cambridge, two years earlier. Francis W. Davis took an active role in the discussions during which representatives of New England business and industry exchanged views with members of the scientific and academic community of the entire nation, and at which a delegation headed by Daniel V. DeSimone and Dr. Donald A. Schon of the U. S. Department of Commerce presented the government point of view.

While most everyone attending the working conference agreed that the challenge was to apply the nation's growing scientific and engineering resources to new socially and commercially profitable uses, Davis argued that this did not call for establishing more research institutions. "More important is the need to adapt and use existing technology and existing technical advances. The problem is national in scale but the application is largely on a local level.

"A New England university or research center may have already conducted a program which would be of great technical service to a small Oregon industry. But unless New England has some special need for this program, it would be far better in the future if the research is carried out at some Oregon facility working closely with local industry and its problems."

Dr. Lan Jen Chu, Webster professor of electrical engineering at Massachusetts Institute of Technology, and president of Chu Associates, a leading firm in the microwave antenna field, credits Davis' arguments, prestige and activity with firmly linking local industry needs with local technological research that became the predominate feature of the 1965 State Technical Services bill when it was enacted.

In 1947, all inventors expectantly awaited the report of the specially appointed Presidential Commission on sadly-needed and long-overdue changes in the United States Patent System. Instinctively many turned to Davis, who became the unofficial dean of the inventors community in Congressional matters for his interpretation of the Presidential Commission's recommendations.

In 1965 the United States Department of Commerce and every other government agency was pressing for a rapid enactment of the Commission's recommendations into law. While Francis W. Davis favored an increase in the length of patent life such as the Presidential Commission proposed, he was dubious of many of the other recommendations. He mildly suggested that, in his opinion, additional hearings by the House Ways and Means Committee might reveal serious inadequacies in the proposed statute. A few hours after Davis voiced this opinion, Gerald Mossinghoff, director of the Office of Legislative Planning in the United States Patent Office, quietly announced that the Patent Office was no longer pressing for immediate enactment but was recommending that the new patent legislation be held over for the next session of Congress and that additional hearings should be scheduled.

This caused Nelson H. Shapiro, a former assistant examiner in the United States Patent Office, and now a distinguished patent attorney in Washington, D.C. who was familiar with the American Bar Association's vigorous but up to then unsuccessful efforts to delay the bill, to inquire, "Just who is this Francis W. Davis?"

Under the circumstances what appears to be a most appropriate answer was supplied by Robert H. Rines, president of the Academy of Applied Science, also a patent attorney and a member of the National Inventors Council (1963-66), who played a considerable role in urging the President to appoint a Presidential Commission to study the patent situation. Rines said, "Oh, Davis is a man whose whispers sound like thunderclaps to a lot of people these days. But it wasn't always that way."

"No, I'll say it wasn't always that way," Francis W. Davis chuckled when he heard about Rines' statement.

❊   ❊   ❊

One recent afternoon, the inventor of power steering was sitting on the lawn in front of his Nantucket cottage that faces Nantucket Harbor. Suddenly he indicated a seagull that was swooping down for a run at the deck of a float that is moored in front of the Davis cottage. The bird's intentions were most plain. He was planning to drop a shell fish onto the hard deck of the float, hoping to break it open so he could swoop back to a two-point landing and voluptuously enjoy the meat inside. The gull had every intention of leaving the deck covered with cracked shell and other debris for human menials to attend to as best they could.

The "human menials" in question settled Nantucket three centuries ago. Their ancestors were sea captains who roamed all the world's oceans, conquered and processed every kind of whale, invented and developed tools and equipment that enabled them to make millions of dollars in the whaling trade. Testimonials to their inventive ingenuity fill countless whaling museums today.

Yet, during the entire three hundred years of settlement, Nantucket residents have been ceaselessly tormented by their seagull population. Even when the gulls do not use their floats or roofs to crack shells, the birds playfully drop rocks on them.

Sailing captains, skillful enough to navigate the Magellan Straits, to outwit Malay pirates, Australian jailbirds and Hawaiian kings, to develop processes to extract the last ounce of oil and bone from Nature's largest mammal, were completely outmatched by the gulls.

The whalers and their descendants tried to protect their mansions, fabulously furnished with rugs, tapestries and other treasures from Europe and the Orient, with roof scare-crows, or rather, *scare-gulls*. But the gulls only added insult to injury by perching on these devices and, in leaving, spattering their marble steps and splendid wrought iron fences with gull guano.

The seagull that Davis had been watching that day made a second puzzled pass at the Davis float, and then angrily swooped off to the float moored in front of the next bayside cottage. He dropped his shell burden on a deck already littered with cracked shells, and guano, and then coasted in to a landing. Fastidiously, the bird stepped through the litter and pecked at the meat in the newly-cracked shell. The bird was plainly annoyed that it had not been able to bounce the shell open on the clean Davis float.

. The first recorded victory in the three-century conflict of Nantucket residents vs. Nantucket Sound sea gulls occurred in this manner.

Francis W. Davis had observed that seagulls are most afraid of the slightest obstruction that might brush their wings. He first experimented by stringing a taut fish-line about a foot above the flat roof of one wing of his cottage. The next morning he realized that for the first time since he took up residence on the island, he had not been awakened by the gulls' bouncing shells on his roof. Encouraged, he then proceeded to work out design patterns for these lines which would not interfere with human utilization of his boat landing and diving float and the gangway that leads to them.

With autumn turning into winter, the summer residents have left Nantucket. The windows of the cottages that line the harbor are boarded up, ready for the blast of Atlantic winter gales. The fish-lines on the float in front of the Davis cottage sag a little, but it is the only float or dock in the mile-long row that is not littered with cracked shell fragments, and gull-deposited debris.

The gulls have probably noticed that the fish-lines on the Davis float are not as taut as they were in the spring, but not one beaked bombadier has dared to make a run of it as yet.

As Francis W. Davis observed, put a problem under an inventive man's nose, plop him down in an environment favorable to creativity—which really means "walk away and let him alone"—and he's got to start trying to solve it.

"Inventing isn't a vocation; it's a compulsion."

AFTERWORD

We have explored some of the challenges that confront the independent inventor as he travels his long and difficult journey. He must be an iconoclast, challenging the accepted way of doing things; yet he must be a winsome advocate for the disruption he proposes. He must persuade others that he has what they have been waiting for; but they probably haven't been waiting at all. He must overcome the skepticism of potential sponsors as to the workability of his invention; but he is unusual if he can convince them that the inevitable defects are merely the rough edges of early development, soon to be smoothed away. And if he really has a winner, he must ward off imitators at every corner. In short, he must fight one battle after another, and the chances of ultimate triumph would get him fifty to one odds at Monte Carlo. If he fails, society loses nothing. But if he wins society benefits handsomely. He ought, therefore, to be encouraged, not repressed. Society ought always to be solicitous about giving him the opportunity to spread his wings.

—DANIEL V. DE SIMONE[17]
Director, National Inventors' Council
Director, Office of Invention
and Innovation, National Bureau
of Standards

DAVIS PATENTS

(Owned and Controlled)

Covering Power Steering Gears and
Pumps for Operating Same

U. S. PATENTS (Power Steering Gears)

Davis	1,790,620	Jan. 27, 1931	Open Center Valve

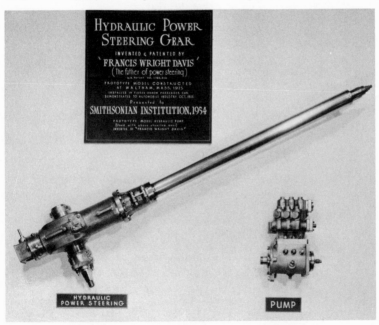

Aikman	1,817,903	Aug. 11, 1931	(Assigned to Davis)
Davis	1,874,248	Aug. 30, 1932	Centering Spring
Davis	1,937,470	Nov. 28, 1933	Hydraulic Reaction
Davis	1,937,485	Nov. 28, 1933	Integral (In-Line)
Davis	1,947,973	Feb. 20, 1934	Nested valve
Jessup	1,947,991	Feb. 20, 1934	(Assigned to Davis)
Stelzer	2,151,998	Mar. 28, 1939	(Assigned to Davis)
Davis	2,213,271	Sept. 3, 1940	"Davis Valve" G.M., etc.

Davis	2,410,049	Oct. 29, 1946	Integral (In-Line)
Davis	2,627,187	Feb. 3, 1953	Hour Glass Worm
Davis	2,634,708	Apr. 14, 1953	Closed Valve
Davis	2,784,611	Mar. 12, 1957	Hy. Balance of Piston
Presnell	2,719,511	Oct. 4, 1955	Reaction Limiting (Assigned to Davis)
Davis	2,824,314	Feb. 25, 1958	Reaction Limiting (Assigned to Davis)

Covering Power Steering Gears and Pumps for Operating Same

U. S. PATENTS (Pumps)

Davis	2,206,079	July 2, 1940	Pump
Davis	2,251,664	Aug. 5, 1941	Fluid Booster
Davis	2,261,143	Nov. 4, 1941	Pump Gear
Davis	2,385,129	Sept. 18, 1945	Gear Lapping Machine

FOREIGN PATENTS (Power Steering Gears) (Partial List)

Davis—British	371,816	Jan. 19, 1931
Davis—French	709,967	Jan. 26, 1931
Davis—German	583,901	Jan. 27, 1931
Davis—Canadian	328,751	Dec. 27, 1932
Davis—British	618,457	June 7, 1949
Davis—French	930,411	Sept. 26, 1944
Davis—British	713,786	Jan. 8, 1952

Additional Davis Patents

U. S. PATENTS (Other Than Steering Gear Series)

Davis	1,186,291	June 6, 1916	Cigar cutter
Davis	1,389,580	Sept. 6, 1921	Locking Differential
Davis	1,552,119	Sept. 1, 1925	Fuel Consumption Indicator
Davis	1,572,519	Feb. 9, 1926	Steering Gear Coupling
Davis	1,846,089	Feb. 23, 1932	Servomotor (Brake)
Davis	1,944,002	June 16, 1934	Multiple Hydraulic System
Davis	2,007,423	July 9, 1935	Double Acting Servomotor
Davis	2,446,909	Aug. 10, 1948	Knife Sharpener
Davis	2,539,993	Jan. 30, 1951	Retractable Wheel Supports for Luggage
Davis	2,661,220	Dec. 1, 1953	Wheel Assembly for Suitcases
Davis	2,696,990	Dec. 14, 1954	Carriage for suitcases, etc.
Davis	3,265,074	Aug. 9, 1966	Vented cigarette holder

FOREIGN PATENTS

Davis—British	655-641	July 1, 1948	Retractable Wheel Supports for Laggage
Davis—Canadian	472-399	Mar. 27, 1951	Retractable Wheel Supports for Laggage
Davis—British	1,074,188	June 28, 1967	Vented cigarette holder

202

APPENDIX II

LIST OF ILLUSTRATIONS

LIST OF DIAGRAMS AND TECHNICAL DRAWINGS

BIBLIOGRAPHY

[1] WHEELS FOR A NATION. Frank Donovan. New York: Thomas Y. Crowell Co., 1965. (Ch. I, p. 15).

[2] "I Have a Rendezvous with Death," Alan Seegar (poem). (Ch. IV, p. 34).

[3] MY YEARS WITH GENERAL MOTORS. Alfred P. Sloan. New York: Doubleday, 1963. (Ch. IX, p. 107).

[4] CREATE OR PERISH. The Case for Inventions and Patents. Robert H. Rines. Cambridge, Mass.: Academy of Applied Science, 1964. (Ch. IX, p. 108).

[5] TECHNOLOGY AND CHANGE: The New Heraclitus. Donald A. Schon, 1967. (Ch. IX, pp. 113-114).

[6] "Power Steering for Automotive Vehicles," Francis W. Davis. Presented to the Society for Automotive Engineers, January 9, 1945, p. 240. (Ch. XII, p. 145).

[7] "Power Steering in 1952," W. K. Creson, Vice President, Engineering, Ross Gear & Tool Co. Presented at annual SAE meeting, January, 1952. (Ch. XIII, p. 158).

[8] THE WIND AND BEYOND. Theodore Von Karman, Pioneer in Aviation and Pathfinder in Space. Theodore Von Karman and Lee Edson. Boston: Little, Brown & Co., 1967. (Ch. XIV, p. 167).

[9] THE NEW INDUSTRIAL STATE. John Kenneth Galbraith. Boston: Houghton Mifflin, 1967. (Ch. XIV, p. 170).

[10] Charles E. Wilson, Secretary of Defense (1953-57), President of General Motors (1941-1953). Columbia Encyclopedia notes: "As Secretary of Defense, he attempted to effect a "New Look" in defense policy, which, involving cuts in the military budget. . . , led to much controversy." N.Y.: Columbia University Press, 1963, Third Edition, p. 2333. (Ch. XIV, p. 173).

[11] THE ROLE OF THE INDEPENDENT INVENTOR. Some Case Histories of Selected Commercial Inventions. Daniel V. De Simone, Director, Office of Invention & Innovation, National Bureau of Standards, U.S. Dept. of Commerce; presented before the Subcommittee on Antitrust and Monopoly of the Committee on the Judiciary, U.S. Senate, May 18, 1965. (Ch. XIV, p. 177).

[12] Ibid. (Ch. XIV, p. 178).

[13] WINGS AT WORK, the Story of Business Aviation. Film presented by the Academy of Applied Science; released in 1966. (Ch. XIV, p. 180).

[14] John Kenneth Galbraith, *op. cit.* (Ch. XIV, p. 184).

[15] UNSAFE AT ANY SPEED. Ralph Nader. New York: Grossman Publishing, 1965. (Ch. XIV, p. 185).

[16] Saturday Evening Post, editorial by William A. Emerson, Jr. December 2, 1967. (Ch. XIV, p. 193).

[17] Conclusion. De Simone, *op. cit.* (p. 199).

INDEX

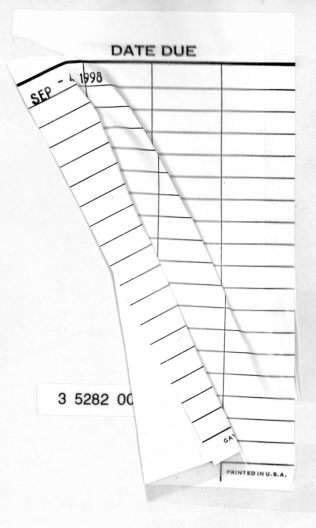

DATE DUE

SEP - 4 1998

3 5282 00

PRINTED IN U.S.A.

Acknowledgments. _____

Editorial Supervision . . . Morgan Branch

Photo, page 157 . . . courtesy of Boston Museum of Science.

Route followed by Francis Davis in trans-continental trip for Pierce Arrow in 1921.

GENERAL MAP OF
TRANSCONTINENTAL ROUTES
WITH PRINCIPAL CONNECTIONS